A MAP HISTORY OI United States

Brian Catchpole

HEINEMANN
EDUCATIONAL

Heinemann Educational,
a division of Heinemann Educational Books Ltd
Halley Court, Jordan Hill, Oxford OX2 8EJ

OXFORD   LONDON   EDINBURGH
MELBOURNE   SYDNEY   AUCKLAND
IBADAN   NAIROBI   GABORONE   HARARE
KINGSTON   PORTSMOUTH NH (USA)
SINGAPORE   MADRID

ISBN 0 435 31158 1
© Brian Catchpole 1972
First published 1972
Reprinted 1976, 1977, 1979
Reprinted with additions 1981
Reprinted 1987, 1989

Other books by the same author
A MAP HISTORY OF THE MODERN WORLD
A MAP HISTORY OF THE BRITISH PEOPLE
1700 to the Present Day
A MAP HISTORY OF RUSSIA
A MAP HISTORY OF MODERN CHINA
A MAP HISTORY OF OUR OWN TIMES

Photoset by Interprint Ltd, Malta
and printed in Great Britain by
Butler & Tanner Ltd, Frome and London

PREFACE

In less than 400 years the American people have achieved a standard of living higher than that of any other nation in the world. Theirs is a remarkable achievement. Admittedly, the Americans have had a great deal of luck; their country is rich in natural resources. But they have also had to face a lot of hardship. The first white men established their tiny colonies on an unfriendly coastline 3000 miles from home. They had to survive Indian attack, plague and famine. They had to throw off British rule by means of revolution. They had to explore and open up their huge continent, a process littered with human misery on a massive scale. There was the near-annihilation of the American Indian; the enslavement of millions of Africans; the exploitation of generations of hopeful immigrants; and a Civil War fought with an intensity rarely equalled in the recent history of other countries. Yet it was a united and democratically governed nation that emerged at the beginning of the twentieth century. With its vast industrial potential and almost unlimited manpower, the United States gave valuable help to the Allies in World War I and, in the unhappy post-war years, managed to preserve her democratic principles. In World War II, the United States played a decisive rôle in the defeat of Nazi Germany and Imperial Japan and emerged a *super-power*—to face all the anxieties and responsibilities that this new status brought.

The aim of this history is to tell these and other stories by means of maps and diagrams related directly to the text. Each self-contained page of narrative faces illustrations and source material designed to contribute to the understanding and further study of a specific topic. Many spreads relate to matters of universal interest. For example, the racial problem may be traced from its roots in the seventeenth century to the struggle for Civil Rights and the beginning of true social integration. Themes such as *The Preservation of Democracy in America* or *America and the Cold War* offer opportunities for centre of interest studies; while the use of *related* spreads (such as 38, 41, 42, 43, 44, 46, 52 and 54 on Viet Nam) provides rapid guidance for the development of project work. Throughout, there is special reference to the working of the United States Constitution, the text of which is included (pp. 124–32). Each theme, moreover, is arranged so that it may be used in conjunction with the companion volume *A Map History of Russia*.

CONTENTS

ABBREVIATIONS

AAA	Agricultural Adjustment Act/Administration
ABM	Anti-Ballistic Missile
ARVN	Army of the Republic of South Viet Nam (troops were usually termed 'Arvins')
AVG	American Volunteer Group
BEF	Bonus Expeditionary Force
CCC	Civilian Conservation Corps
CIA	Central Intelligence Agency
COMINFORM	Communist Information Bureau
CORE	Congress of Racial Equality
CWA	Civil Works Administration
DC	District of Columbia
FBI	Federal Bureau of Investigation
GI	Government Issue – slang for an American soldier – 'a GI'.
G-men	Government men or agents
GNP	Gross National Product
HOLC	Home Owners Loan Corporation
ICBM	Intercontinental Ballistic Missile
IRBM	Intermediate Range Ballistic Missile
MIRV	Multiple Independently-targeted Re-entry Vehicle
MLR	Main Line of Resistance
NAACP	National Association for the Advancement of Coloured People
NASA	National Aeronautics and Space Administration
NATO	North Atlantic Treaty Organization
NRA	National Recovery Administration
NVN	North Vietnamese (NVA = North Vietnamese Army)
OAS	Organization of American States
OPEC	Organization of Petroleum Exporting Countries
PWA	Public Works Administration
RDF	Rapid Deployment Force
ROK	Republic of Korea – 'Roks' = South Korean troops
SAC	Strategic Air Command
SALT	Strategic Arms Limitation Talks
SEATO	South East Asia Treaty Organization
TVA	Tennessee Valley Authority
USAAF	United States Army Air Force
USIS	United States Information Service
USS	United States Ship
USSR	Union of Soviet Socialist Republics
V-1	German World War II pilotless bomb – the 'doodle-bug'
V-2	German World War II supersonic rocket
WASP	'White Anglo-Saxon Protestant'
WPA	Works Progress Administration
WPB	War Production Board

THEME 1

Starting Points

About 40,000 years ago the first 'Indians' crossed the Bering Strait from Asia to begin their slow settlement of the Americas; by 1000 A.D. Viking sailors had landed in Canada; and during the sixteenth century Spaniards based on Cuba and Mexico explored much of Texas and the Deep South. Yet it would be fair to say that the history of North America truly began in 1607 when the British sailed up the James River to build a permanent settlement at Jamestown. Twelve years later the citizens of Jamestown bought twenty Negroes from the captain of a Dutch ship. Red men, white men and black men had now all arrived in the land which one day would be the United States of America.

But first it was to be part of the British Empire in America, an impressive collection of colonies stretching from Quebec in the north down to the rich sugar islands of the Caribbean. Thirteen of these colonies were on the eastern seaboard of America and, in Westminster, the British government treasured every one as a lucrative source of tobacco or timber, furs or fish. Because these Thirteen Colonies were such a profitable part of their mercantile empire, the British were ready to fight Indians, Frenchmen and smugglers in order to preserve it. They introduced Navigation Laws which gave their merchant ships a near monopoly of the North Atlantic trade and imposed an irksome array of commercial and political restrictions on the American colonists whose numbers, by 1763, were approaching 2.5 million people.

Between 1763 and 1775 these 'Americans' developed a new sense of unity and a sudden awareness that they were becoming a nation in their own right—though when they clashed with British troops at Lexington in 1775 King George III of England called them rebels and traitors. Within a year these rebels had proclaimed their national sovereignty and transformed a civil war in America into a struggle for American independence.

1 : The first white men

Vikings in North America

Viking sailors landed in North America just under a thousand years ago. They had already colonized parts of Iceland and Greenland when the climatic conditions of the tenth century were rather more favourable for settlement than they are today. One of them, Bjarni Herjolfson, was at sea between Iceland and Greenland in the late summer of 986. Severe gales drove him westwards where he sighted a low-lying, well-forested land. He had seen the eastern coastline of Canada. But Bjarni did not land; the first European to set foot in North America was probably Leif Eriksson who made three landfalls which he named Helluland, Markland and Vinland.* His brother, Thorvald, followed him and beached his longboat on a shore called 'Keelness' where he had the bad luck to be ambushed by local natives. In the fight which followed, Thorvald was the only Viking to die—killed by an arrow. The rest of his crew returned to base where their news did not dishearten other enthusiastic Greenlanders who wanted to settle in Vinland. According to the Norse sagas, one group 'took with them all kinds of livestock for it was their intention to colonize the country, if they could do so. . .'. They landed in Vinland, built a settlement and began trading with the natives whom they called 'Skraelings.' After three difficult winters and more than one fight with the Skraelings, the settlers had had enough. They abandoned their camp and returned to Greenland. After 1020 there are no more records of Viking colonies in North America. But it is very likely that those original settlers had penetrated as far south as what is today the eastern seaboard of the United States. And it is almost certain that Greenlanders continued to visit North America for supplies of tall timbers and furs. Two fascinating pieces of evidence exist: the Icelandic Annals state that in 1347 a Greenland ship sought shelter in an Icelandic harbour. The crew said they had been to Markland. And a few years ago, American historians discovered the controversial 'Vinland Map'. At first it was thought to be genuine—its date was assumed to be around 1450. However, scientific tests suggested it was a forgery and it is no longer thought that Columbus knew about the early Viking voyages.

The Spaniards in America

When Christopher Columbus sailed from Spain in 1492 his task was to 'discover and acquire islands and mainland in the Ocean Sea'. He reached the Canaries—then headed into the unknown. After 33 days he made landfall at San Salvador. Turning north, he discovered other islands and to his dying day—he made three other transatlantic voyages—maintained that he had found the short sea route to eastern Asia. Thousands of Spaniards followed him, seeking their fortune in the rich lands of the 'Indies' and over the next 70 years they carved out a vast empire in Central and South America. Gradually, their explorers edged northwards: in 1513 Juan de León led an expedition into Florida; in 1539 Hernando de Soto explored the lands east of the Mississippi; while in 1541 Francisco de Coronado entered the Great Plains to the west of the Mississippi and reported that vast numbers of 'cows'—presumably herds of buffalos—were roaming there. But it was a generation later before the first Spanish colony at St Augustine (1565) was founded in what is today the United States of America.

The American Indians

When the first Spanish explorers arrived, there were approximately half a million 'Indians' living in North America. They were quite unlike the image of the Redskin projected on our cinema and television screens in the twentieth century. American Indians were for the most part farmers. They had no horses. They lived in villages composed of timber and earthen huts—not wigwams—and had reached a cultural level roughly equivalent to the late neolithic period in British prehistory. The Indians could weave, make pottery and work copper and precious metals. They had well-defined social systems and could build huge temple mounds. Most tribes led a peaceful, settled, agricultural life though a few—notably the Apaches, Comanches and Kiowas—lived in the Plains and raided the Hopis. There was very little tradition of scalping or war bonnets except in the south-east where the fierce tribes of Creeks, Choctaws, Chickasaws and Cherokees were to be unrelenting enemies of the white man. The Spaniards made very little impression on the Indians—save in one important respect. They had brought horses with them across the Atlantic. Some escaped and multiplied on the Great Plains. The Apaches tamed them and were therefore ready to pounce on the white men when, many years later, settlers began to move westwards across America.

*Identified by some historians as Baffin Island, Labrador and Newfoundland.

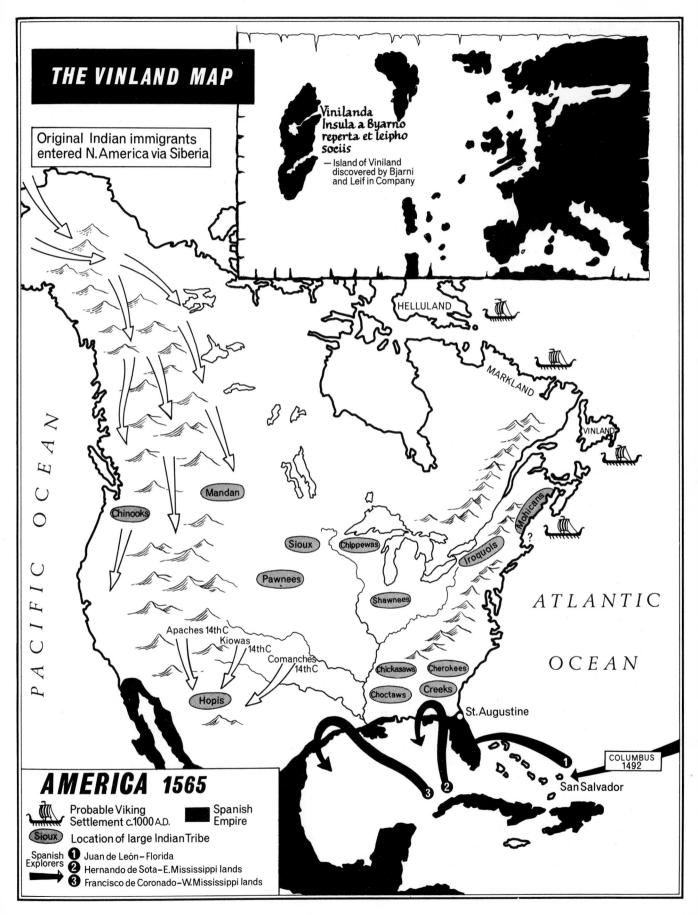

THE VINLAND MAP

Original Indian immigrants entered N.America via Siberia

Vinilanda Insula a Byarno reperta et leipho sociis
— Island of Viniland discovered by Bjarni and Leif in Company

HELLULAND

MARKLAND

VINLAND

PACIFIC OCEAN

ATLANTIC OCEAN

Chinooks

Mandan

Sioux

Chippewas

Mohicans

Iroquois

?

Pawnees

Shawnees

Apaches 14th C

Kiowas 14th C

Comanches 14th C

Chickasaws

Cherokees

Choctaws

Creeks

Hopis

St. Augustine

COLUMBUS 1492

San Salvador

1

2

3

AMERICA 1565

Probable Viking Settlement c.1000 A.D.

Spanish Empire

Sioux — Location of large Indian Tribe

Spanish Explorers
1 Juan de León – Florida
2 Hernando de Sota – E.Mississippi lands
3 Francisco de Coronado – W.Mississippi lands

2: The early settlers

The first of the English

At Sir Walter Raleigh's suggestion, 150 people settled on Roanoke Island in 1587. Four years passed by before the supply ships arrived; and by then not a single colonist was left. One had scratched the word 'Croatan' on a wall, but no-one has ever discovered what happened to them. The next band of settlers arrived in Chesapeake Bay during 1607. They were all employees of the Virginia Company (formed in 1606) and they were looking forward to a favourable site and a pleasant climate. They found neither: the Indians were hostile and malarial mosquitos infested the river banks. But they had a resourceful leader in Captain John Smith and he persuaded them to build a settlement at Jamestown. Slowly, they began to establish themselves. There was never enough food and the Indians were always dangerous. Then prospects improved when they found they could grow tobacco, a highly profitable cash crop. By 1627 they exported 500,000 lbs annually and the Company now simply acted as a sales distributor. The settlers were no longer mere Company servants. They were freemen with their own land—and it was this prospect of land ownership that attracted first hundreds and then thousands of English colonists. Families who could pay for the transatlantic voyage received 50 acres of land for each man, woman or child entering Virginia. Others came as 'indentured servants' prepared to serve their masters until they too could claim a share of freehold land. It could all be made to sound very attractive; and talk of seeking one's fortune in Virginia was commonplace in seventeenth century England.

The 'Pilgrim Fathers'

Everyone* was welcome in Virginia—including religious fanatics. One group of extremist Puritans had already broken away from the Anglican Church and lived in exile in Holland. The Virginia Company offered the exiles the chance of a better life in America and they crossed the Altantic in 1620. This group of settlers—later called the 'Pilgrim Fathers'—made landfall at Cape Cod, which was well to the north of their original objective. This did not deter them. They set up their base at Plymouth and solemnly agreed to '. . . *combine ourselves together into a body politic, for our better ordering and preservation . . . for the general good of the colony*.' This covenant became known as the 'Mayflower Compact'—named after their famous ship. As in Virginia, the first few years were difficult; but they survived. And because they wished to remain as congregations of their churches, the colonists in 'New England' did not try to expand far into the interior. They also had a healthy respect for a nearby colony of aggressive Dutchmen as well as for the Indians! So they tended to develop—just as the Spaniards did in the far south—a preference for an *urban* way of life. The New England settlers found a livelihood in trading and fishing. Moreover, as they were not simply trying to amass wealth, they set out to create something unique, something they could not built in England. First and foremost they wanted to see a people's commonwealth grow up in a spirit of religious unity, guided always by their own—rather bigoted—interpretation of Christian ideals. Therefore it is easy to see that the New England settlements were quite different in character from those further south—an important feature of English colonial life in Eastern America. Though they were all of the same culture and all spoke the same language, each colony was to develop its own individual attitudes towards life.

Rival settlements

After 1624 Dutch fur traders were operating in the Delaware valley and two years later a brand new port—New Amsterdam—was busily exporting the pelts to Holland. Nearby, Swedish troops, aided by labouring Finns, built Fort Christina by 1638. But this did not prosper and the Dutch absorbed the settlement in 1655. Yet even the Dutch, brilliant colonisers elsewhere in the world, were no match for the English. Charles II of England awarded the Dutch colony to his brother, the Duke of York, in 1664 and the small party of Dutch settlers could put up no effective resistance. This meant a change of name for New Amsterdam—which became New York. Much more dangerous were the ambitious French explorers operating out of their bases in Quebec and Montreal. They paddled across the Great Lakes and discovered the Mississippi River. In 1679 La Salle followed the river south until he sailed through the delta into the Gulf of Mexico. Within a short time his discovery would encourage the French, in alliance with the Spaniards, to conceive a plan to *outflank* the English coastal settlements and drive them into the sea.

*This was true of all the colonies throughout the seventeenth century—as a contemporary verse illustrates:
   'The Planter old did thus me greet,
   "Whether you come from jail or college,
   You're welcome to my certain knowledge . . ."'

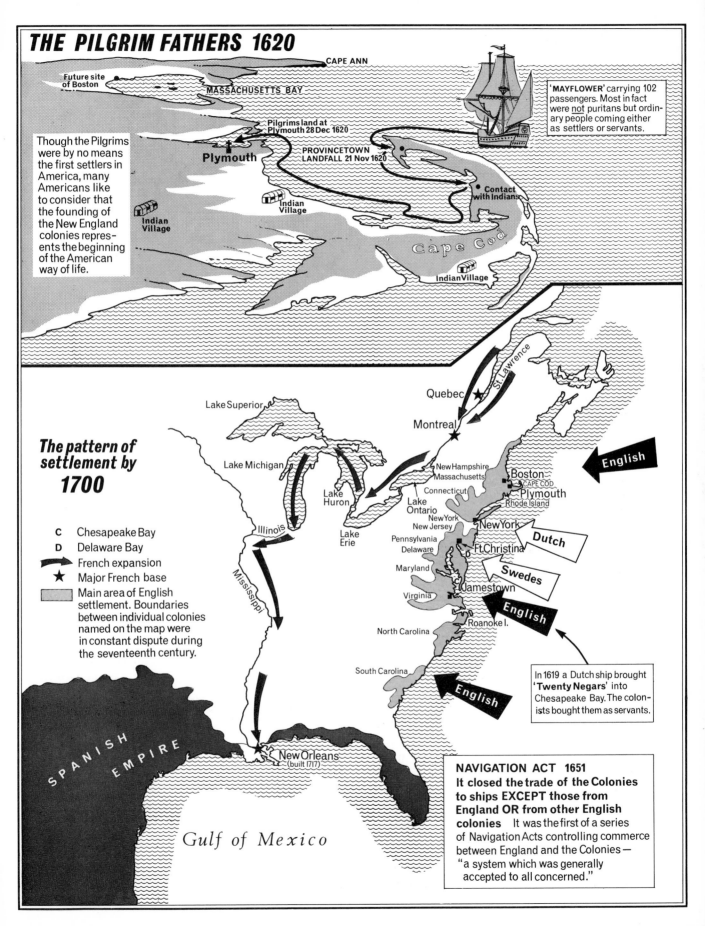

THE PILGRIM FATHERS 1620

CAPE ANN

Future site of Boston

MASSACHUSETTS BAY

'MAYFLOWER' carrying 102 passengers. Most in fact were not puritans but ordinary people coming either as settlers or servants.

Pilgrims land at Plymouth 28 Dec 1620

Plymouth

PROVINCETOWN LANDFALL 21 Nov 1620

Though the Pilgrims were by no means the first settlers in America, many Americans like to consider that the founding of the New England colonies represents the beginning of the American way of life.

Indian Village

Indian Village

Contact with Indians

Cape Cod

Indian Village

The pattern of settlement by 1700

Lake Superior

Quebec ★

St. Lawrence

Montreal ★

Lake Michigan

English

New Hampshire
Massachusetts

Boston
CAPE COD
Plymouth

Lake Huron

Connecticut

Rhode Island

Lake Ontario

New York
New Jersey

New York

Lake Erie

Illinois

Pennsylvania
Delaware

D Ft. Christina

Dutch

C   Chesapeake Bay
D   Delaware Bay
➤   French expansion
★   Major French base

   Main area of English settlement. Boundaries between individual colonies named on the map were in constant dispute during the seventeenth century.

Maryland

Swedes

C Jamestown

Virginia

English

North Carolina

Roanoke I.

Mississippi

South Carolina

English

In 1619 a Dutch ship brought **'Twenty Negars'** into Chesapeake Bay. The colonists bought them as servants.

SPANISH EMPIRE

New Orleans
(built 1717)

Gulf of Mexico

NAVIGATION ACT 1651
It closed the trade of the Colonies to ships EXCEPT those from England OR from other English colonies It was the first of a series of Navigation Acts controlling commerce between England and the Colonies — "a system which was generally accepted to all concerned."

3: The King's American Empire

The Thirteen Colonies

By 1750 the Hanoverian Kings of England ruled over thirteen colonies on the eastern American seaboard. Nearly two million colonists—including about 190,000 African Negro slaves—made up the 'American people' whose numbers increased with every boatload of immigrants sailing in from Europe. Colonists pushed inland until their farms, townships, forts and log-cabins were mushrooming in the Appalachian foothills. Here the Indians were often on the war-path but along the broad coastal fringe the people were now feeling reasonably secure. Most Americans worked on the land, in the lumbercamps and in the fishing and whaling fleets. Britain's Navigational Acts discouraged industrial enterprise so most merchants in Boston and New York exported primary products such as wheat, flax, hemp, cattle, horses, timber and furs in exchange for British manufactures. As few Americans desired factory jobs, the colonial economy depended upon agriculture supplemented by some profitable smuggling. Anyway, the *1750 Iron Act* banned new iron industries in America and though the colonial assemblies accepted this sort of legislation they simply turned a blind eye when an ambitious industrialist wanted to build a small factory. Most of these colonial assemblies—made up of successful planters and farmers, lawyers and merchants—were self-willed, accepting London's rule only when it coincided with their own interests. Nevertheless, they were perfectly willing to take advantage of Britain's expertise, as in the case of the Pennsylvania-Maryland border dispute. Two London astronomers, Charles Mason and Jeremiah Dixon, came to survey the disputed territory. Between 1763 and 1767 they mapped a new frontier, abandoning their task only when unfriendly Shawnees interfered. Two years later King George III ratified the 'Mason-Dixon Line'.

The French and Indian War

By 1756 the French and British were fighting battles all over the world in their struggle for imperial supremacy. Desultory fighting broke out even earlier in America when the French tried to move into the Ohio valley during 1751. George Washington, then a colonel in the Virginian army, tried to stem their advance but he and his men surrendered to the French at Fort Necessity in 1754. Next year the British sent in their regular troops but they died in an ambush set by the French and their Indian allies. So by 1756 the war—which the British called the Seven Years' War—was being fought in earnest. General Montcalm, the French commander, began his drive to push the colonists into the sea; the British retaliated by sending Generals Amherst and Wolfe to attack the French base at Quebec. There, at the *Heights of Abraham (1759)*, Wolfe defeated Montcalm and destroyed French power in North America. Quebec Province became a British colony and American settlers began to stream into former French territory, undeterred by a temporary setback in May 1763 when the Ottawa chief Pontiac led a short but savage rebellion against them.

Trouble over taxes

Meanwhile, the British government issued a *Royal Proclamation* (October 1763) temporarily forbidding colonial settlements beyond the crest of the Alleghanies. Though some settlers had already passed this point, the British wanted to stabilize their western frontier with the retreating Indians. This in turn raised a major policy problem: who would pay for the ten thousand men needed to police the new frontier territories? Not unreasonably they decided that taxpayers on both sides of the Atlantic could share the costs of basing extra troops in America. And while they were about it, they tightened the somewhat lax Navigation Laws so often flouted by the merchants of New England. *The 1764 Revenue Act* (sometimes called the Sugar Act) empowered revenue officers to collect sugar duties and to haul unwilling taxpayers before local admiralty courts. Next year the British introduced a *Stamp Act* to extend one of their own established taxes to the unenthusiastic Americans who now had to pay extra duty on newspapers, legal documents, cargo clearances and even on 'pub' licences. They tried to soften the blow by appointing Americans to supervise the collection of duty, but so violent was the outcry that every one of the stampmasters resigned. Wealthy members of a group called the *Sons of Liberty* organized protest up and down the colonies; while the colonial assemblies sent representatives to a 'Stamp Act Congress' in New York to denounce the stamp tax and the admiralty courts which they considered to be unconstitutional impositions. Soon the cry of 'No taxation without representation' (i.e. no representation in the Westminster Parliament*) was common and a wave of violence so surprised the British that they repealed the Stamp Act in 1766. However, they also passed a *Declaratory Act* which confirmed Parliament's right 'to make law . . . to bind the colonies and the peoples of America'. Rather than accept this principle the Americans would, in less than a decade, deliberately choose the path of revolution.

---

*In 1764 an American lawyer called James Otis claimed that Parliament had no right to tax unrepresented subjects . . . no more right than to 'make 2 and 2, 5 . . .' He was inaccurate in his view of the British Parliament as it then existed, but his sentiments captured plenty of American support.

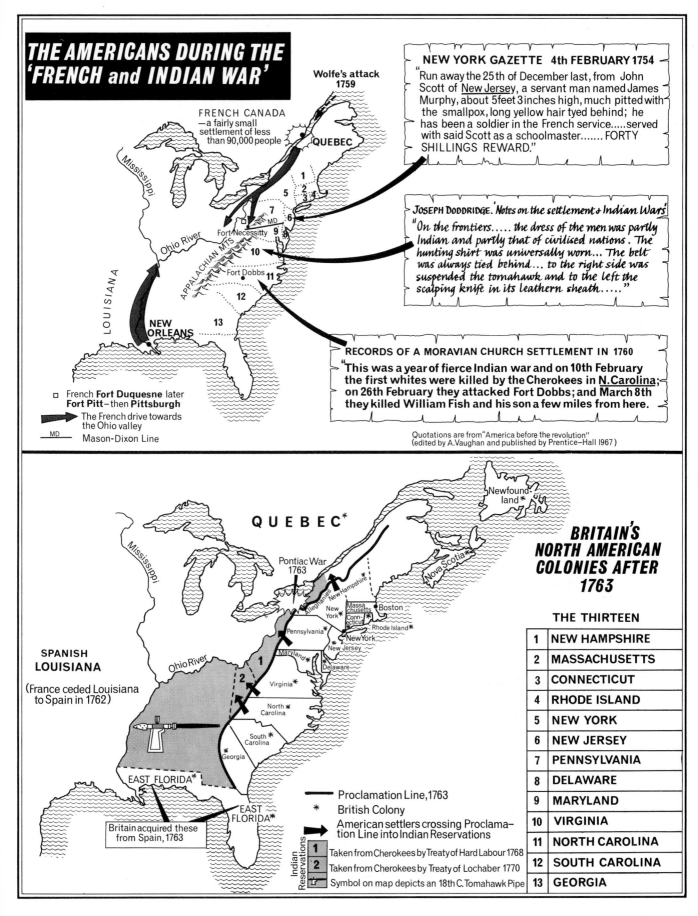

THE AMERICANS DURING THE 'FRENCH and INDIAN WAR'

Wolfe's attack 1759

FRENCH CANADA — a fairly small settlement of less than 90,000 people

QUEBEC

Mississippi

Ohio River

Fort Necessitty

APPALACHIAN MTS

Fort Dobbs

LOUISIANA

NEW ORLEANS

MD

□ French **Fort Duquesne** later **Fort Pitt** – then **Pittsburgh**

➤ The French drive towards the Ohio valley

—MD— Mason-Dixon Line

NEW YORK GAZETTE 4th FEBRUARY 1754

"Run away the 25th of December last, from John Scott of <u>New Jersey</u>, a servant man named James Murphy, about 5 feet 3 inches high, much pitted with the smallpox, long yellow hair tyed behind; he has been a soldier in the French service.....served with said Scott as a schoolmaster....... FORTY SHILLINGS REWARD."

JOSEPH DODDRIDGE. Notes on the settlement & Indian Wars

"On the frontiers..... the dress of the men was partly Indian and partly that of civilised nations. The hunting shirt was universally worn... The belt was always tied behind... to the right side was suspended the tomahawk and to the left the scalping knife in its leathern sheath....."

RECORDS OF A MORAVIAN CHURCH SETTLEMENT IN 1760

"This was a year of fierce Indian war and on 10th February the first whites were killed by the Cherokees in <u>N.Carolina</u>; on 26th February they attacked Fort Dobbs; and March 8th they killed William Fish and his son a few miles from here.

Quotations are from "America before the revolution"
(edited by A. Vaughan and published by Prentice–Hall 1967)

BRITAIN'S NORTH AMERICAN COLONIES AFTER 1763

QUEBEC*

Newfoundland *

Pontiac War 1763

Mississippi

Alleghanies

New Hampshire

Massachusetts

Boston

Nova Scotia *

New York

Connecticut

Rhode Island *

Pennsylvania *

New York

New Jersey

SPANISH LOUISIANA

(France ceded Louisiana to Spain in 1762)

Ohio River

Maryland *

Delaware

Virginia *

North Carolina *

South Carolina *

Georgia *

EAST FLORIDA *

EAST FLORIDA *

Britain acquired these from Spain, 1763

— Proclamation Line, 1763

* British Colony

➤ American settlers crossing Proclamation Line into Indian Reservations

Indian Reservations

1 Taken from Cherokees by Treaty of Hard Labour 1768

2 Taken from Cherokees by Treaty of Lochaber 1770

Symbol on map depicts an 18th C. Tomahawk Pipe

THE THIRTEEN

1	NEW HAMPSHIRE
2	MASSACHUSETTS
3	CONNECTICUT
4	RHODE ISLAND
5	NEW YORK
6	NEW JERSEY
7	PENNSYLVANIA
8	DELAWARE
9	MARYLAND
10	VIRGINIA
11	NORTH CAROLINA
12	SOUTH CAROLINA
13	GEORGIA

4: The American Revolution, 1775

The deeper issues

Most of the crises leading up to the American Revolt involved the rights and wrongs of taxing the settlers. Yet it was not simply the financial squabbles which made the colonists rebel. By 1775 there were more than $2\frac{1}{2}$ million Americans in the Thirteen Colonies. They were a tough, determined people; they had at the outset little sense of national unity but were perfectly willing to believe that the British Parliament was threatening both their wealth and their liberty. After all, it was the prospect of wealth and liberty that had attracted many of them to America in the first place. That was why they resented the Revenue Act, the Stamp Act, the Mutiny Act*; and that was why American leaders such as Sam Adams were able to fasten on the taxation issue as a means of changing resentment into something bigger—a sense of patriotism.

The growth of ill-will 1767–75

The British were nothing if not persistent. Quite unwittingly they aided the growth of American patriotism. Their Chancellor, Lord Townshend, tried to raise revenue in America during 1767 by taxing certain imported goods. But this simply boosted the American smuggling trade and forced the Royal Navy to step up its coastal patrols; in the ports the revenue officers became even more diligent. All of this created tension: merchants boycotted British goods; mobs tarred and feathered revenue officers; workers in Boston and New York came out on strike. By 1768 Boston was the worst trouble spot and, inevitably, the British stationed troops there. Before long, a mob provoked a patrol into opening fire and five patriots—including one Negro—died in the *Boston Massacre 1770*. Prime Minister Lord North agreed to repeal most of the Townshend duties, but retained the tax on tea. As smugglers brought in 90% of American tea the colonists didn't object to this. However, other incidents escalated the ill-will on both sides. In 1772 the British revenue schooner *Gaspée* had the bad luck to run aground off Providence. Out rowed a boatload of patriots who shot up the crew and set fire to the schooner. More trouble came in 1773 when Lord North permitted the East India Company to sell tea in America well below the price charged by the smugglers. More patriots boarded three tea ships berthed in Boston harbour and tipped the cargoes overboard. When Lord North heard about the 'Boston Tea Party' he resolved to coerce the citizens of Boston into submission. He shut down the port's trade with the *1774 Boston Port Act*: he dissolved the local assembly with the *1774 Massachusetts Government Act*; and he sent out General Gage to restore law and order within the turbulent colony.

Lexington, Concord and Bunker Hill 1775

General Gage arrived to find that his authority barely extended beyond Boston's city limits. Local farmers were forming a resistance movement; in September 1774 all the colonies except Georgia sent representatives to an illegal 'Continental Congress' in Philadelphia. While the Congress was in session, Paul Revere** rode in from Suffolk County with a resolution that the people there were going to disobey the British rules and regulations. Congress contemplated using force but emphasized that it was 'for the present only resolved to pursue . . . peaceful measures'. In fact, it was General Gage who took the initiative. In April 1775 intelligence reports stated that the patriots had hidden explosives in nearby Concord. Gage decided to destroy these and set out from Boston on the mission. When he reached Lexington Common the road was barred by American 'minutemen'. There was a skirmish and several Americans died. During the return march from Concord snipers killed or wounded 244 British troops. Next month the patriots captured two forts at Crown Point and Ticonderoga and in June they fought their spectacular battle on top of Breed's Hill at Charlestown. This engagement, against a large number of British regulars, is usually called the Battle of Bunker Hill 1775. Clearly, the revolution was in earnest. All thirteen colonies sent delegates to a second Continental Congress at Philadelphia where American leaders such as Sam and John Adams, Thomas Jefferson and George Washington came forward to create the army and navy that would fight and ultimately win the War of American Independence 1775–83.

*Passed in 1765 and sometimes called the Quartering Act. Disliked by the colonists because they had to provide 6000 British troops with barracks and food supplies.
**Paul Revere's most famous ride was in 1775 when he galloped out of Charlestown to warn the Lexington minute men that Gage's troops were approaching.

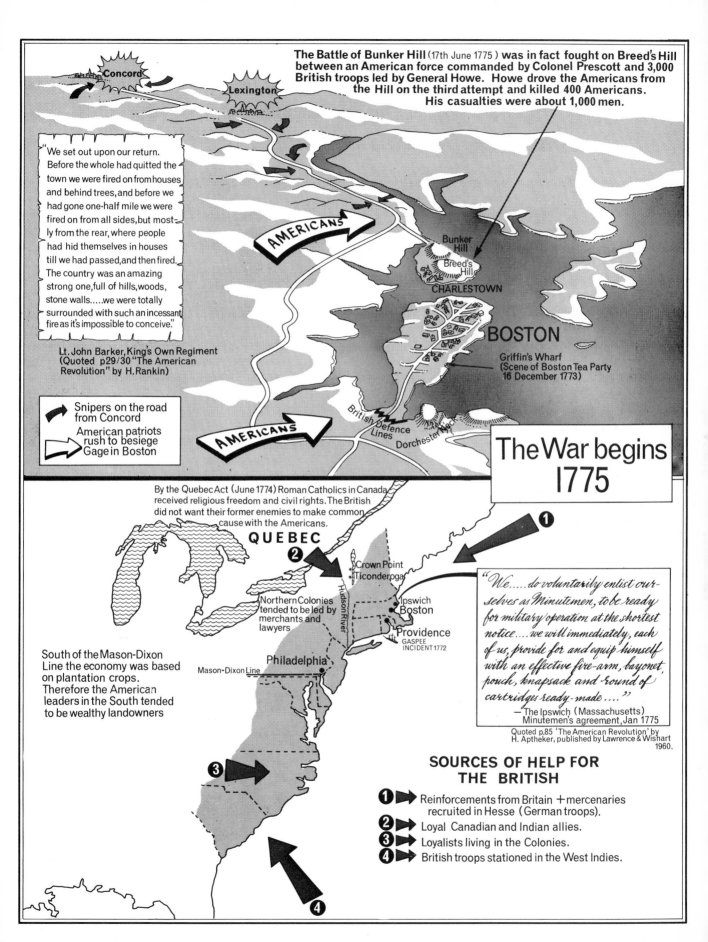

The Battle of Bunker Hill (17th June 1775) **was in fact fought on Breed's Hill between an American force commanded by Colonel Prescott and 3,000 British troops led by General Howe. Howe drove the Americans from the Hill on the third attempt and killed 400 Americans. His casualties were about 1,000 men.**

"We set out upon our return. Before the whole had quitted the town we were fired on from houses and behind trees, and before we had gone one-half mile we were fired on from all sides, but mostly from the rear, where people had hid themselves in houses till we had passed, and then fired. The country was an amazing strong one, full of hills, woods, stone walls.....we were totally surrounded with such an incessant fire as it's impossible to conceive."

Lt. John Barker, King's Own Regiment (Quoted p29/30 "The American Revolution" by H. Rankin)

Snipers on the road from Concord

American patriots rush to besiege Gage in Boston

Concord

Lexington

AMERICANS

AMERICANS

Bunker Hill

Breed's Hill

CHARLESTOWN

BOSTON

Griffin's Wharf (Scene of Boston Tea Party 16 December 1773)

British Defence Lines

Dorchester Neck

The War begins 1775

By the Quebec Act (June 1774) Roman Catholics in Canada received religious freedom and civil rights. The British did not want their former enemies to make common cause with the Americans.

QUEBEC

❷

Crown Point

Ticonderoga

Northern Colonies tended to be led by merchants and lawyers

Hudson River

Ipswich

Boston

Providence

GASPEE INCIDENT 1772

❶

South of the Mason-Dixon Line the economy was based on plantation crops. Therefore the American leaders in the South tended to be wealthy landowners

Mason-Dixon Line

Philadelphia

❸

"We.....do voluntarily enlist ourselves as Minutemen, to be ready for military operation at the shortest notice....we will immediately, each of us, provide for and equip himself with an effective fire-arm, bayonet, pouch, knapsack and round of cartridges ready-made...."

— The Ipswich (Massachusetts) Minutemen's agreement, Jan 1775

Quoted p.85 'The American Revolution' by H. Aptheker, published by Lawrence & Wishart 1960.

SOURCES OF HELP FOR THE BRITISH

❶ Reinforcements from Britain + mercenaries recruited in Hesse (German troops).

❷ Loyal Canadian and Indian allies.

❸ Loyalists living in the Colonies.

❹ British troops stationed in the West Indies.

❹

Further Reading

Theme 1 – Starting Points

Spread

1. The first white men
2. The European settlements

3. The Thirteen Colonies

4. Revolution 1775

The Vikings, Gwyn Jones, OUP, 1968
The Golden Door, Roger Thompson, Allman & Son, 1969
The American Revolution, H. Aptheker, Lawrence and Wishart, 1960
The American War of Independence, Peter Wells, ULP, 1967

THEME 2

Imperial Power and Democracy

By 1787 the Americans had thrown off British rule, established world-wide trading contacts and created a unique form of republican government on a continental scale. They had always been great traders and with their first-class merchant marine and an audacious navy (an elusive foe, as the British would discover in the War of 1812) they brought home cargoes from ports as far apart as China and the Mediterranean. They settled along the Pacific seaboard before they had fully explored the interior or tamed the 'Wild West'. And they attracted immigrants escaping from the poverty endemic in Central Europe and Ireland. 'Amerika, du hast es besser', wrote Goethe in 1831. Millions agreed and swarmed across the Atlantic to seek happiness in the 'land of the free'.

But not all men were free. Every year the number of Negro slaves increased; every year the United States moved closer towards a grave political crisis. Men who favoured the 'peculiar institution' based their spurious arguments on a belief in the racial inferiority of black people. Those who disagreed sought to abolish slavery absolutely. Yet the problem seemed to defy any sort of democratic solution. Until 1850 Northern and Southern politicians compromised by admitting equal numbers of *free* and *slave* states into the Union. Then the 1854 Kansas-Nebraska Act, which allowed settlers to make the decision whether to permit slavery in the new territory, provoked open warfare between rival groups in 'Bleeding Kansas'. Finally, in 1857, the Supreme Court destroyed the artificial balance between *free* and *slave* states with its famous decision in the Dred Scott case. Scott was a slave whose master had taken him into Illinois, where slavery was illegal. Scott therefore claimed to be free. But the Supreme Court not only decided that Dred Scott would be a slave forever; it ruled that any law limiting slavery—such as the 1820 Compromise*—was unconstitutional. This meant that the entire democratic structure of America was at risk; or, as Lincoln put it, a house divided against itself would not stand.

Civil War between the North and South began in 1861. Though it was fought by the North to preserve the Union and not to abolish slavery, Lincoln adopted the cause of abolition in 1863 for political reasons. Victory for his side resulted in the destruction of the South and the end of slavery—'the Negro became a freedman but not a free man'.** Now the nation had to recover from the vicissitudes of war and, in technological and commercial terms if not in human terms, it did this remarkably quickly. By the beginning of the twentieth century, the United States had overtaken both Britain and Germany in steel production and had acquired the trappings of contemporary imperial power. The American people had revealed an astonishing capacity for reconstruction and progress.

*See page 24.
**P. 12 *The History of the Negro in the United States* Alan Conway (Historical Association, 1968).

5: The American War of Independence, 1775–1783

Commonsense and Independence

In January 1776 a British emigrant named Tom Paine published an emotion-charged piece of propaganda entitled 'Commonsense'. Paine argued that the cause of America's troubles was that 'royal brute' in England— King George III. Though the reasons he gave were far from sound, they were enough to persuade the colonists to demand their independence. Within a matter of weeks, Thomas Jefferson was busily drafting a revolutionary document, America's Declaration of Independence. In this unanimous 'Declaration of the Thirteen United States of America' (4 July 1776), Jefferson listed the complaints, ambitions and beliefs of the American people—most of whom approved the words he used. They went wild with delight in New York but, even as they celebrated, a huge fleet nosed into the Narrows that separate Long Island from Staten Island. Dozens of troopships disgorged thousands of British redcoats under the command of General Howe. As they gazed at their foe from the banks of the Hudson River, the American rebels must have wondered what chance they had against the armed might of Great Britain.

The fighting on land

'English Mastiffs be not scar'd at the Barking of American Curs': the redcoats had very little respect for the rabble that opposed them. George Washington, commander of the American forces, knew that his troops were 'a people in arms' and not a professional army. He would have to devise tactics to tempt the redcoats inland where they would be easy prey for his guerrilla fighters. But for the time being, he could only glare at Howe across the Narrows. Then Howe attacked and defeated Washington at the *Battle of Long Island*. Washington retaliated on Boxing Day 1776 and won the *Battle of Trenton*. Skirmishes such as these proved nothing: Howe was planning a series of elaborate flanking movements along America's east coast. One depended on General Burgoyne's 9,500 troops stationed in Canada. These moved south during 1777 but soon ran into trouble. Burgoyne survived two battles at *Freeman's Farm* but, with his forces down to less than 5000 men, soon found himself surrounded at *Saratoga*. Here he surrendered to the American General Gates on 17 October 1777. This disaster at Saratoga persuaded the French to form an open alliance with the Americans in 1778; while in 1779 the Spaniards also joined in the war against Britain. Yet there was relatively little fighting. Washington's army holed up at Valley Forge where it endured a harsh winter and the even harsher tongue of Baron von Steuben, a highly efficient training officer from Germany. The months passed by with no decisive action; though the Comte de Rochambeau arrived with 8000 French troops while Admiral de Grasse sailed in with 36 ships of the line. 1781 saw a combined Franco-American attack upon British troops in Virginia. The British fell back on *Yorktown* where, outnumbered by the enemy and threatened in the rear by de Grasse's fleet, they had no option but to surrender on 19 October 1781. Though there were other British forces in America, the American Revolution had in effect succeeded. Britain lost the war on the land because of her brief but conclusive failure to command the sea.

The war at sea

Yet the British had managed to rule the waves for most of the war. The Royal Navy patrolled American coastal waters and captured scores of blockade runners. The tiny American navy—equipped with some very fast and well-armed frigates—was usually helpless. It did inflict some damage, though. John Paul Jones, another British emigrant, commanded a small force of warships that raided the British coasts and defeated a British flotilla off *Flamborough Head* during the evening of 23 September 1779. But the moment of truth in the naval war was undoubtedly 1781. The Royal Navy was trying to discourage a French cross-Channel invasion and at the same time holding off a Spanish attack upon Gibraltar. It hadn't enough ships to contain de Grasse's fleet at the crucial moment of Yorktown. The following year saw the main combat area shift from America to the West Indies. Admiral Rodney intercepted de Grasse at the *Battle of the Saints* (April 1782), outfought the French warships and in the process managed to capture the French Admiral.

Peace: the Treaty of Versailles 1783

1782 had seen the fall of Lord North in Britain. Lord Shelburne replaced him and negotiated the Peace Treaty of Versailles during 1783. Britain ceded Florida to Spain but kept her colonies in Canada and the West Indies. In return, she recognized the independence of the Thirteen United States of America. So the colonists had won by force of arms the independence they had demanded in 1776. Their victory meant that they could now set off in 'pursuit of happiness', though nearly two hundred years would pass before even the majority of Americans managed to catch up with it.

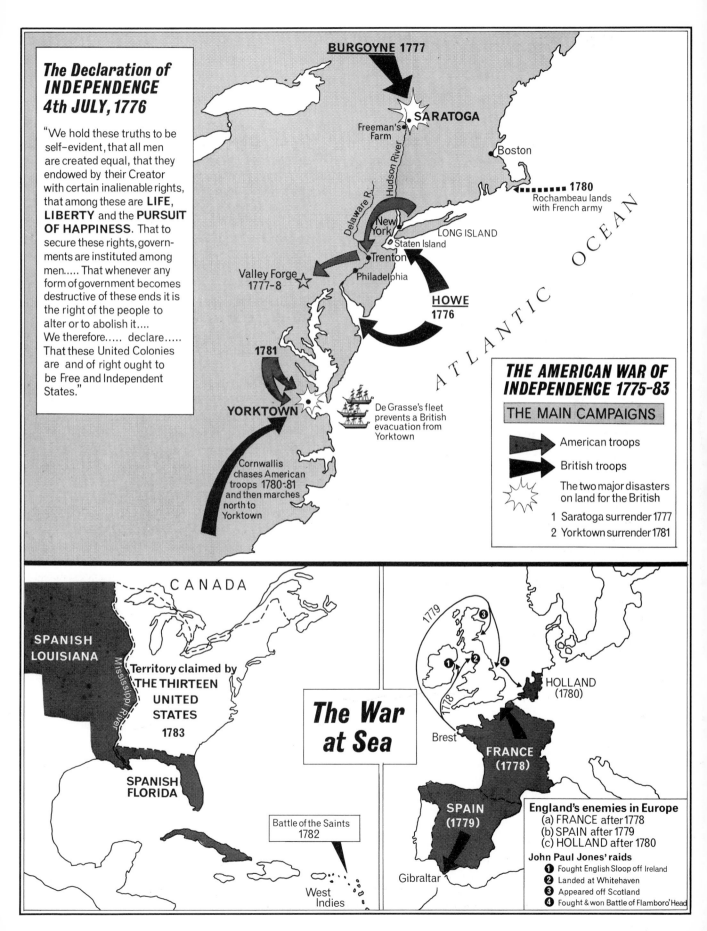

The Declaration of INDEPENDENCE 4th JULY, 1776

"We hold these truths to be self-evident, that all men are created equal, that they endowed by their Creator with certain inalienable rights, that among these are **LIFE**, **LIBERTY** and the **PURSUIT OF HAPPINESS**. That to secure these rights, governments are instituted among men..... That whenever any form of government becomes destructive of these ends it is the right of the people to alter or to abolish it....
We therefore..... declare..... That these United Colonies are and of right ought to be Free and Independent States."

BURGOYNE 1777

SARATOGA

Freeman's Farm

Boston

Hudson River

1780
Rochambeau lands with French army

Delaware R.

New York

LONG ISLAND

Staten Island

Trenton

Valley Forge 1777-8

Philadelphia

HOWE 1776

1781

ATLANTIC OCEAN

YORKTOWN

De Grasse's fleet prevents a British evacuation from Yorktown

Cornwallis chases American troops 1780-81 and then marches north to Yorktown

THE AMERICAN WAR OF INDEPENDENCE 1775-83

THE MAIN CAMPAIGNS

➡ American troops

➡ British troops

✴ The two major disasters on land for the British
1 Saratoga surrender 1777
2 Yorktown surrender 1781

CANADA

SPANISH LOUISIANA

Mississippi River

Territory claimed by THE THIRTEEN UNITED STATES 1783

SPANISH FLORIDA

Battle of the Saints 1782

West Indies

The War at Sea

1779

1778

③

HOLLAND (1780)

Brest

FRANCE (1778)

SPAIN (1779)

Gibraltar

England's enemies in Europe
(a) FRANCE after 1778
(b) SPAIN after 1779
(c) HOLLAND after 1780
John Paul Jones' raids
① Fought English Sloop off Ireland
② Landed at Whitehaven
③ Appeared off Scotland
④ Fought & won Battle of Flamboro' Head

6: The United States of America

The Union

During 1781 the Americans had drawn up their 'Articles of Confederation' to provide a working form of government in the midst of their struggle for independence. Now the war was over and many Americans paid scant respect to their new Confederation. Some states went their own way so that open rivalry replaced the wartime unity. They argued over state boundaries, refused to pay taxes and imposed taxes on all sorts of commercial activities. New York taxed New Jersey's ships; New Jersey promptly slapped a tax on New York's lighthouses; there was even a rebellion during 1786–87 when Daniel Shay led a band of desperate farmers who stood to lose their land if they couldn't meet their tax demands. Some form of central government would have to sort these matters out; otherwise the title 'Thirteen United States' would become a mockery and the freedoms for which so many Americans had died would be squandered. Benjamin Franklin, who had worked so hard to bring France into the war, remarked that 'when a broad table is to be made and the edges of the planks do not fit, the artist takes a little from each and makes a good joint'. The Thirteen States saw the point; their delegates assembled in Philadelphia where they agreed that each state must sacrifice some of its sovereign powers for the good of the American Union. In this mood, they created in 1787 the constitution of the 'United States of America'. Their country would be a Republic. Each member state would send elected congressmen to a *House of Representatives* and elected senators to a *Senate*. Together they would form a legislative assembly called *Congress*. Executive power would be in the hands of an elected *President*—in this way the legislative and executive powers of the Republic would be quite separate. In the event of dispute, there could be an appeal to a *Supreme Court* where judges would reach a verdict based upon a study of the supreme arbiter—the *written constitution* of the United States.

The people

George Washington was America's first President. He served two terms of office from 1789 until he retired in 1797. He was a legend in his own lifetime—the man who steered the colonists to victory in war and then guided them through the first difficult years of peace. For America inherited a host of problems and most people enjoyed very little improvement in their lives. Half a million American Negroes were still slaves. Some had slipped away on British ships; others escaped to states that had no love for slavery; a few won their freedom by joining the American army. They were the lucky ones. By 1790 the slave states imported enough slaves from Africa to replenish their stocks of cheap labour. Less tragic was the fate of the Loyalists—colonists who remained loyal to George III. They lost their lands and fled abroad and this meant that the USA lost about 60,000 of its wealthiest and most talented people. Almost everybody suffered from the post-war depression. The British closed the West Indies to American merchants who, before their rebellion, had sold their timber and grain products there. Other merchants found that Britain refused to buy fish and whale-oil from them. Fortunately, these setbacks were temporary. By 1790, when America's population reached 4 million people, trade began to prosper, new manufactures began and the movement westwards was once more in full swing.

The west

By 1783, the Spaniards blocked any American expansion across the Mississippi while Indian tribes such as the Shawnee and Piankashaw contested any attempts to settle north of the Ohio. In 1791 the Indians defeated one expedition led by General St. Clair. But their triumph was shortlived. It was their turn to suffer defeat in 1794 when 'Mad Anthony' Wayne won the Battle of Fallen Timbers. Now the Indians had no option but to concede a large tract of the North-West by the Treaty of Greenville (1795). Yet this was by no means America's most spectacular gain in this period. Her next acquisition was Louisiana which she secured without any bloodshed. Spain had secretly ceded Louisiana to France during some protracted negotiations 1800–1801; but within two years this vast territory had become a positive embarrassment to Napoleon, poised as he was on the brink of war with not only Britain but half of Europe as well. He therefore agreed to sell the territory to President Thomas Jefferson who paid just over $15,000,000 for the 'Louisiana Purchase'. For about 3 cents an acre Jefferson had doubled the size of the USA! Simultaneously, Jefferson authorized two explorers, Meriwether Lewis* and William Clark, to seek a route across Louisiana to the Pacific. Following the course of the Missouri River, they built a base at Fort Mandan and then pushed on through the rocky lands of the Flat Head and Nez Percé Indians. They reached the Columbia River and arrived on the Pacific coast in November 1805 after a journey lasting well over eighteen months.

*He had been Jefferson's Private Secretary between 1801 and 1803.

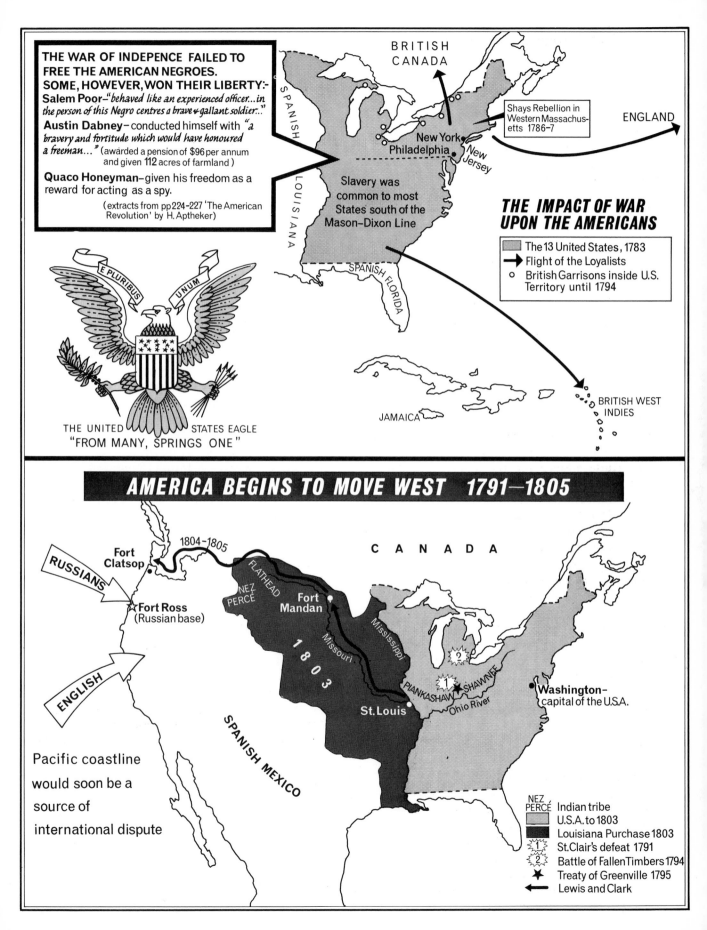

THE WAR OF INDEPENCE FAILED TO
FREE THE AMERICAN NEGROES.
SOME, HOWEVER, WON THEIR LIBERTY:-
Salem Poor–*"behaved like an experienced officer...in the person of this Negro centres a brave & gallant soldier..."*
Austin Dabney–conducted himself with *"a bravery and fortitude which would have honoured a freeman..."* (awarded a pension of $96 per annum and given 112 acres of farmland)
Quaco Honeyman–given his freedom as a reward for acting as a spy.
(extracts from pp 224-227 'The American Revolution' by H. Aptheker)

BRITISH CANADA

Shays Rebellion in Western Massachus-etts 1786-7

ENGLAND

New York
Philadelphia
New Jersey

SPANISH LOUISIANA

Slavery was common to most States south of the Mason–Dixon Line

SPANISH FLORIDA

THE IMPACT OF WAR UPON THE AMERICANS

The 13 United States, 1783
➤ Flight of the Loyalists
○ British Garrisons inside U.S. Territory until 1794

E PLURIBUS UNUM

THE UNITED STATES EAGLE
"FROM MANY, SPRINGS ONE"

JAMAICA

BRITISH WEST INDIES

AMERICA BEGINS TO MOVE WEST 1791–1805

Fort Clatsop
1804–1805
CANADA

RUSSIANS
★ Fort Ross (Russian base)

FLATHEAD
NEZ PERCE
Fort Mandan

ENGLISH

1803
Missouri
Mississippi

SPANISH MEXICO

St. Louis

PIANKASHAW
① SHAWNEE
Ohio River
②

Washington- capital of the U.S.A.

Pacific coastline would soon be a source of international dispute

NEZ PERCÉ Indian tribe
U.S.A. to 1803
Louisiana Purchase 1803
① St. Clair's defeat 1791
② Battle of Fallen Timbers 1794
★ Treaty of Greenville 1795
◀— Lewis and Clark

7: The War of 1812

The Chesapeake Incident 1807

Aboard the USS *Chesapeake*, one of America's 38 gun frigates, the crew was relaxed and content. It was mid-June and their destination was a patrol station in the Mediterranean. In the distance appeared HMS *Leopard*, a British frigate. First it shadowed them and then urged them to heave-to. Then came the command: 'Surrender all deserters!' When the Americans refused, the *Leopard*, opened fire. With three dead and many wounded, the US skipper struck his flag and handed over four protesting deserters. HMS *Leopard* then sailed away.

Causes of war

This incident highlighted lots of problems facing the USA. Ever since 1803 Britain and France had been locked in the Napoleonic Wars. In 1806 Napoleon swore to starve out the British by publishing his *Berlin Decrees*. The Royal Navy, backed by the 1807 *Orders in Council*, promptly blockaded Napoleon's Continental coastline. Woe betide any US ship that tried to beat the blockade, for neither Britain nor France respected the rights of neutral countries. France seized scores of US vessels. So did Britain, but she also added the indignity of impressing captured seaman to replace the thousands of British sailors who had deserted the foul conditions found aboard ships in the Atlantic fleets. And as the British were none too particular about whom they impressed an incident such as the *Chesapeake* affair could easily spark off trouble. Yet there were even deeper issues at stake. Many Americans resented their present lack of economic independence. British frigates were everywhere, denying Americans their freedom of trade.* Why not take Canada from the British? It would not only act as a lever to force the British to relax their blockade; it might reduce any Canadian tendency to stir up Indian trouble east of the Mississippi. So lots of Americans were 'War Hawks', supporting a war against Britain. However, Congress tried to resolve these complex issues peacefully. It imposed an embargo on British and French goods; then it tried to dissuade US merchants from trading with the belligerents. But when these tactics failed, President James Madison asked Congress to declare war on Britain. Ironically, the British repealed their *Orders in Council* on 16 June 1812. But the Americans did not know this. They were three thousand miles away and declared war two days later.

The War 1812–1814

The Americans had deliberately taken on the strongest navy in the world. They had to beat the Atlantic blockade, protect their whalers and merchantmen in the Pacific, intercept British convoys en route to Quebec and, simultaneously, run the risk of battle with the convoy escorts. The *Chesapeake* managed to break out of Boston and then had the bad luck to meet HMS *Shannon* which overpowered the US ship and towed it to Halifax! But the USS *Constitution* defeated HMS *Guerrière* in a fight off the St. Lawrence. Similar sea battles took place elsewhere in the Atlantic, in the Pacific and even around the coasts of Britian; in the end the Royal Navy drove the Americans from the seas and exposed the US coastline to amphibious attack. On land, the war was a battle for the frontiers. Most of the fighting occurred around the Great Lakes where the Americans took control of Lake Erie and burnt York—later named Toronto. Britain retaliated by attacking American forts before launching a seaborne assault upon Washington (1814) where they burnt the Capitol, the White House and other public buildings. A second force fought and lost the *Battle of New Orleans* where 700 British troops died in vain—the war was already over!

The Peace

Britain and America signed the Peace of Ghent on Christmas Eve 1814. They agreed to restore the 1812 frontiers; the USA secured a small stretch of Spanish Florida. It seemed an inconsequential peace. In fact, the War of 1812 had a profound effect upon American thought and attitudes. American leaders realized that it was vital to reach a friendly understanding with Canada—nobody could defend such a long frontier; equally important was the need to work *with* rather than *against* British naval power. Therefore America's first taste of international warfare forced her to create a foreign policy which, for the next hundred years, would allow her to enjoy both the profits of commercial expansion and a sense of security. For both she would be in considerable debt to Britain and the Royal Navy.

*There was no unity among Americans on this point. After all, Britain was fighting for survival. She could hardly be sympathetic to a selfish American trading policy. This was why some New England states would not support the war and tried to keep on trading with Britain. Some even went so far (at the 1814 Hartford Convention) to talk about breaking up the American Union on this point!

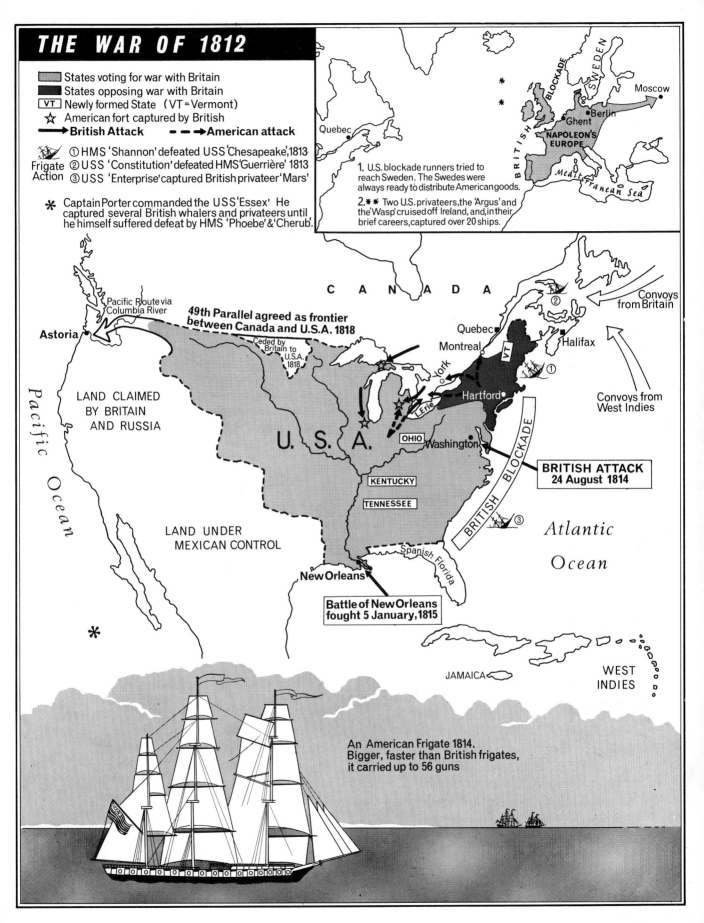

THE WAR OF 1812

States voting for war with Britain
States opposing war with Britain
VT Newly formed State (VT = Vermont)
★ American fort captured by British
→ **British Attack** - - → **American attack**

Frigate Action
① HMS 'Shannon' defeated USS 'Chesapeake', 1813
② USS 'Constitution' defeated HMS 'Guerrière' 1813
③ USS 'Enterprise' captured British privateer 'Mars'

∗ Captain Porter commanded the USS 'Essex' He captured several British whalers and privateers until he himself suffered defeat by HMS 'Phoebe' & 'Cherub'.

Quebec

SWEDEN
BRITISH BLOCKADE
Moscow
Berlin
Ghent
NAPOLEON'S EUROPE
Mediterranean Sea

1. U.S. blockade runners tried to reach Sweden. The Swedes were always ready to distribute American goods.

2. ∗∗ Two U.S. privateers, the 'Argus' and the 'Wasp' cruised off Ireland, and, in their brief careers, captured over 20 ships.

C A N A D A

Convoys from Britain

Pacific Route via Columbia River

49th Parallel agreed as frontier between Canada and U.S.A. 1818

Quebec
Montreal
VT
Halifax

Astoria

Ceded by Britain to U.S.A. 1818

York
②
X ①

Convoys from West Indies

Pacific Ocean

LAND CLAIMED BY BRITAIN AND RUSSIA

Hartford

L.Erie

U. S. A.

OHIO
Washington

BRITISH ATTACK 24 August 1814

BRITISH BLOCKADE

KENTUCKY

LAND UNDER MEXICAN CONTROL

TENNESSEE

③

Atlantic

Ocean

Spanish Florida

New Orleans

Battle of New Orleans fought 5 January, 1815

∗

JAMAICA

WEST INDIES

An American Frigate 1814. Bigger, faster than British frigates, it carried up to 56 guns

8: An empire of commerce

The Asian trade

In 1784, just one year after their War of Independence had ended, the Americans began to found an empire of trade in the Orient. Optimistically named the *Empress of China*, a converted privateer sailed out of New York harbour bound for Canton. In her hold was a cargo of furs, lead bars and ginseng.* Within a year she was back with a rich consignment of chinaware, spices, tea and silks—and a cool profit of $38,000. Other ships followed to lay the foundations of a commercial empire in the east; yet it was not to be the work of settlers and colonists. Instead it was built by intrepid sailors and hard-headed businessmen whose trade with the east began long before the pioneers' wagon-trains had even reached the Pacific coastline, long before the central land mass of America had been fully explored. It was no easy task to build up this Asian trade. It took the Americans sixty years to reach a formal trade relationship with the reluctant and suspicious Chinese. Even so, by the 1844 Wanghia Treaty the Americans made a better deal with the Chinese than had any of the other 'foreign devils' from Europe. By 1850 many American merchants and missionaries were at work on the Chinese mainland.

The Mediterranean trade

Barbary coast pirates infested the Mediterranean at the beginning of the nineteenth century. Already the USA had tried to buy protection for its merchantmen by negotiating expensive treaties with the North Africans. But one of them, the Bashaw of Tripoli, repudiated his treaty in 1801 and began raiding the American trade routes. He even captured a frigate— the USS *Philadelphia*—and towed it into Tripoli Harbour. President Jefferson sent out a fleet and a force of marines. The marines attacked Tripoli Harbour in 1804 and set fire to the *Philadelphia*—a show of force which soon persuaded the Bashaw to respect his treaty obligations.**

Japan

Meanwhile, the Asian trade suffered from the sheer distances involved. Designed for transatlantic routes, the new steamships would have to carry far more coal than cargo in order to cross the Pacific. This was one reason why Commodore Perry made his famous expedition to Japan in 1853; if he could persuade the Japanese to open up coaling-stations then America's profits from the Asian trade might well increase. Though the Japanese had never seen steamers before they were not over-awed by Perry's 'Black Ships'. So he sailed away to return the next year with warships. Though the Japanese had no wish to trade with the US they had even less desire to become a Russian colony; and as a Russian naval squadron had visited Japan in 1853, they decided to let Perry have the use of Hakodate and Shimoda in exchange for whisky and guns.

Securing the Pacific coastline

As America pursued her varied trading contacts she became aware that other nations shared her interest in the Pacific coastline. Britain coveted the Oregon territory. Not until 1846 would she accept the extension of the 49th Parallel as the frontier between Canada and the USA. Russia also pressed her claims in this area; already she had whaling crews and fur trappers based in California. In 1821 the Tsar claimed the Pacific coastline as far south as the 51st Parallel. President Monroe retorted with his famous doctrine: no European power had any right to colonize the American hemisphere. Britain sided with the President over this matter and the Tsar backed down in 1824. But to secure control of California the Americans had to resort to war. President Polk deliberately created a 'border incident' on the Rio Grande in 1846; he ordered American troopers to provoke Mexican fire so that he could inform Congress that Mexico 'had invaded our territory and shed American blood on American soil'. Congress declared war and US forces began their attacks. From the Pacific an amphibious force captured California. US marines marched on Mexico City and gazed in awe on the Halls of Montezuma. By 1848 the Mexicans had no alternative but to surrender and make massive territorial concessions to the USA. Polk argued that California would bring 'vast benefits to the USA, to the commercial world and . . . to mankind'. It certainly did. Within a year there occurred the great Californian gold strike and thousands of 'Forty-niners' swarmed in to seek their fortunes.

*Ginseng: a root found in eastern American forests. Believed (quite wrongly) by the Chinese to be a cure for most diseases.
**The USS *Chesapeake* was in fact sailing to take up her patrol station off North Africa when, in 1807, the British frigate *Leopard* intercepted her. See Page 16.

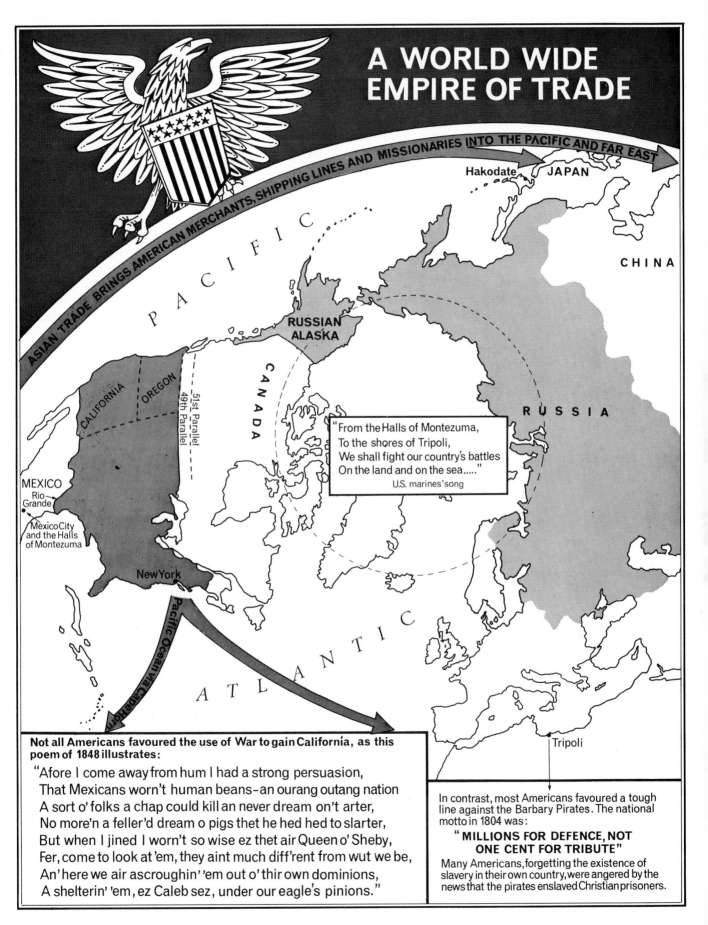

A WORLD WIDE EMPIRE OF TRADE

ASIAN TRADE BRINGS AMERICAN MERCHANTS, SHIPPING LINES AND MISSIONARIES INTO THE PACIFIC AND FAR EAST

Hakodate JAPAN

CHINA

PACIFIC

RUSSIAN ALASKA

CANADA

CALIFORNIA

OREGON

51st Parallel
49th Parallel

RUSSIA

"From the Halls of Montezuma,
To the shores of Tripoli,
We shall fight our country's battles
On the land and on the sea....."
U.S. marines' song

MEXICO
Rio Grande

Mexico City
and the Halls
of Montezuma

New York

Pacific Ocean via Cape Horn

ATLANTIC

Tripoli

Not all Americans favoured the use of War to gain California, as this poem of 1848 illustrates:

"Afore I come away from hum I had a strong persuasion,
That Mexicans won't human beans – an ourang outang nation
A sort o' folks a chap could kill an never dream on't arter,
No more'n a feller'd dream o pigs thet he hed hed to slarter,
But when I jined I worn't so wise ez thet air Queen o' Sheby,
Fer, come to look at 'em, they aint much diff'rent from wut we be,
An' here we air ascroughin' 'em out o' thir own dominions,
A shelterin' 'em, ez Caleb sez, under our eagle's pinions."

In contrast, most Americans favoured a tough line against the Barbary Pirates. The national motto in 1804 was:

"MILLIONS FOR DEFENCE, NOT ONE CENT FOR TRIBUTE"

Many Americans, forgetting the existence of slavery in their own country, were angered by the news that the pirates enslaved Christian prisoners.

19

9: A changing land

A new home market

American merchants* were making fortunes out of foreign commerce well before the War of 1812. New York, Philadelphia, Baltimore and Boston were now busy centres of expanding population where merchant families followed a life style very similar to that of their British counterparts. They built impressive houses in select suburbs well away from the labouring poor. They installed sanitation and the new gaslighting. And then they set about producing the manufactured goods for sale to the settlers out west. Of course, the pioneers could build their own houses and make their own clothes. In fact, the period 1820–1850 actually saw an *increase* in domestic industry. But the frontiersmen had to send east for the new ploughs and reapers and for the millions of nails so vital for construction work. In exchange, they offered their produce. Trundling across the Alleghanies came the big 'Conestoga wagons', each one holding up to two tons of grain. Trade soon forged a firm link between the well-established coastal settlements and the fast-growing population of the interior. These circumstances created a demand for better communications so that from the beginning the American people were in the forefront of the nineteenth century's transport revolution.

Roads and canals

One American politician observed in 1817 that 'We are greatly and rapidly growing ... Let us, then, bind the Republic together with a perfect system of roads and canals'. A few canals and turnpikes already existed. Engineers completed the Cumberland Road in 1818; seven years later the remarkable Erie Canal linked Buffalo with New York; and a horde of puffing steam-boats plied their trade along the coast and river systems of the eastern states. Many canal operators showed a quick profit on their investment and their success led to a wave of 'canal mania'—just as there had been in Britain. By 1840 the Americans had built more than 3,500 miles of canals. When the weather was good the canal boats took most of the freight away from the Conestoga wagons; but snow and ice could render them useless for several months of the year. Steamboats were rather more flexible. You could travel from Pittsburgh to New Orleans for 45 dollars in 1840; and if you travelled on a boat owned by the business tycoon Cornelius Vanderbilt you enjoyed splendid comfort as well as reliability. Unfortunately, rivers did not always run in the desired direction and it was not long before Americans sought to build an efficient railroad system.

The railroads

On Christmas Day 1830 a steam locomotive named *The Best Friend of Charleston* hauled 141 passengers on a scheduled trip in South Carolina. Over the next ten years most states in the Union acquired locomotives—some imported from Britain, others made in the USA. There were plenty of investors in America and Britain ready to put up the cash so that engineers could surmount the technical and physical difficulties facing railway builders in the USA. American engineers disliked the heavy British engines and gradually introduced important modifications such as swivelling bogie wheels, cow-catchers, sandboxes, whistles, headlights and bells. The legendary Davy Crockett** rode in a locomotive during 1836 and was amazed by its speed. American designers boosted the power of their engines; one, William Norris, was selling his engines as far afield as Austria. By 1860 the steam locomotive had acquired its characteristic silhouette and was pulling a variety of carriages and freight cars—including sleeping cars designed by George M. Pullman. The railroads were ready to open up America. Not everyone was enthusiastic. Farmers pointed out that the cowcatchers usually killed the cow; when one group of Michigan farmers failed to secure adequate compensation for their losses, they put grease on the tracks and set fire to the local rail depot.

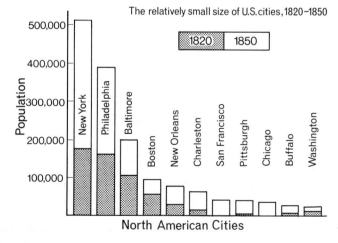

The relatively small size of U.S. cities, 1820–1850

1820 · 1850

Population / North American Cities

New York · Philadelphia · Baltimore · Boston · New Orleans · Charleston · San Francisco · Pittsburgh · Chicago · Buffalo · Washington

*They were remarkable men. For example, Frederic Tudor (1783–1864) was in business on his own account at 13. He invented ice-packing so that he could export perishable goods; he imported coffee in an effort to popularize an alternative drink to tea.

**Davy Crockett died the same year when Texas, then a part of Mexico, declared its independence. He was part of a small force defending the Alamo, a mission building in the town of San Antonio. The Mexicans attacked the Alamo and wiped out every one of its defenders.

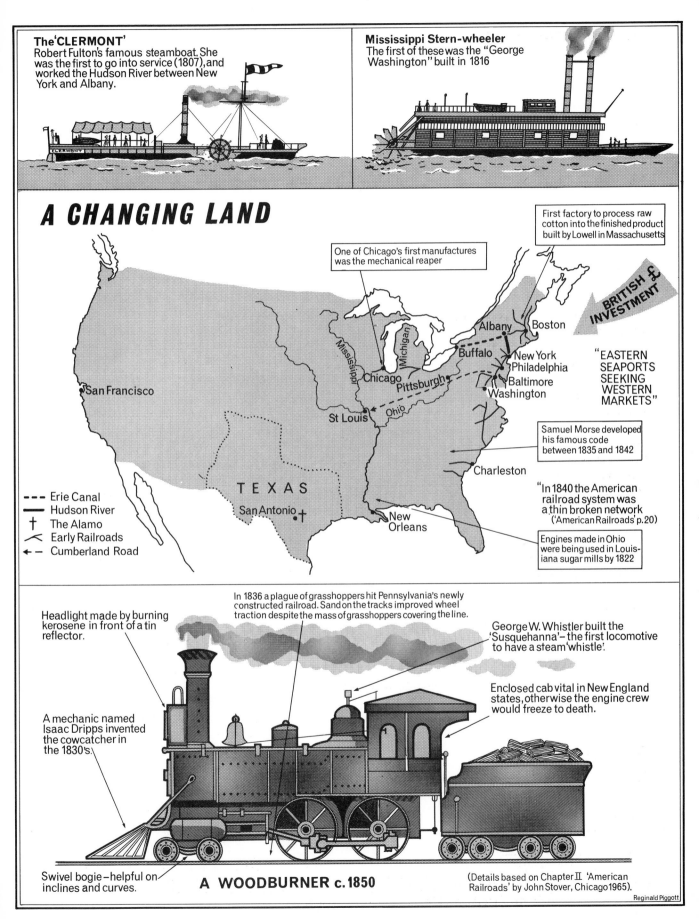

The 'CLERMONT'
Robert Fulton's famous steamboat. She was the first to go into service (1807), and worked the Hudson River between New York and Albany.

Mississippi Stern-wheeler
The first of these was the "George Washington" built in 1816

A CHANGING LAND

First factory to process raw cotton into the finished product built by Lowell in Massachusetts

One of Chicago's first manufactures was the mechanical reaper

BRITISH £ INVESTMENT

"EASTERN SEAPORTS SEEKING WESTERN MARKETS"

Albany   Boston
Buffalo
Chicago   New York
Pittsburgh Philadelphia
Baltimore
Washington

Michigan
Mississippi

San Francisco

St Louis   Ohio

Charleston

Samuel Morse developed his famous code between 1835 and 1842

"In 1840 the American railroad system was a thin broken network ('American Railroads' p.20)

T E X A S

San Antonio ✝

New Orleans

Engines made in Ohio were being used in Louisiana sugar mills by 1822

- - - Erie Canal
——— Hudson River
✝ The Alamo
⟨ Early Railroads
←- Cumberland Road

In 1836 a plague of grasshoppers hit Pennsylvania's newly constructed railroad. Sand on the tracks improved wheel traction despite the mass of grasshoppers covering the line.

Headlight made by burning kerosene in front of a tin reflector.

George W. Whistler built the 'Susquehanna'– the first locomotive to have a steam 'whistle'.

Enclosed cab vital in New England states, otherwise the engine crew would freeze to death.

A mechanic named Isaac Dripps invented the cowcatcher in the 1830's.

Swivel bogie – helpful on inclines and curves.

A WOODBURNER c. 1850

(Details based on Chapter II 'American Railroads' by John Stover, Chicago 1965).

Reginald Piggott

10: Absorbing an empire: the USA 1814–1860

Manifest destiny

Between 1814 and 1860 the American people were in effect colonizing an empire. They made two distinct thrusts to gain control of the Pacific coastline. The first was towards Oregon which they won by treaty with the British in 1846; the second was towards California which they took from Mexico by force of arms in 1848. With substantial lengths of the North American coastline under its control the USA could absorb the rest of its land empire at leisure. So, while the Americans streamed westwards, they were in fact heading for lands already claimed by the USA. As one British naval officer exclaimed, when his ship anchored in San Francisco Bay in 1845, 'Dammit! Is there nothing but Yankees here?'

The immigrants

During the nineteenth century about 30 million people abandoned their homes in Europe to seek a better life in America. About a third of these arrived before the Civil War began in 1861. They came mainly to avoid the increasing economic misery prevalent in their homelands. Most pitiful were the Irish, fleeing from the potato blight which, between 1845 and 1851, led to the death of a million people. Germans, Scandinavians, Scots, Welsh and English all reacted in the same way to the decline of agriculture, unemployment and the appearance of industrial slums. They swarmed aboard any vessel which offered a cheap transatlantic passage. The captains of big timber-carriers would willingly fill their empty holds with any number of families at twenty shillings per head; tiny trawlers, returning to the Newfoundland fisheries, could undercut even this low price. On board ship, conditions were foul. Sometimes the passengers mutinied; more often, they endured any privation if it would get them to America. By 1840, the steamships began to compete with the sailing vessels for the more expensive passenger trade; this left the full-rigged ships, the barques and brigantines to compete among themselves for the immigrant trade. It was now the shipping companies' turn to seek their customers. Accommodation aboard ship improved, fares became more reasonable and by 1860 a regular transatlantic scheduled service was in full swing.

The Donner tragedy 1846–7

Many immigrants joined the ox-drawn wagon-trains as they jolted across the well-worn trails to the west. Among the mass of personal experiences, the story of the Donner party stands unique. But though it is untypical, it nevertheless underlines the hardships facing the pioneer families. It began on the Oregon Trail in 1846 when a horseman galloped in with the news that Mexico and the USA were at war. The pioneers debated the wisdom of a change of route and several families decided to take a cut-off south and approach California via the Great Salt Lake. Under the leadership of George Donner, a 62 year-old farmer from Illinois, 87 people with twenty wagons set off on 20 July 1846. They were racing against time. They had to be over the mountains by the end of September, otherwise they would be trapped in the first snow-drifts. Luck was against the Donner party. Trapped in the Sierra Nevada they starved and then resorted to cannibalism. Relief parties reached them in 1847 only to be horrified by the extent of the disaster—the 'most spectacular in the record of western migration'. Of the 87 people who set out, nearly half were dead.

The democratic ideal

Democracy does not mean the same thing in America as it does in Britain. For the nineteenth century American, democracy meant respect for an individual's basic rights, especially his property. It also meant the rule of the majority—which does not always respect an individual's rights. American were therefore always anxious to devise additional guarantees of individual freedom. Americans conducted their politics in this climate of opinion and educated their children—and the immigrants—to adopt these beliefs so that wherever Americans went they would take the democratic ideal with them. There was just one grave weakness—the 'peculiar institution' of slavery. Was the American Negro, born and bred in a nation which epitomized the liberty of the individual, doomed to be a slave forever because the country was also dedicated to the protection of property rights?

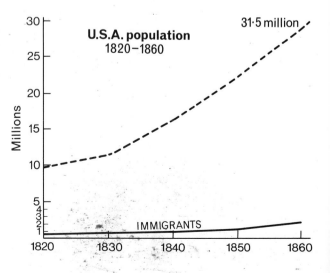

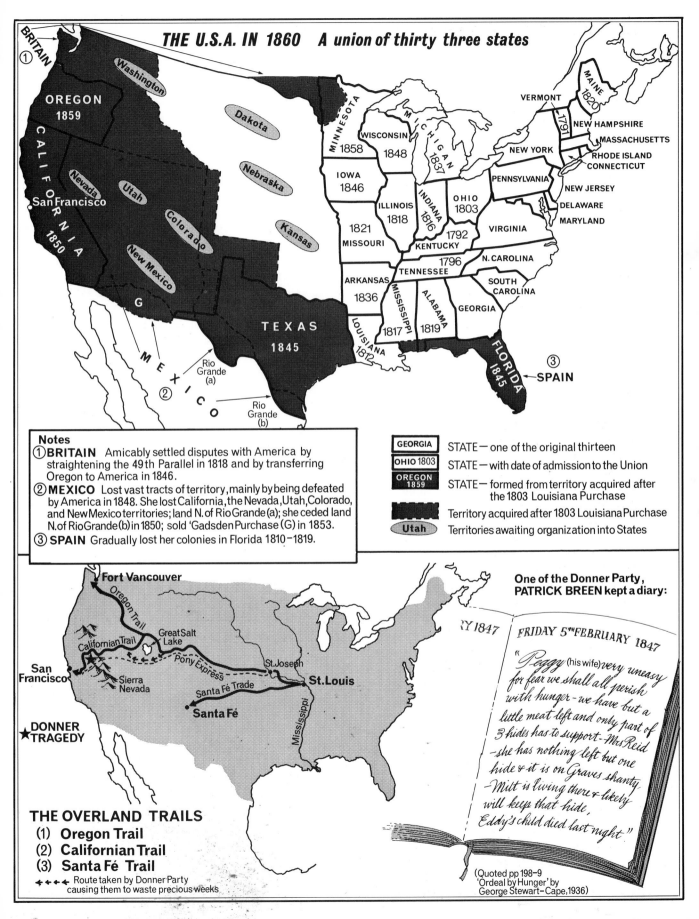

THE U.S.A. IN 1860   A union of thirty three states

① BRITAIN

OREGON 1859

WASHINGTON

C A L I F O R N I A

Nevada   Utah

San Francisco

Colorado

New Mexico

Dakota

Nebraska

Kansas

G

M E X I C O

Rio Grande (a)

②

Rio Grande (b)

T E X A S 1845

MINNESOTA 1858

WISCONSIN 1848

IOWA 1846

MICHIGAN 1837

ILLINOIS 1821

INDIANA 1816

MISSOURI

OHIO 1803

KENTUCKY 1792

VERMONT

NEW HAMPSHIRE

MASSACHUSETTS

RHODE ISLAND

CONNECTICUT

MAINE 1820

1791

NEW YORK

PENNSYLVANIA

NEW JERSEY

DELAWARE

MARYLAND

VIRGINIA

N. CAROLINA

TENNESSEE 1796

ARKANSAS 1836

MISSISSIPPI 1817

ALABAMA 1819

GEORGIA

SOUTH CAROLINA

LOUISIANA 1812

FLORIDA 1845

③ SPAIN

Notes

① **BRITAIN** Amicably settled disputes with America by straightening the 49th Parallel in 1818 and by transferring Oregon to America in 1846.

② **MEXICO** Lost vast tracts of territory, mainly by being defeated by America in 1848. She lost California, the Nevada, Utah, Colorado, and New Mexico territories; land N. of Rio Grande (a); she ceded land N. of Rio Grande (b) in 1850; sold 'Gadsden Purchase (G) in 1853.

③ **SPAIN** Gradually lost her colonies in Florida 1810–1819.

GEORGIA	STATE — one of the original thirteen
OHIO 1803	STATE — with date of admission to the Union
OREGON 1859	STATE — formed from territory acquired after the 1803 Louisiana Purchase
	Territory acquired after 1803 Louisiana Purchase
Utah	Territories awaiting organization into States

THE OVERLAND TRAILS

Fort Vancouver

Oregon Trail

Great Salt Lake

Californian Trail

Pony Express

San Francisco

Sierra Nevada

Santa Fé Trade

St. Joseph

St. Louis

Santa Fé

Mississippi

★ DONNER TRAGEDY

(1) **Oregon Trail**
(2) **Californian Trail**
(3) **Santa Fé Trail**

◆◆◆◆ Route taken by Donner Party causing them to waste precious weeks

One of the Donner Party, PATRICK BREEN kept a diary:

RY 1847   FRIDAY 5ᵗʰ FEBRUARY 1847

" *Peggy* (his wife) *very uneasy for fear we shall all perish with hunger – we have but a little meat left and only part of 3 hides has to support – Mrs Reid – she has nothing left but one hide & it is on Graves shanty, – Milt is living there & likely will keep that hide, Eddy's child died last night"*

(Quoted pp 198–9 'Ordeal by Hunger' by George Stewart–Cape, 1936)

11: The Slavery Crisis

The captive South

South of the Mason-Dixon Line, 4½ million Negro slaves stood condemned to permanent racial and intellectual inferiority. They had no rights: no right to a family, to an education, or to citizenship. They were highly prized—a good fieldworker fetched up to $1800 in 1860—and most planters treated them accordingly. Of course, there were some brutal slavemasters while most planters felt that the threat or the use of punishment was the best way of making a Negro work. However, just as the slave was shackled to his master so the South was shackled to a slave-economy. Slavery had increased with the growing demand for cotton; by 1850 the 'captive South' was dependent for its existence on the progressive exploitation of a helpless mass of humanity.

Slaves and politics

Despite the fine words in the Declaration of Independence, there was nothing in the constitution of the USA that condemned slavery. Very few Americans actively opposed it before 1850. Rich Southerners depended on it; poor Southerners prayed for the day when they too might own some slaves; Northerners might oppose it in principle but remained racially biased against Negroes. Some favoured the abolition of slavery; others wanted to export the problem lock, stock and barrel and send the Negroes to Africa. Slavery became a political issue when it involved the territorial expansion of the USA. An Ordinance of 1787 had forbidden slavery in the 'Old North West'; the 1820 Missouri Compromise admitted Maine as a *free* state and Missouri as a *slave* state. It also ruled that new states admitted north of 36° 30′ would be *free*. Victory over Mexico in 1848 changed the entire situation: would America's newly won empire in the south and west be carved into *slave* states? If so, they would dominate the Union's politics—and this was the last thing that Northerners wanted. Eventually, the politicians produced the 1850 Compromise. California became a *free* state; Utah and New Mexico would remain Territories for the time being and no rules about slavery would operate there. In return, the Northerners would restore any escaped slaves to the South.

Crisis

This last point led to the most heart searching. Two years after the 1850 Compromise, Harriet Beecher Stowe published her *Uncle Tom's Cabin* in which she drew on her experiences of helping runaway slaves. She described the American Negro's fears and frustrations and soon characters—especially the loveable Uncle Tom, the charming Topsy and the evil Simon Legree—became household names*. Northerners gained a new—if somewhat inaccurate—view of slavery. Meanwhile, implementation of the 1850 Compromise brought the inhumanity of slavery to the Northerners' doorsteps. Though few slaves managed to escape, those who did ran the risk of being pursued not only by their masters but by police and marines also. An ordinary American might see this happen; it horrified him. He heard tales about the 'Underground Railway', a secret organization giving aid to runaway slaves, and about the extraordinary John Brown who, in 1858, led a raid into Missouri to rescue 12 slaves and kill a slavemaster. Next year Brown and his supporters occupied an arsenal at Harper's Ferry and tried to raise a slave rebellion. He was hanged.

Secession

By now the Southern states felt their future lay not with the *free* industrial North but with a new and separate America whose destiny was to spread the slave economy into Mexico and even into Cuba. In the 1860 Presidential Elections all the cotton states voted for John C. Breckenridge, member of the Southern Democrat Party. All the *free* states voted for the Republican, Abraham Lincoln. The issue at stake was *not* the abolition of slavery. Lincoln had made this clear two years previously: 'I have no purpose directly or indirectly to interfere with the institution of slavery in the States where it exists. I believe I have no lawful right to do so, and I have no inclination to do so.' He refused to allow any extension of slavery to the Territories. The election result decided South Carolina: on 20 December 1860 she seceded from the Union. The rest of the cotton states followed suit and met at Montgomery, Alabama to create the Confederacy. War between the Confederacy and the remaining states of the Union officially began on 12 April 1861 when Confederates opened fire on the federal base at Fort Sumter. The North fought to preserve the Union; the South fought to create a Confederacy which was incompatible with the democratic ideal of the American people.

*Even in Tsarist Russia, where some landowners were reported to be so impressed by the message of *Uncle Tom's Cabin* that they released serfs previously bound to their estates.

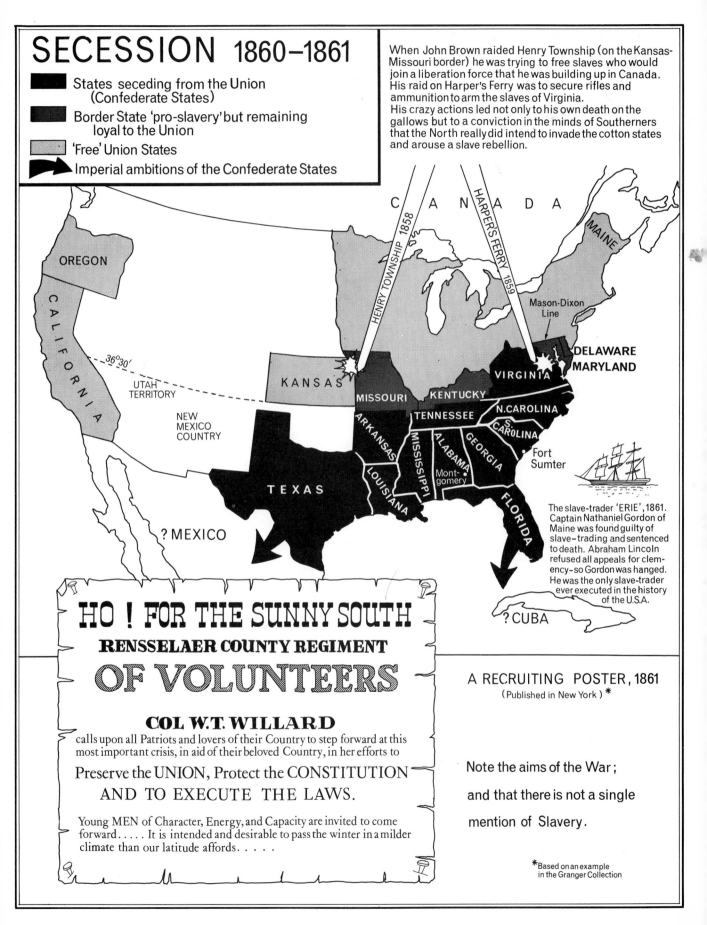

SECESSION 1860–1861

- ■ States seceding from the Union (Confederate States)
- ▨ Border State 'pro-slavery' but remaining loyal to the Union
- ▢ 'Free' Union States
- ➤ Imperial ambitions of the Confederate States

When John Brown raided Henry Township (on the Kansas-Missouri border) he was trying to free slaves who would join a liberation force that he was building up in Canada. His raid on Harper's Ferry was to secure rifles and ammunition to arm the slaves of Virginia.

His crazy actions led not only to his own death on the gallows but to a conviction in the minds of Southerners that the North really did intend to invade the cotton states and arouse a slave rebellion.

CANADA

HENRY TOWNSHIP 1858

HARPERS FERRY 1859

MAINE

Mason-Dixon Line

OREGON

CALIFORNIA

36°30'

UTAH TERRITORY

KANSAS

NEW MEXICO COUNTRY

MISSOURI

KENTUCKY

TENNESSEE

ARKANSAS

MISSISSIPPI

ALABAMA

GEORGIA

LOUISIANA

Mont-gomery

TEXAS

? MEXICO

DELAWARE

MARYLAND

VIRGINIA

N.CAROLINA

S.CAROLINA

Fort Sumter

FLORIDA

The slave-trader 'ERIE', 1861. Captain Nathaniel Gordon of Maine was found guilty of slave–trading and sentenced to death. Abraham Lincoln refused all appeals for clemency–so Gordon was hanged. He was the only slave-trader ever executed in the history of the U.S.A.

? CUBA

HO ! FOR THE SUNNY SOUTH

RENSSELAER COUNTY REGIMENT

OF VOLUNTEERS

COL W.T. WILLARD

calls upon all Patriots and lovers of their Country to step forward at this most important crisis, in aid of their beloved Country, in her efforts to

Preserve the UNION, Protect the CONSTITUTION AND TO EXECUTE THE LAWS.

Young MEN of Character, Energy, and Capacity are invited to come forward . . . . . It is intended and desirable to pass the winter in a milder climate than our latitude affords . . . . .

A RECRUITING POSTER, 1861
(Published in New York) *

Note the aims of the War;

and that there is not a single

mention of Slavery.

*Based on an example in the Granger Collection

12: The American Civil War, 1861–1865

Ill-prepared for war

Neither side was ready for a full-scale modern war. President Lincoln mismanaged the first recruiting campaign and resorted to conscription in 1863. But as he allowed a drafted recruit to find a substitute or buy exemption for $300 this led to both corruption and violence in Northern cities. Some men joined up, deserted and then rejoined just to collect recruiting bounties. Those who couldn't raise $300 complained that it was a rich man's war but a poor man's fight; some rioted for three days in New York. The Confederacy was even less well-off. It was short of men—a mere 1½ million of military age lived in the South compared with nearly 6 million in the North—and after the first rush of enthusiastic volunteers it had few reserves of strength. The saddest irony of the war came in 1865 when the South began to draft its slaves. Despite its weaknesses, the Confederates displayed initiative when it came to naval matters. They commandeered Union ships and converted merchantmen into commerce raiders and blockade runners. They also planned a few surprises for the Yankees and one of these turned out to be the *Hunley*, the first submarine to sink an enemy warship.

The fighting men

A quarter of all American who saw combat lost their lives—due partly to the greater efficiency of small arms. Samuel Colt had already begun to mass-produce his famous revolvers; deadly repeater rifles came into use in 1865. Said one Confederate: 'the Yankees now have a gun that they load on Sundays and fire all the week.'* Half the combat troops suffered wounds or disease and they didn't have much chance in the primitive field-hospitals. Doctors knew something about anaesthetics—when they could lay their hands on them—but very little about antiseptic surgery. And apart from this, the Americans had a lot to learn about the logistics of modern warfare. Some troops complained that their sugar wouldn't dissolve in boiling coffee, but their coats dissolved on their backs when it rained! Yet in some respects this was a sophisticated war: electrically detonated *torpedoes* (they were really mines), the electric telegraph, mobile railway guns and air observation balloons were all in use during the American Civil War.

The war at sea

While the Union Navy blockaded the Southern ports, the Confederates harried the Northern shipping lanes and built massive ironclads to blast enemy ships out of the water. Southern raiders captured about 280 enemy ships; the notorious *Alabama* eventually fell victim to the guns of the USS *Kearsage*; while the *Shenandoah* was still happily sinking Pacific whalers after the war was over. The most famous sea-battle of the Civil War took place in Hampton Roads during 1862 when two extraordinary vessels called the *Monitor* and the *Merrimac* fought the first duel between ironclad warships. However, it was the blockade that proved decisive in the long run. Cut off from its European cotton markets, lacking allies and a stable currency as well as an effective industrial war machine, the rebel states had little hope of victory.

The war on the land

Infantrymen settled the issue between North and South. From the outset, the North intended to capture Richmond and then smash Southern resistance in a series of rapid thrusts. Confederates hoped for a spectacular victory calculated to wreck Union morale and win a grudging recognition of Southern independence. Union armies launched the first big attack at Bull Run in July 1861—and suffered total defeat. They tried again at Second Bull Run in August 1862—and lost. Under General Robert E. Lee the grey-clad Confederates pushed north in an attempt to capture a Northern city—preferably Pittsburgh or Philadelphia. They clashed with Union troops at the Battle of Gettysburg (July 1863) where, despite the heroic charge by General Pickett's 13,000 troopers, the Confederates were beaten. Meanwhile, General Ulysses Grant led the armies of the west into Confederate territory, won the Battle of Shiloh (1862) and then swung south to take Vicksburg in 1863. Grant then sent Sherman to march through Georgia with orders to cripple the South's economy and slice the Confederacy in half. Grant himself moved east to seek out Lee. He fought hideous battles at Wilderness, Spotsylvania, Cold Harbor and Petersburg. Lee's army shrunk to less than 60,000 men, most of whom lacked food and ammunition. Richmond fell on 4 April 1865; Lee formally surrendered his army at Appomattox on 9 April. Five days later John Wilkes Booth shot and killed President Abraham Lincoln.

*Quoted by Shannon in his *America's Economic Growth*, p. 322. Richard Gatling, a North Carolina planter, had just invented his famous quick-firing gun. The United States army adopted it one year after the Civil War ended.

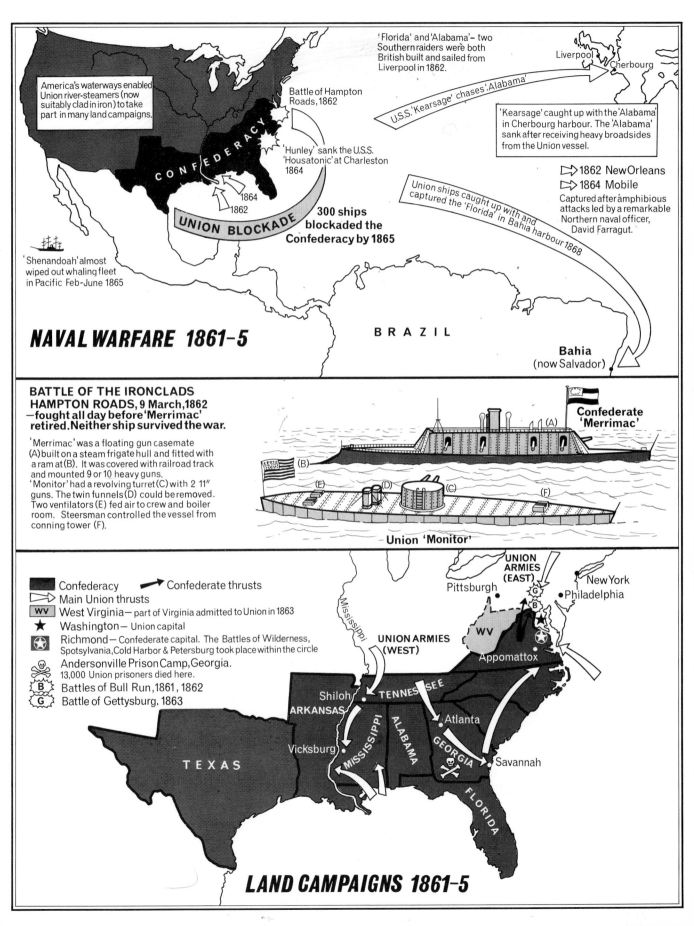

NAVAL WARFARE 1861-5

'Florida' and 'Alabama'– two Southern raiders were both British built and sailed from Liverpool in 1862.

U.S.S. 'Kearsage' chases 'Alabama'

America's waterways enabled Union river-steamers (now suitably clad in iron) to take part in many land campaigns.

Battle of Hampton Roads, 1862

'Hunley' sank the U.S.S. 'Housatonic' at Charleston 1864

'Kearsage' caught up with the 'Alabama' in Cherbourg harbour. The 'Alabama' sank after receiving heavy broadsides from the Union vessel.

Liverpool   Cherbourg

1862 New Orleans

1864 Mobile

Captured after amphibious attacks led by a remarkable Northern naval officer, David Farragut.

Union ships caught up with and captured the 'Florida' in Bahia harbour 1868

CONFEDERACY

1864
1862

UNION BLOCKADE

300 ships blockaded the Confederacy by 1865

'Shenandoah' almost wiped out whaling fleet in Pacific Feb-June 1865

BRAZIL

Bahia (now Salvador)

BATTLE OF THE IRONCLADS
HAMPTON ROADS, 9 March, 1862
—fought all day before 'Merrimac' retired. Neither ship survived the war.

'Merrimac' was a floating gun casemate (A) built on a steam frigate hull and fitted with a ram at (B). It was covered with railroad track and mounted 9 or 10 heavy guns.
'Monitor' had a revolving turret (C) with 2 11" guns. The twin funnels (D) could be removed. Two ventilators (E) fed air to crew and boiler room. Steersman controlled the vessel from conning tower (F).

Confederate 'Merrimac'

Union 'Monitor'

Confederacy   Confederate thrusts

Main Union thrusts

WV West Virginia— part of Virginia admitted to Union in 1863

★ Washington— Union capital

Richmond—Confederate capital. The Battles of Wilderness, Spotsylvania, Cold Harbor & Petersburg took place within the circle

Andersonville Prison Camp, Georgia. 13,000 Union prisoners died here.

B Battles of Bull Run, 1861, 1862

G Battle of Gettysburg, 1863

UNION ARMIES (EAST)

Pittsburgh   New York
Philadelphia

UNION ARMIES (WEST)

WV
Appomattox

Mississippi

TENNESSEE
Shiloh
ARKANSAS

Atlanta

Vicksburg

MISSISSIPPI   ALABAMA   GEORGIA   Savannah

TEXAS

FLORIDA

LAND CAMPAIGNS 1861-5

13: The post-war South

The death of slavery 1865

By leading the North to victory in the Civil War, President Lincoln had saved the American Union; by issuing an Emancipation Proclamation in 1863 he guaranteed the freedom of the American Negro. In December 1865, some months after Lincoln's assassination, Congress passed the *Thirteenth Amendment* to the United States' constitution—slavery was now illegal; in 1868 the *Fourteenth Amendment* made the ex-slaves American citizens; in 1870 the *Fifteenth Amendment* guaranteed their right to vote.

Reconstruction 1865–77

The Civil War devastated the South. Banks, railroads, plantations and local government were simply just not functioning. Dejected soldiers—many of whom resented Lee's surrender at Appomattox—returned to find their homes destroyed, their families dispersed or dead, and their own future bleak in the extreme. Around them wandered the thousands of freed slaves. Droughts, a shortage of seed and a lack of equipment caused food shortages. Men died of starvation in the grim winter of 1866–67. Inevitably there were riots and gunfights. Congress decided to act positively: in March 1867 the *Reconstruction Act* divided the rebel states into five military districts under the control of Federal occupation troops. Their task was to restore law and order, aid the reorganization of local government and prepare for the re-admission of the rebel states to the American Union. Not until April 1877 did the last blue-clad troops withdraw; and Americans label this period 1865–77 the years of 'Reconstruction'. Meanwhile, Republican politicians from the North (including the self-seeking carpet-baggers) used the newly enfranchised Negroes to support their plans for rebuilding the economy of the South. Congressmen such as Thaddeus Stevens were anxious to give Negroes their chance of self-advancement as soon as possible; the Bureau of Freedmen* (created by Lincoln as early as 3 March 1865) offered food, clothing, medical supplies as well as providing millions of dollars for schools and colleges; missionaries flocked south to lend a hand in educating the Negro. Before long, the first Negroes had entered politics— and ever since some historians have fumed about their inexperience and their tendency to become involved in crooked deals. Negroes certainly entered State legislatures—one became Lieutenant-Governor of Louisiana —and for a time they controlled North Carolina's state assembly. They pushed through ridiculously high taxes and dipped their fingers into local revenues. Some South Carolina Negro politicians bought their wives party dresses and reimbursed a colleague who had a bad day at the races out of public funds. But generally examples of Negro corruption pale beside some of the frauds perpetrated by white politicians during the late nineteenth century. Moreover, the Negroes had to raise substantial revenues in order to provide welfare services for the thousands who could not cope with the responsibilities of a white man's world. It was a bizarre period of American history, stacked with stories of corruption; but at least in the process Americans discovered that they had a duty to care for the needs of the underprivileged.

Hostility of the Negro

In theory, the Negro now possessed civil rights and the protection of the law; in practice, he soon lost the vote and any claim to racial equality. Southern Democrats had no intention of letting Yankee carpet-baggers run their affairs. They began a resistance movement against Reconstruction using secret societies such as the Ku Klux Klan. The Klan terrorized Negroes and threatened them with mutilation or worse if they dared to vote. There were serious race riots and several thousand lynchings between 1866 and 1900. The Colfax Riot (1873) led to a Supreme Court decision that murder was a matter for the State rather than Federal law. It now became difficult to convict a white man who murdered a Negro; while at the same time several states modified their voting laws, which led to political discrimination against the poorly educated Negro. So serious did matters become that Booker T. Washington, a prominent Negro leader, advised his people—rather unwisely, according to some critics—to abandon their quest for civil rights: 'The opportunity to *earn* a dollar in a factory just now is worth infinitely more than the opportunity to *spend* a dollar in the opera house.'** The American Negro usually accepted his lot with docility; in contrast, the wars against the Red Indian intensified as the dispute for America's 'Last Frontier' reached a climax.

*The Bureau of Freedmen, Refugees, and Abandoned Lands gave aid to poor whites and Negroes alike.
**Quoted in Alan Conway's *The History of the Negro in the United States*, page 18 (published by the Historical Association 1968).

The State Assembly of ILLINOIS (Lincoln's own State) were horrified by the President's Emancipation Proclamation. They called it a gigantic usurpation.

"....at once converting the war.....into a crusade for the sudden, unconditional and violent liberation of 3,000,000 Negro slaves, a result which would not only be a subversion of the Federal Union but a revolution in the social organisation of the Southern States.....the present and far-reaching consequences of which to BOTH RACES cannot be contemplated without the most dismal foreboding of horror and dismay....."

RECONSTRUCTION IN THE SOUTH
1865 — 1877

President Lincoln emancipated the slaves by proclamation in 1863, and established the Bureau of Freedmen in March 1865.

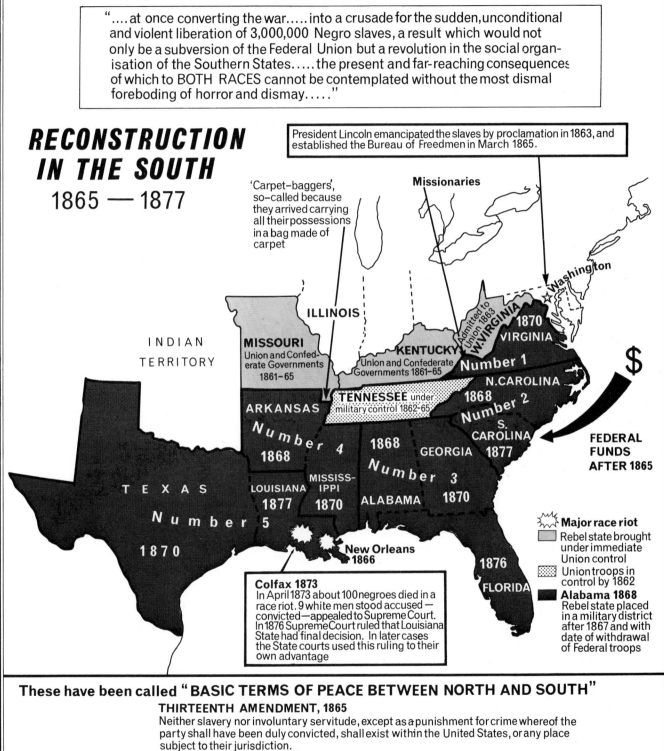

'Carpet-baggers', so-called because they arrived carrying all their possessions in a bag made of carpet

Missionaries

ILLINOIS

INDIAN TERRITORY

MISSOURI
Union and Confederate Governments 1861–65

KENTUCKY
Union and Confederate Governments 1861–65

Admitted to Union 1863 W.VIRGINIA

VIRGINIA

1870

Number 1

N.CAROLINA
1868
Number 2

Washington

$

ARKANSAS

TENNESSEE under military control 1862–65

Number 4
1868

1868

MISSISS-IPPI

GEORGIA

Number 3

S. CAROLINA
1877

FEDERAL FUNDS AFTER 1865

TEXAS

Number 5

1870

LOUISIANA
1877

1870

ALABAMA

1870

Major race riot

Rebel state brought under immediate Union control

Union troops in control by 1862

New Orleans 1866

1876
FLORIDA

Alabama 1868
Rebel state placed in a military district after 1867 and with date of withdrawal of Federal troops

Colfax 1873
In April 1873 about 100 negroes died in a race riot. 9 white men stood accused — convicted—appealed to Supreme Court. In 1876 Supreme Court ruled that Louisiana State had final decision. In later cases the State courts used this ruling to their own advantage

These have been called "BASIC TERMS OF PEACE BETWEEN NORTH AND SOUTH"

THIRTEENTH AMENDMENT, 1865
Neither slavery nor involuntary servitude, except as a punishment for crime whereof the party shall have been duly convicted, shall exist within the United States, or any place subject to their jurisdiction.

FOURTEENTH AMENDMENT, 1868
All persons born or naturalized in the United States.....are citizens of the United States and of the State wherein they reside.

FIFTEENTH AMENDMENT, 1870
The right of citizens of the United States to vote shall not be denied or abridged by the United States or by any State on account of race, colour, or previous condition of servitude.

14: The Wild West and the 'Last Frontier'

The Indian problem

By 1860, the American Indian had his back to the wall. White settlers had either penned him inside reservations or pushed him into the Great Plains—the so-called 'Last Frontier'. Americans had always promised to guarantee the buffalo herds, but the cowboys, homesteaders, prospectors and railroad men did not keep their word. As Sitting Bull, Chief of the Sioux Nation, said in 1877: 'I have never taught my people to trust Americans. I have told them the truth. The Americans are great liars . . .'*

Indian Wars

Sitting Bull's tragedy was that his people, from the Dakotas down to Apache country, lay in the path of the new railroads destined to link the Union with its Pacific coastline. Normally, the Sioux made war against the Pawnees, Snakes and Crows but once their way of life was under attack they raided the white man. Santee Sioux swooped down on Minnesota's settlers in 1862; two years later the US army slaughtered 300 Indians at Sand Creek and forced a truce on the Sioux. Almost immediately, the Cheyenne and Arapaho went on the warpath and devastated large tracts of Kansas and Colorado during 1867–8. This led to Colonel Custer's 'search and destroy' mission of 1868 in which he massacred scores of unsuspecting Indians at the *Battle of the Washita River*. Now the Indians decided to sell their land dearly; 3000 Cheyenne and Sioux warriors met and annihilated Custer and his five troops of cavalry in the celebrated 'Last Stand' fought out at the *Battle of the Little Big Horn (1876)*. It was a great victory, but brought no solution to the Indians' problem. The Sioux Wars continued while in the south Geronimo's Apaches fought out their last battles against soldiers armed with six-shooters, carbines, Gatling guns and artillery. Geronimo surrendered in 1886; the Americans killed Sitting Bull in 1890; the last Sioux War ended in 1891. And by then the railways had changed the face of the land; the 'Last Frontier' had virtually disappeared.

Railways and cattlemen

After the Civil War American and foreign investors poured money into railway projects. The problem of transcontinental transport had to be solved in a hurry. Jefferson Davis† had once proposed camel-trains; Wells Fargo had its efficient horse-drawn coaches. But the railway would provide the best if not the cheapest answer. By 1867 the Kansas Pacific Railroad had reached Abilene and this encouraged Texas cattlemen to drive their herds to the new railheads. Over the next ten years more than 4 million cattle came north to be taken by rail to the slaughter-houses and canning-factories of Chicago and Milwaukee. Statistics are unreliable, but 1884 was thought to be a peak year when 4000 cowboys brought a million head from Texas.

Railways and immigrants

Meanwhile, the Union Pacific Railroad met the Central Pacific at Promontory Point, Utah in 1869, an event which led to a fever of railway speculation. The 1873 economic crisis—brought on by a series of shady railway deals—delayed work for several years but by 1883 the Texas and Southern Pacific, the Northern Pacific and the famous Atchison, Topeka and Santa Fé all completed their transcontinental routes. It is hard to over-estimate the effect this railway revolution had upon America's striking development as a modern industrial state. With about 40% of the world rail mileage, the USA rapidly completed the colonization of her land-empire. More immigrants came swarming in. About 11 million arrived from Western Europe during 1865–1914 while a new flood—about 10 million—appeared from the Balkans and Eastern Europe. Most of the East Europeans were impoverished—and often persecuted—peasants seeking their fortune in a city or a better way of life on a cheap American homestead. They came west by rail, raised their crops and sent them east by rail. The railroads delivered their farm machinery, their barbed wire, their letters from Russia or Greece and their household goods from Chicago mail-order firms. The railroads enabled the American people to sell their beef and their grain to the world. Some men became millionaires and their money from agriculture and transportation helped pay for industrial plant so that, by 1900, the United States of America was the most powerful industrial nation in the world.

*Reported in the *New York Herald*, October 1877 and quoted in *History Today*, January 1962, page 96.
†Jefferson Davis was President of the Confederacy during the American Civil War.

The Pre-Emption Act, 1841
Any person who squatted for six months on Government land may buy 160 acres at $1.25 an acre.

The Homestead Act, 1862
American citizens could have 160 acres of Plains free (after 5 yrs. residence). Indians did not become American citizens until 1924.

The Timber Culture Act, 1873
Any settler who would plant 40 acres of timber on the Plains could have a 160 acre homestead free.

The 'LAST FRONTIER'

San Francisco

Japanese and Chinese immigrants

SIOUX

CHEYENNE

ARAPAHO

Goodnight-loving trail

Western trail

Chisholm trail

Abilene

1876

1890

1862

Milwaukee

Chicago

Millions of immigrants after 1865

1864

1868

1886

MEXICO

TEXAS

Indian Battles

- 1862 Santee Sioux raid Minnesota
- 1864 Sand Creek Massacre (Colorado Territory)
- 1868 Battle of Washita (Indian Territory)
- 1876 Battle of Little Big Horn, Montana
- 1886 Surrender of Geronimo (on border of Arizona and New Mexico Territories)
- 1890 Death of Sitting Bull (South Dakota)

The Great Plains

→ Cattle trails

- - → Advancing railroads

➤★ Advancing prospectors and gold strikes

The 0·45 Colt known as 'The Peacemaker' or 'Frontier' (1873 model)

The Winchester Repeater (1866 model)

GUNS THAT "WON THE WEST"

Most Indians had been moved to west of the Mississippi by 1840. They had to live side by side with the Plains Indians and suffered from inter-tribal warfare. Most tragic were the FIVE CIVILISED TRIBES (Cherokees, Chickasaws, Choctaws, Creeks and Seminoles) who had their own schools, newspapers and written constitution. They sided with the Confederacy during the Civil War and, together with most Indians, finished up in the 'Indian Territory'. Even this area became open to white settlement in 1890. Eventually the Five Civilised Tribes, other Indian tribes and white settlers became part of the State of Oklahoma, admitted to the Union in 1907.

WASHINGTON 1889
OREGON 1859
MONTANA 1889
NORTH DAKOTA 1889
MINNESOTA 1858
VERMONT 1791
MAINE 1820
NEW HAMPSHIRE 1788
IDAHO 1890
WYOMING 1890
SOUTH DAKOTA 1889
WISCONSIN 1848
MICHIGAN 1837
NEW YORK 1788
MASSACHUSETTS 1788
RHODE ISLAND 1790
CONNECTICUT
NEVADA 1864
Promontory Point
Great Salt Lake
NEBRASKA 1867
IOWA 1846
PENNSYLVANIA 1787
NEW JERSEY 1787
UTAH 1896
COLORADO 1876
ILLINOIS 1818
INDIANA 1816
OHIO 1803
DELAWARE 1787
MARYLAND 1788
CALIFORNIA 1850
KANSAS 1861
MISSOURI 1821
KENTUCKY 1792
W. VIRGINIA 1863
VIRGINIA 1788
ARIZONA 1912
NEW MEXICO 1912
OKLAHOMA 1907
ARKANSAS 1836
TENNESSEE 1796
N. CAROLINA 1789
S. CAROLINA 1788
GEORGIA 1788
MISSISSIPPI 1317
ALABAMA 1819
TEXAS 1845
LOUISIANA 1812
FLORIDA 1845

THE LAND EMPIRE OF THE UNION: 48 States by 1912

Date indicates admission to Union

15: The foremost industrial nation

War and industry

American industry was in the doldrums at the beginning of the Civil War. Both sides bought their guns and uniform abroad. Yet by 1863 the North was almost self-sufficient and in 1865 actually exported weapons to Europe. Such rapid development required capital investment and organizing skill; it meant new industrial plant run by first-class businessmen. John D. Rockefeller was such a man; by 1865 he had combined several oil refineries into a single industrial holding. This would be the post-war pattern; 'big business' would transform America into the world's leading industrial nation.

Big business

America's industrialization went ahead despite the contemporary depression in Britain and Western Europe. During the 1870s American businessmen took advantage of low interest charges to borrow money, modernize factories, buy up stocks of raw materials, open up new mines and promise customers quick, cheap deliveries. Rockefeller now dominated the oil industry, Carnegie built America's first steel plant, Armour created his meat-packing empire. They converted their businesses into 'trusts', monopoly concerns that crushed competitors, strikers and political opponents alike. A small board of directors would dominate the financial affairs of a nation-wide industry. Yet, as Carnegie pointed out: '... the millionaires who are in active control started as poor boys and were trained in the sternest but most efficient of all schools—poverty'. This was very important, for it effected the whole outlook of the American people. They saw nothing wrong in the methods of capitalism. Just as the poor whites had envied the rich planters of the South, so the American workers wanted to join the 'bosses'. Most Americans therefore approved of the system, even though their standard of living in a New York tenement or a Nebraska sod-house might be pretty miserable. If one country boy from the log-cabin could be President, surely another could become a millionaire.

The automobile industry

Moreover, some real social benefits grew out of American capitalism. For example, the automobile industry barely existed before 1896; yet by 1914 there were $3\frac{1}{2}$ million cars on American roads. Much credit goes to Henry Ford, the Detroit mechanic who applied mass-production techniques to consumer products. And, unlike other manufaturers such as General Motors, he marketed one type of car—the Model T. He set out to sell this by the million to the American middle-class, the farmers and ultimately to every American who could afford a few dollars down-payment. More than any product—except perhaps for Edison's phonograph—the Model T reinforced a genuine sense of democracy in the USA.

Labour problems

America's astonishing industrial growth produced plenty of labour problems. Before the Civil War wages stood rather higher than those paid in Western Europe. The worst kinds of misery—such as those experienced by the British handloom weavers—could be avoided in the USA. It meant that trade unionism was fairly slow to develop until the Civil War brought inflation and a reduction in the purchasing power of the dollar. Trade unionists then tended to worry about job security as much as wage increases, however; they feared the unending stream of immigrants who always seemed ready to take a lower wage than existing American workers. Such fears contributed to many strikes after 1875 and there were some serious outbreaks of violence. For example, the secret society of miners (called the Molly Maguires) assassinated several mine bosses in Philadelphia. A Pinkerton* 'undercover' agent managed to expose the ringleaders in 1875. Then in 1886 a Chicago newspaper, the anarchist *Arbeiter-Zeitung*, urged strikers to take reprisals against police brutality. During the Haymarket Riots that year someone threw a bomb and seven policemen died. The police arrested eight 'anarchists' and four were hanged on the flimsiest of evidence. In 1892 the steelworkers in Homestead went on strike against their Carnegie employers. Management called in 300 Pinkerton men and there was a pitched battle; it took the State militia to break the strike. In all, the immigrants, Pinkerton men and state militia meant that labour leaders could make very little impression upon big business before Woodrow Wilson became President in 1912.

---

*Allan Pinkerton formed his detective agency at the end of the Civil War. Never short of a job in the lawless America of 1865–1900, Pinkerton men were involved in tracking down outlaws such as the Reno Gang, the James Brothers and the Dalton Boys—with varying degrees of success.

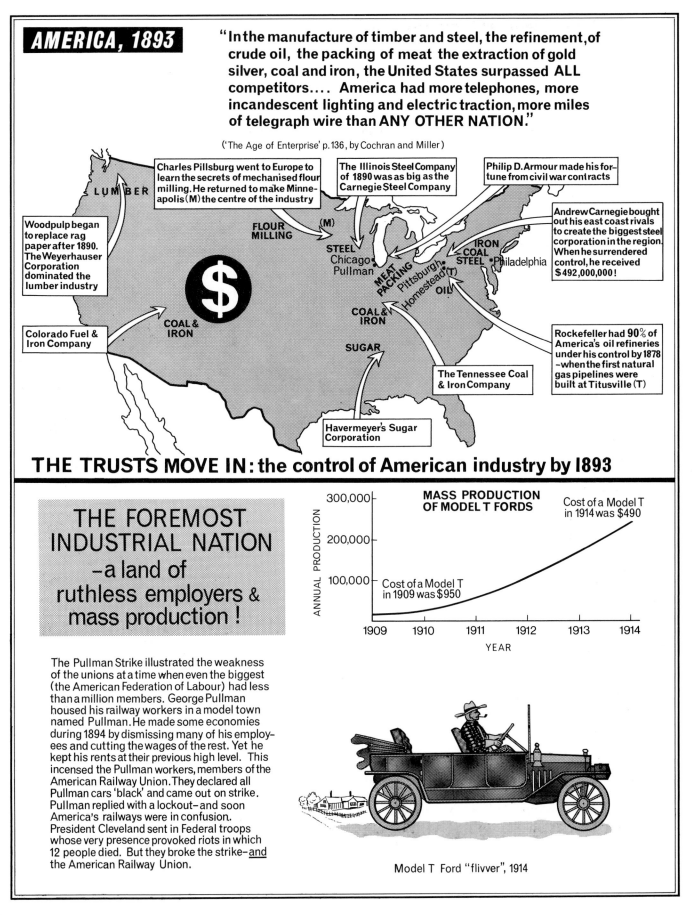

AMERICA, 1893

"In the manufacture of timber and steel, the refinement, of crude oil, the packing of meat the extraction of gold silver, coal and iron, the United States surpassed ALL competitors.... America had more telephones, more incandescent lighting and electric traction, more miles of telegraph wire than ANY OTHER NATION."

('The Age of Enterprise' p.136, by Cochran and Miller)

LUMBER

Charles Pillsburg went to Europe to learn the secrets of mechanised flour milling. He returned to make Minneapolis (M) the centre of the industry

The Illinois Steel Company of 1890 was as big as the Carnegie Steel Company

Philip D. Armour made his fortune from civil war contracts

Woodpulp began to replace rag paper after 1890. The Weyerhauser Corporation dominated the lumber industry

FLOUR MILLING

(M)

STEEL
Chicago
Pullman

MEAT PACKING
Pittsburgh
Homestead (T)

IRON COAL STEEL • Philadelphia

Andrew Carnegie bought out his east coast rivals to create the biggest steel corporation in the region. When he surrendered control, he received $492,000,000!

OIL

Colorado Fuel & Iron Company

COAL & IRON

COAL & IRON

SUGAR

The Tennessee Coal & Iron Company

Rockefeller had 90% of America's oil refineries under his control by 1878 – when the first natural gas pipelines were built at Titusville (T)

Havermeyer's Sugar Corporation

THE TRUSTS MOVE IN: the control of American industry by 1893

THE FOREMOST INDUSTRIAL NATION
– a land of ruthless employers & mass production !

MASS PRODUCTION OF MODEL T FORDS

Cost of a Model T in 1914 was $490

Cost of a Model T in 1909 was $950

ANNUAL PRODUCTION — 300,000 / 200,000 / 100,000

YEAR — 1909 1910 1911 1912 1913 1914

The Pullman Strike illustrated the weakness of the unions at a time when even the biggest (the American Federation of Labour) had less than a million members. George Pullman housed his railway workers in a model town named Pullman. He made some economies during 1894 by dismissing many of his employees and cutting the wages of the rest. Yet he kept his rents at their previous high level. This incensed the Pullman workers, members of the American Railway Union. They declared all Pullman cars 'black' and came out on strike. Pullman replied with a lockout – and soon America's railways were in confusion. President Cleveland sent in Federal troops whose very presence provoked riots in which 12 people died. But they broke the strike – <u>and</u> the American Railway Union.

Model T Ford "flivver", 1914

16: A world-wide empire

Russian America—the Alaska Purchase 1867

Between 1866 and 1904 the United States significantly extended its territorial powers, a process which cost more than a thousand American lives on battlefields as far apart as Cuba and Korea. However, the first major gain came without bloodshed. In 1867 the Russian minister Baron Stoeckl privately indicated to Secretary of State Seward that Russian America was up for sale. Seward paid the Russians $7,200,000 for this frozen land. christened Alaska by Senator Sumner—an ardent imperialist.

Korea and the Pacific

Possession of Alaska convinced many Americans that they now had the Pacific in the palm of their hand. But when they tried to open up Korea, they found how wrong they were. Already one American ship, the USS *Sherman*, had come under attack from Korean fireships. Then Admiral Rodgers' expedition in 1871 led to a fierce firefight between marines and poorly armed Korean soldiers. Rebuffed, the Americans decided to leave Korea to Russian and Japanese exploitation, although they did manage to make a somewhat fruitless trade treaty with the Korean Emperor in 1882. In fact, America gained very little in the Pacific before 1898: her gains added up to tiny Brooks Island, claimed by the captain of the USS *Lackawanna* in 1867 and renamed Midway Island.

The Spanish-American War 1898:
(a) the Caribbean theatre:

During the nineteenth century American businessmen invested about $50,000,000 in the Spanish colony of Cuba. When Cuban revolutionaries began destroying sugar mills, tobacco plantations and other sources of investment profit, the businessmen clamoured for US intervention. A chance came in February 1898; the US battleship *Maine* exploded in Havana harbour. 'Remember the Maine!' was soon on the lips of every bellicose American who was sure that the Spaniards had caused the explosion. Within a month Spain and America were at war. It was essentially a naval war—and the Americans now had some very impressive warships. Their brand-new *Oregon* sailed from California to Santiago Bay where American naval units were blockading the Spanish fleet; while a US invasion force invaded Cuba on 22 June. Led by Roosevelt's famous 'Rough Riders', the troops stormed the Spanish hill positions during a furious two-day battle. On 3 July the Spaniards made a desperate attempt to break out of Santiago Bay. They had not got a chance; led by the

Oregon, the US ships gave chase and either blew them to pieces or forced them to beach. 474 Spaniards were killed or wounded while the Americans had two casualties. In contrast, the US army came off much worse. More than 800 men died in the Cuban campaigns—but 4000 perished *in* America! Yellow fever and typhoid—caused, some said, by tins of contaminated meat—ran riot through the army camps where thousands of enthusiastic volunteers had gathered.

The Spanish-American War 1898:
(b) the Pacific theatre:

During the early hours of 1 May 1898 Admiral Dewey's Asiatic Squadron steamed into Manila harbour. Calmly navigating through the defences, Dewey systematically destroyed the anchored Spanish fleet—for the cost of 8 wounded Americans. Next month, 11,000 American troops arrived and soon brought Spanish resistance on the Philippines to an end. At the same time, the USS *Charleston* lobbed a few shells into the Spanish base on Guam which promptly surrendered. Spain made peace by the *Treaty of Paris* and she conceded the Philippines, Guam and Puerto Rico to the Americans. She also agreed that Americans should remain in Cuba until the people there had devised their own government. And to round off her new colonial empire, America annexed Wake Island and the Hawaiian Islands in 1898; she also acquired parts of Samoa in 1900.

The Panama Canal

Now America felt the need for a canal link between the Pacific and Atlantic Oceans. Panama's revolution* in 1903 gave her another chance to intervene in Latin America's affairs—she backed the revolutionaries and recognized their new government. Next she negotiated the Canal Zone Treaty which gave her the right to build a canal in a ten mile zone across Panama. Construction workers arrived in 1904 and the first ships sailed through the Canal in 1914—the year when war broke out in Europe. But the United States of America, now a world power as well as being the leading industrial nation, decided to adopt a course of unflinching neutrality.

---

*President Roosevelt—the leader of the heroic Rough Riders—had let it be known that he was prepared to support Panama's people in their bid to liberate themselves from Colombia. Roosevelt's motto was: 'speak softly and carry a big stick, and you will go far'. It certainly took the Americans to the Panama Canal Zone.

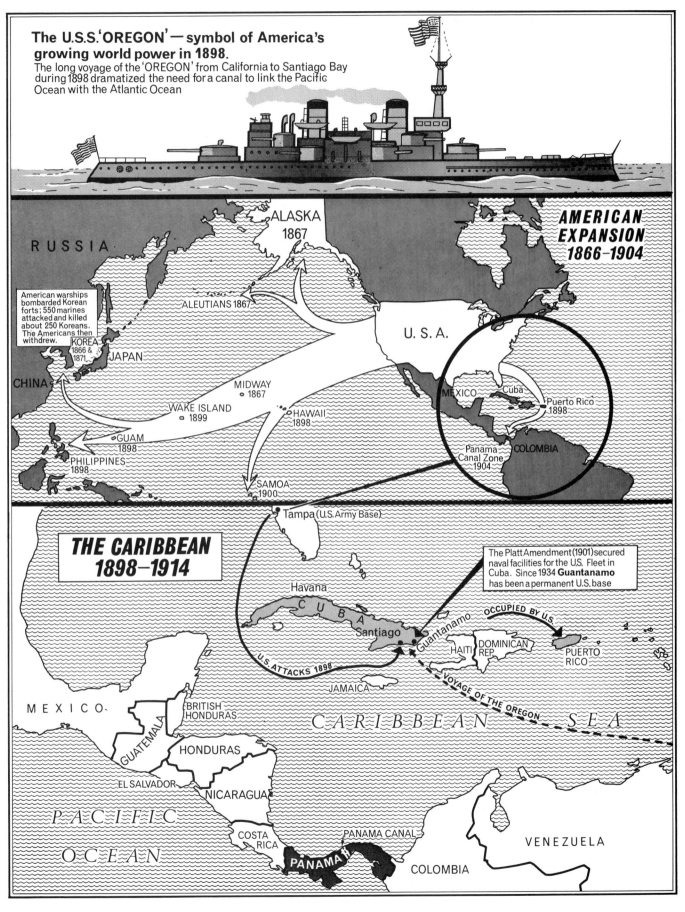

The U.S.S.'OREGON'— symbol of America's growing world power in 1898.
The long voyage of the 'OREGON' from California to Santiago Bay during 1898 dramatized the need for a canal to link the Pacific Ocean with the Atlantic Ocean

AMERICAN EXPANSION 1866–1904

RUSSIA

ALASKA 1867

ALEUTIANS 1867

American warships bombarded Korean forts; 550 marines attacked and killed about 250 Koreans. The Americans then withdrew.

KOREA 1866 & 1871

JAPAN

CHINA

MIDWAY 1867

WAKE ISLAND 1899

HAWAII 1898

GUAM 1898

PHILIPPINES 1898

SAMOA 1900

U.S.A.

MEXICO

Cuba

Puerto Rico 1898

Panama Canal Zone 1904

COLOMBIA

Tampa (U.S. Army Base)

THE CARIBBEAN 1898–1914

The Platt Amendment (1901) secured naval facilities for the U.S. Fleet in Cuba. Since 1934 **Guantanamo** has been a permanent U.S. base

Havana

C U B A

Santiago

Guantanamo

OCCUPIED BY U.S.

DOMINICAN REP.

HAITI

PUERTO RICO

U.S. ATTACKS 1898

JAMAICA

VOYAGE OF THE OREGON

MEXICO

BRITISH HONDURAS

GUATEMALA

HONDURAS

C A R I B B E A N   S E A

EL SALVADOR

NICARAGUA

COSTA RICA

PANAMA CANAL

PANAMA

COLOMBIA

VENEZUELA

P A C I F I C   O C E A N

Further Reading

Theme 2 – Imperial Power and Democracy

Spread

5. War of Independence	*The American Revolution*, Roger Parkinson, Wayland, 1971
6. United States of America	*Thomas Jefferson and American Democracy*, Max Beloff, EUP, 1948
7. The War of 1812	*History of the United States*, Oscar Handlin, Holt, Rinehart & Winston, 1967 (Ch. 32)
8. An empire of commerce	*The Rising American Empire*, Van Alstyne, Quadrangle, 1965
9. A changing land	*Rails West*, G. B. Abdill, Bonanza Books, 1960
	The Great Experiment, Frank Thistlethwaite, CUP, 1965
10. Absorbing an empire	*The Uprooted*, Oscar Handlin, Watts & Co., 1953
	Ordeal by Hunger, George Stewart, Cape, 1935
	Passage to America, Terry Coleman, Hutchinson, 1972
11. The Slavery Crisis	*To be a Slave*, Julius Lester, Longmans, 1970
	The Death of Slavery, Elbert Smith, Univ. of Chicago, 1967
	Origins of the American Civil War, B. J. Dalton, Warne, 1967
12. The Civil War	*The Civil War in America*, Alan Barker, Black, 1961
13. Problems of the post-war South	*The History of the Negro in the United States*, Alan Conway, Historical Association, 1968
	Age of Enterprise, Cochran and Miller, Harper & Row, 1961
14. Wild West and the 'last frontier'	*Concise Dictionary of American History*, Charles Scribner, 1963, pp. 451–477 for detailed account of American Indians.
15. The foremost industrial nation	*Age of Enterprise*, Cochran and Miller, Harper & Row, 1961
16. A world-wide empire	*The Rising American Empire*, Van Alstyne, Quadrangle, 1965

THEME 3

The First World War
and Its Aftermath

When war broke out in Europe in August 1914, President Wilson counselled neutrality. He had no wish to involve the United States in Europe's problems. His overriding interest was in promoting the welfare of the American people; in fact, during his 1913 inaugural address he hadn't bother to mention international affairs. He rapidly persuaded Congress to adopt most of his proposals: the creation of twelve Federal Reserve Banks (1914); the harmonious settlement of American control over the Panama Canal (1914); the reduction of monopolies in big-business (the Clayton anti-Trust Act 1914); the adjustment of railwaymen's pay (the Adamson Act 1916); the pursuit of Mexican raiders across the Rio Grande (1916–1917). He wasn't so successful over the immigration issue. In 1915 Congress excluded all aliens over 16 who couldn't read. Wilson vetoed the bill on humanitarian grounds. But in 1917 Congress passed the bill over Wilson's veto.

Even more important issues were at stake. The U-boat sinkings and the shocking information contained in the Zimmerman Telegram led America to declare war on Germany in April 1917. Wilson's personal impact on the war and its aftermath was immense. His famous Fourteen Points led the Germans—quite wrongly—to assume that they represented a statement of Allied war aims. At the Paris Peace Conference he was probably the most popular figure. And his dream of a 'League of Nations' which would outlaw war as a means of settling international disputes became a reality.

Thousands of Americans saw combat on land, sea and in the air. But while the majority of these were helping to destroy the German Army on the Western Front, others took part in those extraordinary interventions in Russia, interventions officially designed to persuade Lenin and the Bolsheviks— who had already made their peace with Germany—to rejoin the fray. So it was that American soldiers, whose battle honours ranged from the Halls of Montezuma to the shores of Tripoli, from the rivers of Korea to shell-torn Belleau Wood*, found themselves pitched into the confusion of the Russian Civil War. Their stay was brief. Under the brilliant leadership of Lenin and Trotsky the Bolshevik Revolution survived and by April 1920 the last American soldiers had quit the soil of Russia.

*Located north of Château-Thierry, scene of fighting on the Western Front in 1918.

17: 'Be neutral . . . in thought as well as in action'

President Wilson's heritage

Woodrow Wilson, university teacher and historian, became President of the United States in 1913. His mission was to improve the American way of life and he lost no time in telling his people that they had wasted their resources, polluted their environment and caused unnecessary human suffering in their bid for industrial pre-eminence. So while the Allied armies were facing the Germans in the decisive Battle of the Marne, Wilson was persuading Congress to pass two important acts. The Federal Trade Commission Act (September 1914) created machinery to combat 'unfair methods of competition in commerce'; the Clayton anti-Trust Act (October 1914) declared war on the big corporations and gave trade unionists the right to engage in peaceful picketing. Social reform fascinated the President and it irritated him that international events should drive him into the realms of foreign affairs. He objected to any extension of America's role in the world. Already she had endorsed the 'Open Door' by sending 2,500 marines to China in 1900 where they helped to crush the Boxer Rising; she had arranged the 1905 Treaty of Portsmouth which ended the Russo-Japanese War; she had suggested the basis for settling the 1905 Moroccan Crisis; and she had advocated the use of international arbitration at the Hague Conferences of 1899 and 1907. For Wilson, this was the limit of America's involvement. His job was to keep out of Europe's 'Great War'; this was why he told the American people in 1914 that they must remain 'neutral in fact as well as in name . . . impartial in thought as well as in action'.

American attitudes

Americans had no reason to argue with their President. No treaty bound them to the Allies or the Central Powers. They had little sympathy with Europe's problems; in fact, it was to avoid these problems that many immigrants had left their homelands in the first place. Now they believed that the European nations had only themselves to blame, pushed into war by their military alliances and notorious arms race. Of course, there were plenty of emotional* and economic ties with Britain. During 1915–16, America sent half of her exports to the United Kingdom. But these ties were soon forgotten when the Royal Navy stopped and searched American freighters on the high seas. Memories of the 'Chesapeake incident'** flooded back and the newspapers were quick to show how much America resented any British interference with neutral shipping. And yet side by side with this resentment grew an awareness that somehow the future security of the USA was tied up with a British victory in Europe. It was not long before the German habit of sinking unarmed ships changed American indifference into deep concern.

The decline of German-American relations
February 1915–May 1916

Unterseebooten of the Imperial German Navy were the cause of this change. On 4 February 1915 Germany proclaimed a 'war zone' around the British Isles. Submarines would sink enemy ships on sight; and as there was a chance of error creeping into ship-identification any neutral vessel venturing into the zone would be at risk. Wilson regarded this as an affront to the principle of neutrality and promptly warned that the 'Government of the United States would be constrained to hold the Imperial German Government to a strict accountability' for the loss of American ships or American lives. Crisis came with the sinking of the British Cunarder *Lusitania* on 7 May 1915. *U-20* had attacked the huge liner without any warning; 1198 people died—and 128 of them were American citizens. Wilson sent strong protests to Berlin but while these were under review another U-boat sank the *Arabic* and two more Americans died. The Germans, who regretted both sinkings solely on the grounds that they had roused US hostility, apologized and promised that U-boat commanders would signal in advance their intention to attack an *unarmed* liner. This satisfied Wilson who now began to contemplate the role of mediator in the European war. Neither Britain nor Germany relished his intervention for both were now committed to a 'knock-out blow' on the Western Front. This meant that while thousands of French and German soldiers died in the bloodbath at Verdun, American attention riveted on a handful of compatriots injured during a U-boat attack on the Channel steamer *Sussex*. Wilson was irate and threatened to break off relations with Germany. Again the Germans apologized and promised that they would give due warning to merchant ships before firing torpedoes into their unfortunate victims. The incident placed Wilson in a dilemma. He wanted peace, but he would not stop American freighters or American citizens going to Europe. Inevitably, there would be more American deaths. Wilson won the 1916 Presidential campaign on the slogan 'He kept us out of the war!' But what price was he prepared to pay to preserve America's neutrality now?

*In 1859 a US fleet, though strictly neutral, aided a British squadron under attack from Chinese guns. Commodore Tattnall, USN, justified himself with the famous remark: 'Blood is thicker than water'.
**See page 16.

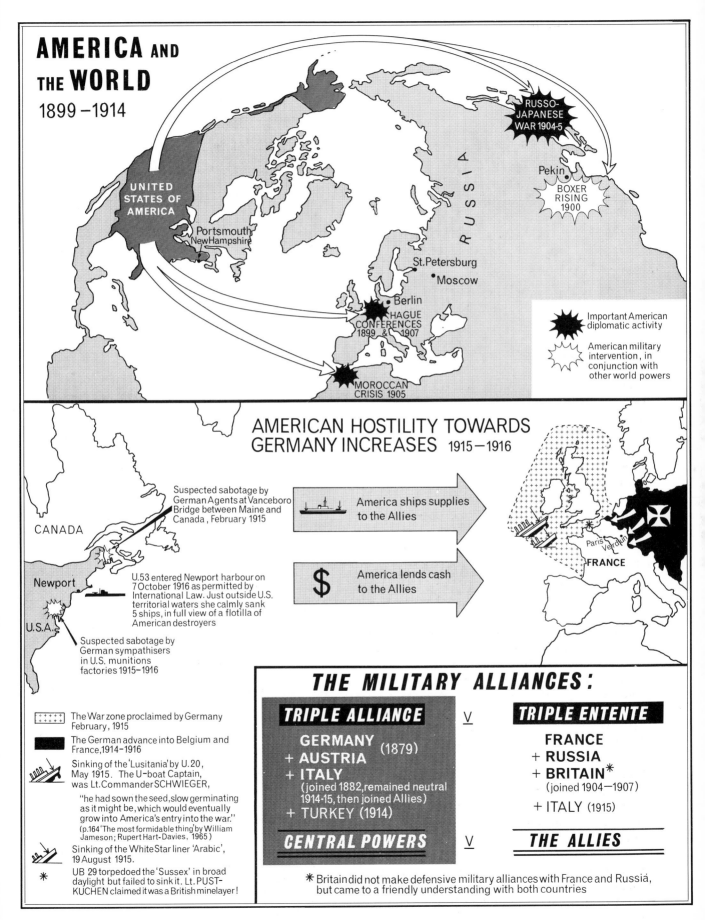

AMERICA AND THE WORLD
1899 – 1914

RUSSO-JAPANESE WAR 1904-5

UNITED STATES OF AMERICA

RUSSIA

Pekin

BOXER RISING 1900

Portsmouth New Hampshire

St. Petersburg
•Moscow

•Berlin
HAGUE CONFERENCES 1899 & 1907

★ Important American diplomatic activity

✦ American military intervention, in conjunction with other world powers

MOROCCAN CRISIS 1905

AMERICAN HOSTILITY TOWARDS GERMANY INCREASES 1915 – 1916

CANADA

Suspected sabotage by German Agents at Vanceboro Bridge between Maine and Canada, February 1915

America ships supplies to the Allies

Newport

U.53 entered Newport harbour on 7 October 1916 as permitted by International Law. Just outside U.S. territorial waters she calmly sank 5 ships, in full view of a flotilla of American destroyers

$ America lends cash to the Allies

Paris Verdun

FRANCE

U.S.A.

Suspected sabotage by German sympathisers in U.S. munitions factories 1915–1916

+++++ The War zone proclaimed by Germany February, 1915

▇ The German advance into Belgium and France, 1914–1916

Sinking of the 'Lusitania' by U.20, May 1915. The U-boat Captain, was Lt. Commander SCHWIEGER,

"he had sown the seed, slow germinating as it might be, which would eventually grow into America's entry into the war."
(p.164 'The most formidable thing' by William Jameson; Rupert Hart-Davies, 1965)

Sinking of the White Star liner 'Arabic', 19 August 1915.

✳ UB 29 torpedoed the 'Sussex' in broad daylight but failed to sink it. Lt. PUST-KUCHEN claimed it was a British minelayer!

THE MILITARY ALLIANCES :

TRIPLE ALLIANCE

GERMANY (1879)
+ AUSTRIA
+ ITALY
(joined 1882, remained neutral 1914-15, then joined Allies)
+ TURKEY (1914)

CENTRAL POWERS

V

TRIPLE ENTENTE

FRANCE
+ RUSSIA
+ BRITAIN✳
(joined 1904–1907)

+ ITALY (1915)

V

THE ALLIES

✳ Britain did not make defensive military alliances with France and Russia, but came to a friendly understanding with both countries

18: America at war

The declaration of war

'I order the unrestricted submarine campaign to begin on 1 February with the utmost energy.' With these ominous words the German Kaiser Wilhelm II sent a hundred U-boats to attack merchant shipping in the war zone. He and his advisers, Ludendorff and Hindenburg, were well aware that indiscriminate sinkings would bring America into the war but they were ready to take this risk if they could starve Britain into an early surrender. 'If Wilson wants war', wrote the Kaiser, 'let him make it and then let him have it'. Now Wilson could no longer, as he put it, 'preserve both the peace and the honour of the United States'. He warned his people of serious Allied weaknesses now that Russia was in the midst of revolutionary turmoil. He spoke of a telegram sent by the German Foreign Secretary Zimmerman and intercepted by British Intelligence: Germany was plotting a Mexican invasion of Texas! Then he revealed that U-boats sank 3 American ships on 18 March—the world was no longer safe for democracy and so America must protect herself against German militarism. He urged Congress to 'exert all its power and employ all its resources to bring the government of the German Empire to terms and end the war'. On 6 April 1917 Congress declared war on Imperial Germany.

The power and resources

For years the Americans had shipped supplies to the Allies and yet they were strangely unprepared for the kind of war now being waged on land, sea and in the air. They had no tanks and little modern artillery. Americans, who had been the first to conquer powered flight, had no aircraft capable of taking on Germany's crack Albatros scouts. The Navy, however, was well-equipped. Thirty-four destroyers sailed to Queenstown for escort duties—they sank a U-boat in November—while several battleships joined the Grand Fleet at Scapa Flow. A token force of US troops arrived in France during June but very few saw action before 1918. Clearly, America's entry into the shooting war could not be decisive until she had recruited, equipped and transported to Europe a very big fighting force. Recruitment was a problem—many Americans remembered the trouble met by Lincoln when he tried to raise an army. However, the Selective Service Act (May 1917) required all men between 21 and 30 to register for military service. Selecting draftees became a ritual; Newton D. Baker, Secretary of War, was solemnly blindfolded before drawing the numbers of the conscripts. Huge training camps—half in the North and half in the South!—rose out of the ground; factories received orders for the mass-production of rifles, gasmasks and uniforms. America's resources were being mobilized in a fast-moving twentieth century industrial revolution—but it could not happen overnight. The shipbuilding industry, for example, had to build new yards and the first prefabricated ship to slide down Hog Island's slipways was as late as August 1918.

The war and the people

Very few Americans questioned the decision to go to war with Germany. They were sure—or at least 67 out of 68 American newspapers *said* they were sure—that there was no other way of dealing with the submarine menace. This explains why they accepted a degree of government control unprecedented in American history. The state took over railways, threatened strikers with the draft, limited free speech and sponsored propaganda films. So that the President could bring America's industrial might to bear, Congress gave him near-dictatorial powers. There was little grumbling. Workers won wage increases; employers saw their profits rise—4000 became millionaires during 1917–18. Negroes left the South to seek work in the North's munition plants but soon encountered plenty of white prejudice. However, they successfully channelled most prejudice into 'Germanophobia'. Despite Wilson's pious statement that 'We have no quarrel with the German people' college and high school students were soon hearing stories about the 'vicious Hun' and discovering that German was dropped from the timetable. Books by German authors disappeared from library shelves and delicatessen coyly renamed their sauerkraut 'liberty cabbage'.* Gradually the Americans found themselves very much in demand. Bolshevik revolutionaries had taken Russia out of the war and Ludendorff was massing his troops on the Western Front. 'The Yanks are coming' might be a popular refrain; but there was some doubt whether they would reach the front line in time.

*The Americans were not unique. The British middle-class had frowned on keeping dachshunds as pets and refrained from drinking hock since 1914.

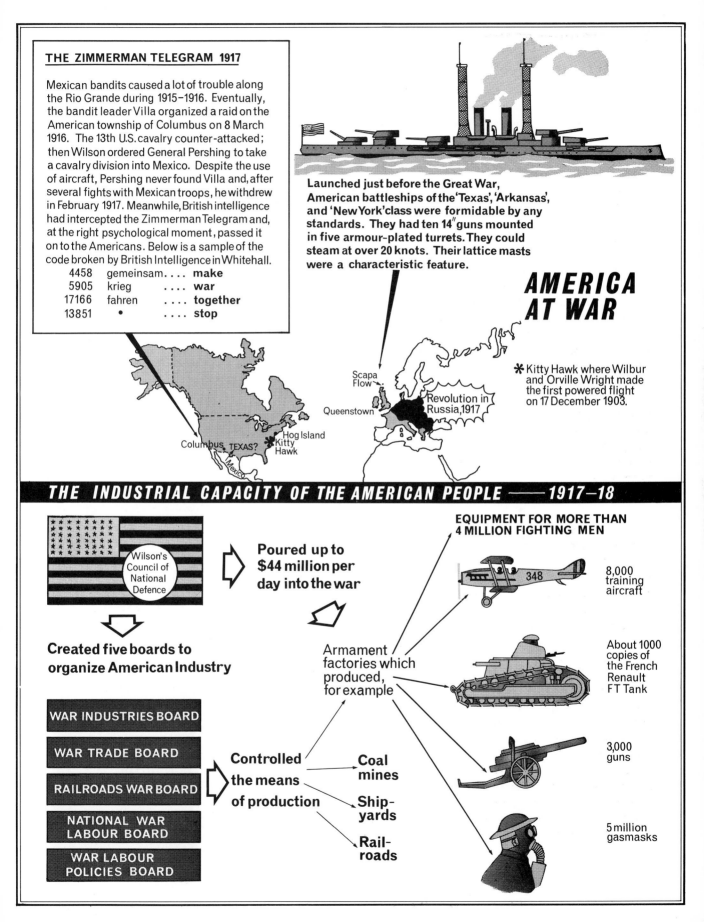

THE ZIMMERMAN TELEGRAM 1917

Mexican bandits caused a lot of trouble along the Rio Grande during 1915–1916. Eventually, the bandit leader Villa organized a raid on the American township of Columbus on 8 March 1916. The 13th U.S. cavalry counter-attacked; then Wilson ordered General Pershing to take a cavalry division into Mexico. Despite the use of aircraft, Pershing never found Villa and, after several fights with Mexican troops, he withdrew in February 1917. Meanwhile, British intelligence had intercepted the Zimmerman Telegram and, at the right psychological moment, passed it on to the Americans. Below is a sample of the code broken by British Intelligence in Whitehall.

4458	gemeinsam	....	**make**
5905	krieg	....	**war**
17166	fahren	....	**together**
13851	•	....	**stop**

Launched just before the Great War, **American battleships of the 'Texas', 'Arkansas', and 'New York' class were formidable by any standards. They had ten 14″ guns mounted in five armour-plated turrets. They could steam at over 20 knots. Their lattice masts were a characteristic feature.**

AMERICA AT WAR

* Kitty Hawk where Wilbur and Orville Wright made the first powered flight on 17 December 1903.

Scapa Flow
Queenstown
Revolution in Russia, 1917
Columbus TEXAS?
Mexico
Hog Island
Kitty Hawk

THE INDUSTRIAL CAPACITY OF THE AMERICAN PEOPLE —— 1917–18

Wilson's Council of National Defence

Poured up to **$44 million per day into the war**

Created five boards to organize American Industry

WAR INDUSTRIES BOARD

WAR TRADE BOARD

RAILROADS WAR BOARD

NATIONAL WAR LABOUR BOARD

WAR LABOUR POLICIES BOARD

Controlled the means of production

Armament factories which produced, for example

Coal mines

Ship-yards

Rail-roads

EQUIPMENT FOR MORE THAN 4 MILLION FIGHTING MEN

8,000 training aircraft

About 1000 copies of the French Renault FT Tank

3,000 guns

5 million gasmasks

19: Over there!

The Fourteen Points

On 8 January 1918 Woodrow Wilson described his Fourteen Points to Congress. They contained a remarkable recipe for the perpetuation of peace in the post-war world. Secret diplomacy, trade barriers and arms races were the root cause of war—in his view—and they must be banned. Freedom of the seas must be guaranteed to all nations. Subject peoples, wherever they might be, must have the right of 'self-determination' and a chance to decide their own destinies. And, above all, there must be a 'general association of nations' for the future ordering of international affairs. None of the Allies objected to the Fourteen Points and most people naturally assumed that they represented a statement of Allied war aims. But the war was far from won. Ludendorff launched *Operation Michael*—the German Army's greatest attack—on 21 March 1918. Under his savage thrusts the British reeled back while American aid was still aboard transports sailing across the Atlantic Ocean. In fact, the Allies stemmed the German attack just outside Amiens before the big contingents of American troops landed in France. Their chance to prove their worth came on 28 May.

Combat

a) *on land*: The large numbers of American troops gave the Allies an enormous advantage though it is doubtful whether, as Ludendorff later maintained, their presence made America 'the decisive power in the war'. US units still lacked the more sophisticated weapons and remained dependent upon Britain and France for their aircraft and artillery. But they relieved their weary allies on large sectors of the front. Their first major attack on *Cantigny* (28 May) was a complete success; in June 200,000 Americans bored into the German salient at *Château-Thierry*. Marshal Foch, Supreme Allied Commander, allowed General Pershing to organize his men into the First American Army and in September they flattened another German salient at *St. Mihiel*. At the end of the month they were ready for their great effort: the attack on the *Argonne*. 1,200,000 troops began their hard slog through heavily defended German positions until they reached the Meuse valley. Here the fighting went on for weeks and, for the cost of 112,000 casualties, two US armies (Pershing formed the 2nd US Army in October) smashed 47 German divisions. By Armistice Day (11 November 1918) the American Expeditionary Force had made a major contribution to the Allied attacks which defeated the German Army on the Western Front.

b) *on sea*: The US Navy concentrated on the U-boat menace. Equipped with new hyrophones and depth-charges, its destroyers and sub-chasers convoyed 2 million troops across the Atlantic and not a single American soldier died en route for France. But the Navy's most remarkable achievement was the colossal minefield sown between Britain and Norway; many a U-boat foundered trying to pierce this underwater screen.

c) *in the air*: Even before the outbreak of war American volunteers joined the French Air Force where they fought in the celebrated *Escadrille Lafayette* which flew Spad and Nieuport *chasers*. Eventually, 45 US squadrons operated on the Western Front. Some, equipped with British D.H.4s and led by General 'Billy' Mitchell, bombed German targets behind the lines; others were *pursuit* squadrons and some fliers—particularly Captain 'Eddie' Rickenbacker—became noted fighter aces.

WILSON'S FOURTEEN POINTS   JANUARY 1918

1 NO MORE SECRET DIPLOMACY

2 ABSOLUTE FREEDOM OF THE SEAS

3 NO MORE ECONOMIC BARRIERS TO BE PLACED IN THE WAY OF INTERNATIONAL TRADE

4 WORLD WIDE REDUCTION OF ARMAMENTS

5 A FAIR SETTLEMENT OF ALL COLONIAL PROBLEMS ESSENTIAL

6 EVACUATE ALL RUSSIAN TERRITORY: GIVE THE PEOPLE A CHANCE TO SORT OUT THEIR OWN PROBLEMS

7 REHABILITATE BELGIUM— a symbol to the rest of mankind.

8 ALL FRENCH TERRITORY, INCLUDING ALSACE & LORRAINE, TO BE RESTORED

9 SETTLE ITALY'S FRONTIERS

10 GIVE INDEPENDENCE TO THE DIFFERENT PEOPLES OF THE AUSTRO-HUNGARIAN EMPIRE

11 EVACUATE THE BALKAN STATES

12 LET THE PEOPLES OF THE TURKISH EMPIRE SEEK THEIR INDEPENDENCE

13 SET UP AN INDEPENDENT POLISH STATE

14 'A GENERAL ASSOCIATION OF NATIONS MUST BE FORMED.'

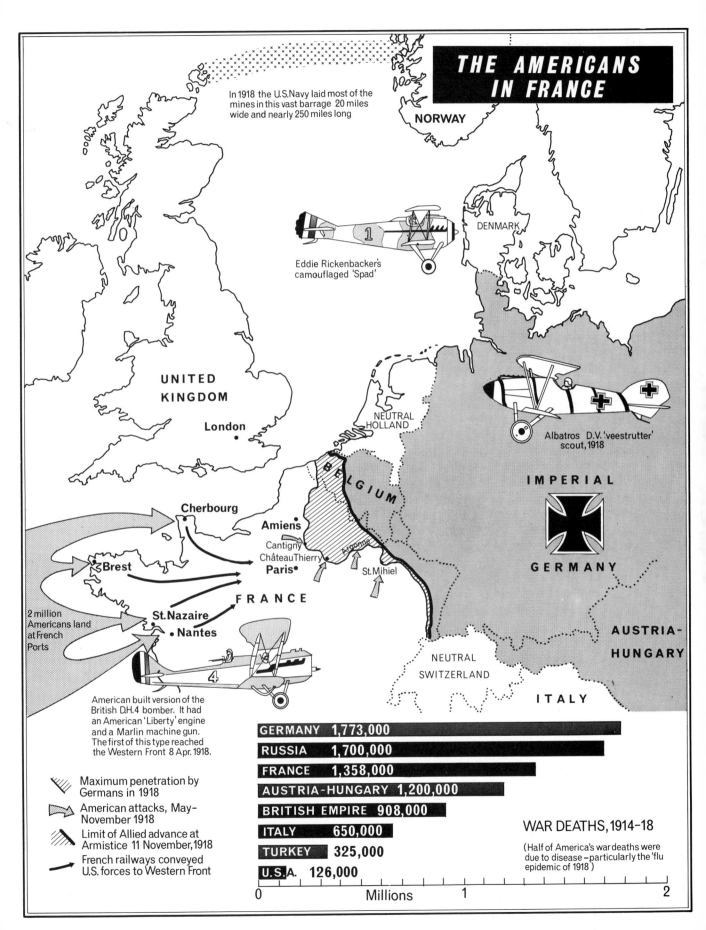

THE AMERICANS IN FRANCE

In 1918 the U.S.Navy laid most of the mines in this vast barrage 20 miles wide and nearly 250 miles long

NORWAY

DENMARK

Eddie Rickenbacker's camouflaged 'Spad'

UNITED KINGDOM

London

NEUTRAL HOLLAND

Albatros D.V. 'veestrutter' scout, 1918

IMPERIAL

GERMANY

Cherbourg

Amiens

Cantigny

Château Thierry

Argonne

BELGIUM

Paris

St. Mihiel

Brest

FRANCE

AUSTRIA-HUNGARY

2 million Americans land at French Ports

St.Nazaire

Nantes

NEUTRAL SWITZERLAND

ITALY

American built version of the British D.H.4 bomber. It had an American 'Liberty' engine and a Marlin machine gun. The first of this type reached the Western Front 8 Apr. 1918.

Maximum penetration by Germans in 1918

American attacks, May–November 1918

Limit of Allied advance at Armistice 11 November, 1918

French railways conveyed U.S. forces to Western Front

GERMANY	1,773,000
RUSSIA	1,700,000
FRANCE	1,358,000
AUSTRIA-HUNGARY	1,200,000
BRITISH EMPIRE	908,000
ITALY	650,000
TURKEY	325,000
U.S.A.	126,000

WAR DEATHS, 1914–18

(Half of America's war deaths were due to disease – particularly the 'flu epidemic of 1918)

0   Millions   1   2

20: The Peacemaker

Wilson goes to Europe

In December 1918 the US troopship *George Washington* nosed into the harbour at Brest. On board was President Wilson, ready to attend the Paris Peace Talks scheduled to start in the New Year. But first he found time to tour the countryside of the Allies—the USA had never formed an alliance but preferred to regard herself as an associated power—and there he told delighted crowds that he had come to Europe to fashion an eternal peace that was both just and right. Other Allied leaders paid lip service to his idealism but never failed to voice their own selfish views. Orlando of Italy wanted to settle his northern frontiers; Clemenceau of France—he was always contemptuous of Wilson—intended to secure France against the threat of another German attack; Lloyd George of Britain was after hard cash. 'When Germany defeated France [*i.e. in 1871*],' said the British Prime Minister, 'she made France pay. That is the principle she herself established. That is the principle we shall proceed upon . . . .' Another politician put it more crudely: 'We'll get out of her all that you can get out of a lemon and a bit more. I would squeeze her until you can hear the pips squeak!' Yet Wilson was the only member of the 'Big Four' who did not speak for all his people. The 1918 Congressional elections had returned Republican majorities to the Senate and the House of Representatives; while a Democrat President conducted America's affairs in Paris his Republican opponents took control of the powerful Senate Foreign Relations Committee. Wilson was in Paris with the hopes of the world on his shoulders; but, as Churchill later observed, behind him lay 'the sullen veto of the Senate'.

The Peace Conference 1919

The 'Big Four' began their talks on 12 January 1919 and after much debate they approved the creation of a League of Nations to be bound by a Covenant that Wilson and his committee members would draft. At the heart of this was Article X: 'The members of the League undertake to respect and preserve the territorial integrity and existing political independence of all members of the League . . .' With this in his pocket, Wilson sailed back to America to test the Senate's reaction. To his disgust, it rejected the Convenant because the wording seemed to require America's constant involvement in world crises. Wilson retorted that he would sew up the Covenant with the final Peace Treaty so tightly that not even the US Senate could unravel it. Then he returned to Paris. There he was confident that the League would be able to handle any territorial problems that might come along. Unfortunately, the complexities of Central European and Middle East politics often escaped him and Wilson soon sacrificed several of his famous Fourteen Points. Nevertheless, he persuaded the Allies not to charge Germany for the entire cost of the war and substituted instead the idea of fixed reparation payments; he persuaded them to mandate all former German and Turkish colonies to the League; and he carved independent nations out of the defunct Austro-Hungarian Empire. Perhaps he was ill-equipped for this last task. Having decided on Czechoslovakia's frontiers, he was appalled to discover just how many Germans lived inside the Sudetenland—a problem that would steer Europe towards World War II twenty years later.

America opts out

By April 1919 Wilson was exhausted. He had constant bouts of 'flu and left Europe as soon as the Germans accepted the dictated *Versailles Treaty* on 28 June. He reached America on 8 July; two days later he took the draft of the Treaty to the Senate. The Senators rejected it*. This made Wilson decide to stump round the country to whip up popular support for the League of Nations. It was against his doctor's advice and soon the effort proved too much. He had a stroke and was out of politics for months. Later on, during 1920, he tried to turn the Presidential election into a referendum on the League. Harding, the Republican candidate, opposed US entry into the League and played on the feelings of all Americans who, though they favoured peace, did not want the USA drawn into every international squabble in the future. They were prepared to be involved up to a point; but Wilson was adamant—this was simply not enough. So the electorate had to choose between Wilson's world involvement** and Harding's offer of a 'return to Normalcy' and a policy of 'Isolation'. They chose Harding and rejected membership of the League. When Harding hear of his victory he said, 'I am just a man of limited talents from a small town. I don't seem to grasp that I am President'. It did not bode too well for the future.

*Germany and America signed the formal Treaty of Berlin in 1921. It contained most of the Versailles clauses apart from references to the League, the International Labour Office and certain territorial changes.
**Wilson was not a Presidential candidate in 1920. The Democrats nominated James C. Cox, Governor of Ohio. Wilson, now permanently crippled, died in February 1924.

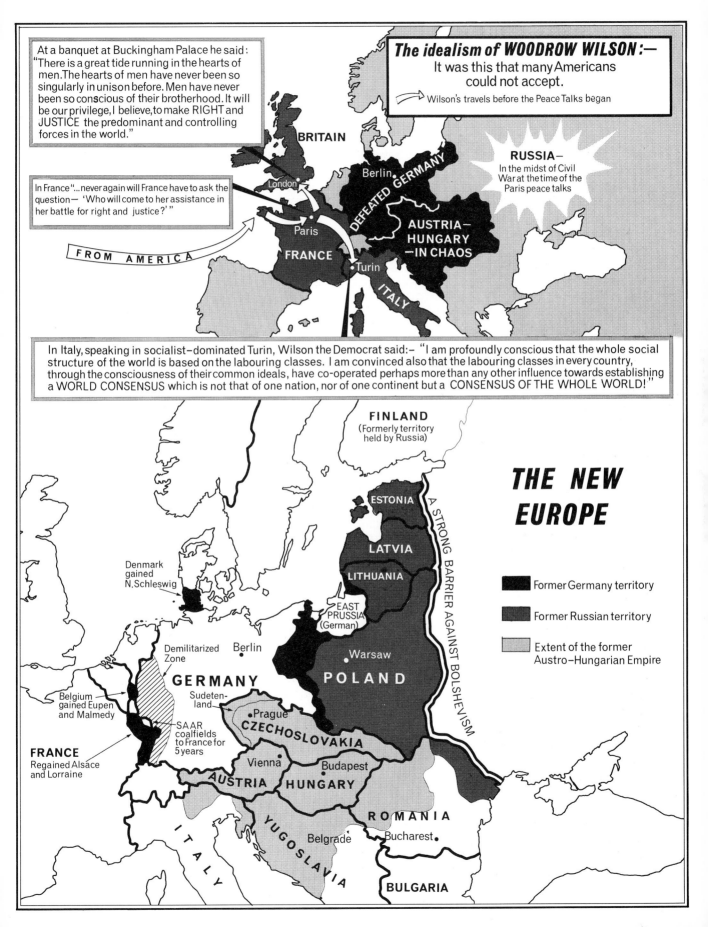

At a banquet at Buckingham Palace he said: "There is a great tide running in the hearts of men. The hearts of men have never been so singularly in unison before. Men have never been so conscious of their brotherhood. It will be our privilege, I believe, to make RIGHT and JUSTICE the predominant and controlling forces in the world."

The idealism of WOODROW WILSON :—
It was this that many Americans could not accept.

Wilson's travels before the Peace Talks began

BRITAIN

London

Berlin

DEFEATED GERMANY

RUSSIA—
In the midst of Civil War at the time of the Paris peace talks

In France "...never again will France have to ask the question— 'Who will come to her assistance in her battle for right and justice?'"

Paris

AUSTRIA–
HUNGARY
—IN CHAOS

FROM AMERICA

FRANCE

Turin

ITALY

In Italy, speaking in socialist–dominated Turin, Wilson the Democrat said:– "I am profoundly conscious that the whole social structure of the world is based on the labouring classes. I am convinced also that the labouring classes in every country, through the consciousness of their common ideals, have co-operated perhaps more than any other influence towards establishing a WORLD CONSENSUS which is not that of one nation, nor of one continent but a CONSENSUS OF THE WHOLE WORLD!"

FINLAND
(Formerly territory held by Russia)

ESTONIA

LATVIA

LITHUANIA

Denmark gained N. Schleswig

EAST PRUSSIA (German)

THE NEW EUROPE

A STRONG BARRIER AGAINST BOLSHEVISM

Warsaw

Demilitarized Zone

Berlin

POLAND

Belgium gained Eupen and Malmedy

GERMANY

Sudeten-land

Former Germany territory

Former Russian territory

SAAR coalfields to France for 5 years

Prague

CZECHOSLOVAKIA

Extent of the former Austro–Hungarian Empire

FRANCE
Regained Alsace and Lorraine

Vienna

Budapest

AUSTRIA

HUNGARY

ITALY

R O M A N I A

YUGOSLAVIA

Belgrade

Bucharest

BULGARIA

45

21: America and the Bolsheviks

The interventions in Russia

Between 1918 and 1922 no less than a dozen nations intervened in the civil war being fought in Russia between Lenin's Bolsheviks and the counter-revolutionaries. American troops served side by side with British, Canadian, French, Chinese and Japanese in what was probably the most confused and discreditable episode in the final stages of the First World War. The interventions were supposed to achieve three aims: to capture large dumps of war materials before the Germans or Bolsheviks could lay their hands on them; to re-establish in Russia a fighting front against the Germans; and to rescue the *Czech Legion*—stranded prisoners-of-war who wanted to fight their own war of independence against Austria. According to the information that filtered through to Woodrow Wilson in Washington, these were the Allies' priorities. Wilson had no wish to intervene—it was a contradiction of his Sixth Point. However, the military situation appeared to warrant some military action in Russia. *Operation Michael* had brought the Germans to within thirty miles of Paris; while the *Peace of Brest-Litovsk*, forced on Russia in March 1918, allowed the Germans to pillage the wheatlands of the Ukraine. It was vital, said the British, to resume the war in Russia; Marshal Foch agreed and assured Wilson that he could spare some US troops from the Western Front. The President yielded to pressure and allowed three battalions of raw recruits to be kitted out in England for a Russian expedition.

Archangel 1918–19

Under British command, these troops reached Archangel on 4 September 1918. Two battalions, moving south in search of the German foe, soon clashed with Bolshevik troops and found themselves to be unwilling participants in the Russian civil war. Nearly 300 miles inland, freezing in sub-zero temperatures, these young Americans built log blockhouses in an effort to keep out both the Russian winter and the Red Army. And they were still there when the war on the Western Front ended in November 1918. With their troopships iced up in Archangel harbour, they waited while the politicians argued about their future. Winston Churchill wanted to reinforce them so they could crush Bolshevism once and for all. 'If we don't put our foot on the egg,' he said, 'we shall have to chase the chicken round the farmyard of the world.' Wilson was not a bit impressed. He wanted his troops out of Northern Russia as soon as possible and in July 1919 the last US soldiers departed.

Siberia 1918–20

Meanwhile, the Czech Legion had occupied Vladivostok where even bigger arms dumps existed. Wilson heard that bands of German prisoners-of-war, armed to the teeth, were roaming eastern Russia at will. He agreed that American and Japanese troops should occupy the port and provide security for Czech soldiers who wished to travel westwards along the Trans-Siberian Railway. Two regiments of US troops—the advance guard of over 7000 men—left Manila in August 1918 and landed at Vladivostok. Their task was to guard sections of the railway and, more important, to keep an eye on the Japanese who might try to carve an empire out of eastern Russia. With the nearest German soldier 5000 miles away, this ridiculous situation continued until the Armistice in November 1918. American units then moved into the interior towards Lake Baikal and though they never made contact with regular units of the Red Army they frequently clashed with partisans and lost 400 men in the process. It was not until 1 April 1920 that the last American soldiers evacuated Russia.

American aid to Russia 1921–3

The interventions were a total failure. Even worse, they actively encouraged resistance against the Bolsheviks so that thousands of Russians lost their lives in a futile cause. They also provided Lenin and the Bolsheviks with propaganda evidence of America's 'imperial ambitions'. Certainly, some of President Wilson's advisers favoured the destruction of Bolshevism. But the President did not; once he saw that the counter-revolutionaries were incapable of providing the Russian people with a democratic form of government he refused to keep his troops in Russia. And with his retirement from politics, other Americans sought to offer the Russian people as much material aid as possible. Lenin accepted an offer of help from the *American Relief Administration* (ARA) and during 1921 the first shipments of food entered Russia. Working with Jewish and Quaker relief organizations, ARA saved 10 million Russians from disease and starvation. Medical teams inoculated about 8 million people; food parcels fed them; tons of seed corn arrived to plant the derelict farmlands; Red Cross equipment stocked thousands of Russian hospitals. It was a practical gesture of humanity from a United States of America that communists everywhere were now labelling an evil, imperialist nation.

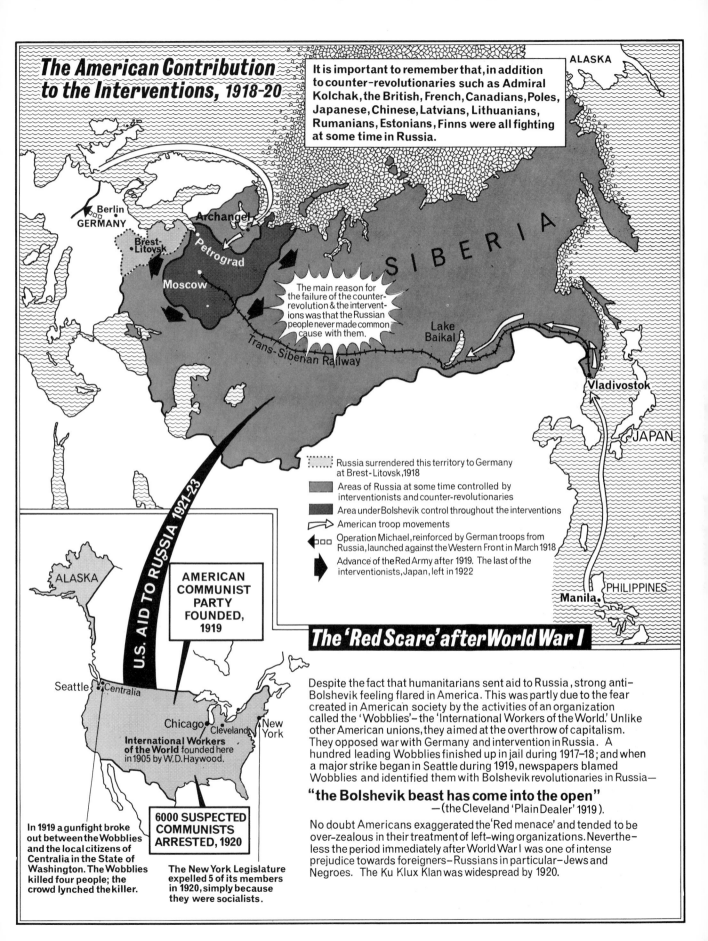

The American Contribution to the Interventions, 1918-20

It is important to remember that, in addition to counter-revolutionaries such as Admiral Kolchak, the British, French, Canadians, Poles, Japanese, Chinese, Latvians, Lithuanians, Rumanians, Estonians, Finns were all fighting at some time in Russia.

ALASKA

Berlin
GERMANY

Brest-Litovsk

Archangel

Petrograd

Moscow

SIBERIA

The main reason for the failure of the counter-revolution & the interventions was that the Russian people never made common cause with them.

Trans-Siberian Railway

Lake Baikal

Vladivostok

JAPAN

PHILIPPINES

Manila

Russia surrendered this territory to Germany at Brest-Litovsk, 1918

Areas of Russia at some time controlled by interventionists and counter-revolutionaries

Area under Bolshevik control throughout the interventions

American troop movements

Operation Michael, reinforced by German troops from Russia, launched against the Western Front in March 1918

Advance of the Red Army after 1919. The last of the interventionists, Japan, left in 1922

U.S. AID TO RUSSIA 1921-23

ALASKA

AMERICAN COMMUNIST PARTY FOUNDED, 1919

Seattle · Centralia

Chicago · Cleveland · New York

International Workers of the World founded here in 1905 by W.D. Haywood.

In 1919 a gunfight broke out between the Wobblies and the local citizens of Centralia in the State of Washington. The Wobblies killed four people; the crowd lynched the killer.

6000 SUSPECTED COMMUNISTS ARRESTED, 1920

The New York Legislature expelled 5 of its members in 1920, simply because they were socialists.

The 'Red Scare' after World War I

Despite the fact that humanitarians sent aid to Russia, strong anti-Bolshevik feeling flared in America. This was partly due to the fear created in American society by the activities of an organization called the 'Wobblies'– the 'International Workers of the World.' Unlike other American unions, they aimed at the overthrow of capitalism. They opposed war with Germany and intervention in Russia. A hundred leading Wobblies finished up in jail during 1917–18; and when a major strike began in Seattle during 1919, newspapers blamed Wobblies and identified them with Bolshevik revolutionaries in Russia—

"the Bolshevik beast has come into the open"
—(the Cleveland 'Plain Dealer' 1919).

No doubt Americans exaggerated the 'Red menace' and tended to be over-zealous in their treatment of left-wing organizations. Nevertheless the period immediately after World War I was one of intense prejudice towards foreigners–Russians in particular–Jews and Negroes. The Ku Klux Klan was widespread by 1920.

Further Reading

Theme 3 – The First World War and Its Aftermath

See *Purnell's History of the First World War* for a detailed and well-illustrated account

Spread

17. 'Be neutral . . . in thought as well as in action' *The Most Formidable Thing*, William Jameson, Rupert Hart-Davis, 1965 (Chapters 9 & 10)

18. America at war *The Great Departure*, Daniel Smith, John Wiley, 1965

19. Over there! *Concise Dictionary of American History*, pp. 1025–1029

20. The Peacemaker *Wilson and the Dream of Reason*, Esmond Wright, History Today, April 1960.

21. America and the Bolsheviks *Russia and the West*, George Kennan, Mentor,

THEME 4

The Preservation of Democracy in America

It had been an unwilling America that had gone to war in 1917 to succour a Europe which millions of its first-generation immigrant citizens had already rejected. Once the war was won, Congress expressed its lack of confidence in Europe by refusing to sign the Versailles Peace Treaty and by opting out of the League of Nations. The American people rejected President Wilson and jumped on the band-wagon of 'normalcy' and set out to have a good time. But the passing of the Eighteenth Amendment cast a blight on the so-called Jazz Age and introduced corruption into all levels of American political life. The 'Roaring Twenties', associated with Prohibition, gang warfare and G-men, were years in which the American way of life became both the most advanced and the most notorious in the world.

Then came the catastrophic and totally unexpected Wall Street Crash. The United States, whose overseas investments and loans propped up the economy of the German Weimar Republic and, to a lesser extent, most of the world's trade, suffered an acute depression which ultimately put 12 million Americans out of a job. The disaster had world-wide effects. It knocked away Germany's economic supports and paved the way for Adolf Hitler's rise to power. There were signs even in America that democracy might totter and perish. Fortunately, at almost the same moment as Adolf Hitler became Chancellor of Germany, Franklin Delano Roosevelt became President of the United States. Roosevelt provided a non-violent answer to most of America's problems during the Thirties. His 'New Deal' gave jobs to millions and alleviated, even if it didn't cure, the misery that had swept over the land. By 1939 there was still a great deal of unemployment—but conditions had became better. Undoubtedly, the main reason for flourishing steel towns and improvements in farm prices was Roosevelt's policy of aiding Britain and China in their struggle against Nazi Germany and Imperial Japan.

Then came the 'day of infamy'. On Sunday 7 December 1941 Japanese carrier aircraft attacked Pearl Harbor. Once more America had become a 'reluctant belligerent'.

22: The search for peace and stability, 1921–1929

Isolationism

America's attitude to world affairs after 1921 is usually described as isolationist. This is true only in so far that she never joined the League of Nations and steadfastly refused to entangle herself in foreign alliances. But isolationist is hardly a reasonable description of a nation that played so decisive a role in world finance as well as in the quest for international peace.

The reduction of armaments

America had specific motives in mind when she urged a reduction in world armaments. President Harding had a very real fear of Japan and rightly assumed that further growth in Japanese military power might encourage this ambitious nation to encroach upon China. In 1921 he invited those countries with economic and military interests in the Pacific to attend the Washington Naval Conference. Here Secretary of State Hughes suggested that navies should scrap their capital ships until the battlefleets of Britain, USA and Japan reached a *tonnage* in the ratio of 5:5:3. At the same time, Britain and the USA shelved plans to fortify their naval bases in the Pacific on the condition that Japan renounced her footholds in China and recognized the long-standing principle of the 'Open Door'. It was a more than generous gesture on the part of America. At the Washington Naval Conference 1921–2 she deliberately abandoned the chance of becoming the strongest naval power in the world and seriously weakened her defences in the Pacific.

The renunciation of war

America had declared war on Germany on 6 April 1917. Exactly ten years later the French suggested that Americans should join them in a general renunciation of war. Secretary of State Kellogg met the French Premier Briand in Paris and the famous *Kellogg-Briand Pact* of 1928 resulted. Eventually, 62 nations—including Soviet Russia—renounced war 'as an instrument of national policies'. It had been a splendid verbal exercise. Unfortunately, the world paid only lip service to the high principles it enshrined.

War debts and reparations

Meanwhile America turned her thoughts to the billions of dollars she had lent the Allied nations since the outbreak of war in 1914. Now she hoped to recover some of her outlay with, wherever possible, some interest. Not all of Washington's financial experts thought this was wise. Obviously, there was no hope of persuading Lenin to return money lent originally to the Tsar. The rest of the Allies were likely to prove difficult too—most suffered from growing unemployment and a shortage of cash. But the USA persisted in its quest and soon discovered that neither Britain nor France intended to repay debts to America until the Germans had paid their reparations. A *Reparations Committee* had already settled the amount Germany was to pay (1921) but the 1919 Versailles Treaty had robbed the Germans of a great deal of vital industrial equipment. Moreover, since the Armistice the Germans had suffered an abortive communist revolution 1918–19, depression, unemployment and inflation. Before long they defaulted on their reparations payments and a Franco-Belgian army promptly invaded the Ruhr at the beginning of 1923. In the resulting political and economic chaos Adolf Hitler carried out his unsuccessful attempt to overthrow the Weimar government of Germany.

Aid to Weimar

These events led to the total collapse of the German monetary system and forced the Americans to intervene. General Dawes and a team of experts drew up their 1924 plan to place Germany's finances on a brand new footing. They devised a new currency and loaned German industrialists 200 million dollars so they could start afresh. After this the Germans paid their reparations faithfully until crisis struck again in 1929. Once more the Americans came to the rescue and another team of experts, led by Owen D. Young, arranged a plan whereby the Germans could meet their reparations by making annual payments over the next 59 years. It was ironical, in the light of events a decade later, that America's efforts to achieve peace and financial stability should bring immediate benefits first to Japan and then to Germany.

Collapse

But within a few weeks of the Young Plan the Wall Street Crash heralded a depression that shattered the world's trading system and demolished the delicate structure of war debts and reparations. Everyone now asserted that they could not possibly meet their payments to America and the USA had to write-off most of her investment in reparations as well as the war debts. It made the American people very bitter about unreliable Europeans and a lot of them went along with President Coolidge's* cutting remark: 'They hired the money, didn't they?'

*Calvin Coolidge was President of the United States from 3 August 1923 until 1929.

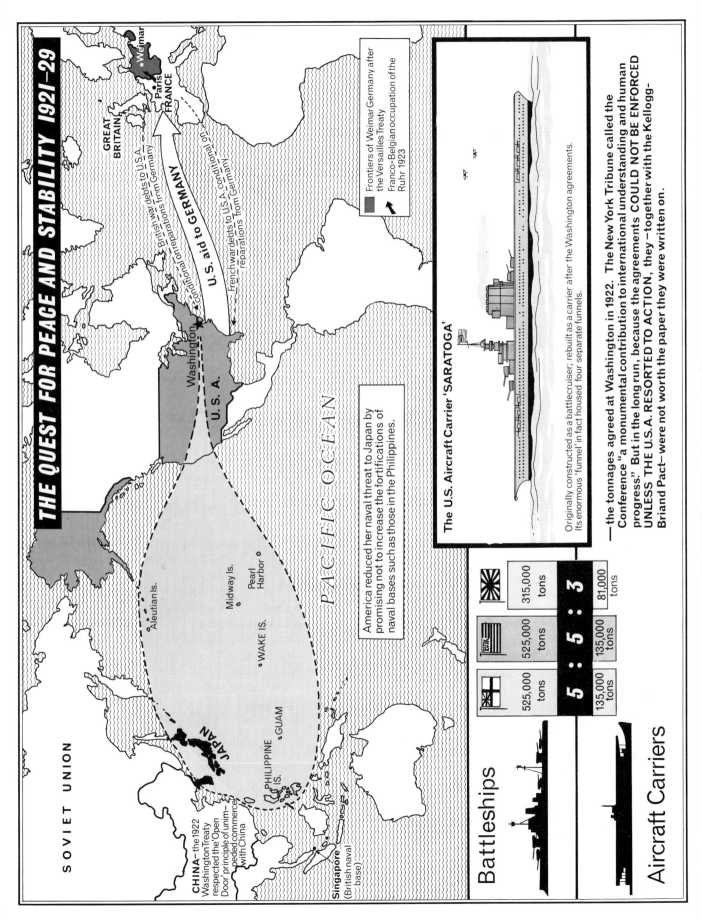

THE QUEST FOR PEACE AND STABILITY 1921–29

SOVIET UNION

GREAT BRITAIN

Paris
FRANCE

Weimar

CHINA – the 1922 Washington Treaty respected the 'Open Door' principle of unimpeded commerce with China

British war debts to U.S.A.
conditional on reparations from Germany
U. S. aid to GERMANY
French war debts to U.S.A. conditional on reparations from Germany

Washington

U. S. A.

Aleutian Is.

Midway Is.

Pearl Harbor

°WAKE IS.

°GUAM

JAPAN

PHILIPPINE IS.

America reduced her naval threat to Japan by promising not to increase the fortifications of naval bases such as those in the Philippines.

PACIFIC OCEAN

Singapore
(British naval base)

Frontiers of Weimar Germany after the Versailles Treaty

Franco-Belgian occupation of the Ruhr 1923

The U.S. Aircraft Carrier 'SARATOGA'

Originally constructed as a battlecruiser; rebuilt as a carrier after the Washington agreements. Its enormous 'funnel' in fact housed four separate funnels.

—the tonnages agreed at Washington in 1922. The New York Tribune called the Conference "a monumental contribution to international understanding and human progress." But in the long run, because the agreements COULD NOT BE ENFORCED UNLESS THE U.S.A. RESORTED TO ACTION, they – together with the Kellogg-Briand Pact – were not worth the paper they were written on.

Battleships

525,000 tons	525,000 tons	315,000 tons

5 : 5 : 3

135,000 tons	135,000 tons	81,000 tons

Aircraft Carriers

23: The Roaring Twenties and the Crash of 1929

The Roaring Twenties

These were the years in which the extraordinary contrasts within American society became more apparent than ever before. For the millions of city-dwellers, life had never been more exciting. With a shorter working week and a bigger pay packet, a new army of consumers bought automobiles, radios and refrigerators. With their increased leisure time, they became movie addicts or cheered themselves hoarse at the local ball-game. They thrilled to Lindbergh's solo transatlantic flight in 1927; they read with fascination the reports of Chicago's gang warfare after the *Eighteenth Amendment* to the US Constitution prohibited 'the manufacture, sale or transportation of intoxicating liquors' (1919). They argued furiously over the rights and wrongs of the 1925 Scopes case in which a biology teacher challenged the Tennessee State ruling that all instruction relating to the creation of the universe had to be based on biblical rather than upon scientific explanations. They aired their prejudices about immigrants and Negroes—though most were sickened by the execution of Sacco and Vanzetti* in 1927 and by the reports of Ku Klux Klan atrocities. But above all these Americans radiated great confidence in the future. The Roaring Twenties were an age of optimism; as far as they were concerned, 'Uncle Sam' was the greatest country in the world.

Poverty

Other Americans, also numbered in millions, were anything but optimistic. Since the war ended in 1918, food prices had dropped until many farmers could not meet their mortgage repayments. Every year, thousands abandoned their farms and headed for the cities—where they swelled the unemployment problem—while the rest struggled on as best they could. But these farmers couldn't afford to wire their homesteads for electricity, let alone buy washing-machines or refrigerators. Nor could they afford to part exchange their wartime Model T for a glistening new Chevrolet. Therefore, a large percentage of the population failed to share in the prosperity that was supposed to characterize the Roaring Twenties. More important, they were potential consumers who could not buy their own country's mass-produced goods. Hire purchase and credit facilities might disguise the need to find ready cash; but they could not *cure* poverty. America's industrial and political leadership ought to have recognized these symptoms of economic unhealthiness; they should have redistributed America's very considerable wealth. But they did nothing; offering to help poor farmers, itinerant workers and unemployed labourers smacked too much of socialism for their liking.

The perils of prosperity

Though the industrialists were reluctant to solve the growing consumer crisis, they spared no effort to extract cash from those who had some spare dollars. They spent fortunes on advertising to persuade the average American family that it was vital to 'keep up with the Joneses'—and, of course, a lot of families responded. But just as many wanted to invest rather than just spend their extra cash. They believed that the road to instant wealth was through investment on the stock exchange—and so a 'get rich quick' craze swept over the country after 1926. Millions of ordinary people spent money on the Wall Street stock exchange and their eagerness to buy encouraged the mushrooming of all sorts of investment companies such as Goldman, Sachs & Co., described opposite. By the beginning of 1929 billions of dollars—an unparalleled investment—inflated the value of shares far beyond their true worth. All of this money rested on a rickety foundation that could so easily collapse.

The Wall Street Crash 1929

During September some stock exchange traders decided to cash in on the abnormally high share prices by unloading large blocks of shares for sale on the open market. Immediately, brokers who had lent clients money to buy shares saw this as a danger signal and called in their loans. Customers naturally tried to raise cash by selling their stock and when this depressed share prices the nation began to panic. Everybody tried to salvage their investment and on 'Black Thursday' (24 October) nearly 13 million shares changed hands. For the next five days, America's horde of speculators scrambled to find purchasers for shares which were virtually worthless. By 29 October, it was all over. The Wall Street Crash had ruined thousands of families and was leading directly to the collapse of industry and the growth of mass unemployment. It also accelerated a worldwide trade recession. This was the beginning of the 'Great Depression', the most shattering experience—if perhaps one excludes Pearl Harbor—in the recent history of the American people.

---

*Nicola Sacco and Bartolomeo Vanzetti were Italian immigrants. They were also atheists and anarchists. Found guilty of a murder at South Braintree, Massachusetts, they protested their innocence at their trial in 1920. Despite scanty prosecution evidence, all appeals failed and they were executed as late as 1927.

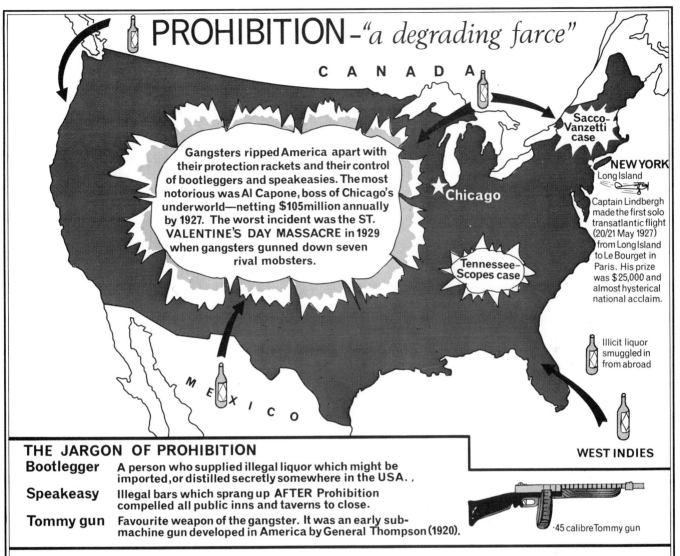

PROHIBITION – *"a degrading farce"*

CANADA

Gangsters ripped America apart with their protection rackets and their control of bootleggers and speakeasies. The most notorious was Al Capone, boss of Chicago's underworld—netting $105million annually by 1927. The worst incident was the ST. VALENTINE'S DAY MASSACRE in 1929 when gangsters gunned down seven rival mobsters.

★ Chicago

Sacco-Vanzetti case

NEW YORK
Long Island

Captain Lindbergh made the first solo transatlantic flight (20/21 May 1927) from Long Island to Le Bourget in Paris. His prize was $25,000 and almost hysterical national acclaim.

Tennessee-Scopes case

MEXICO

Illicit liquor smuggled in from abroad

WEST INDIES

THE JARGON OF PROHIBITION

Bootlegger A person who supplied illegal liquor which might be imported, or distilled secretly somewhere in the USA.

Speakeasy Illegal bars which sprang up AFTER Prohibition compelled all public inns and taverns to close.

Tommy gun Favourite weapon of the gangster. It was an early sub-machine gun developed in America by General Thompson (1920).

·45 calibre Tommy gun

The nation-wide share-buying craze that preceded the CRASH

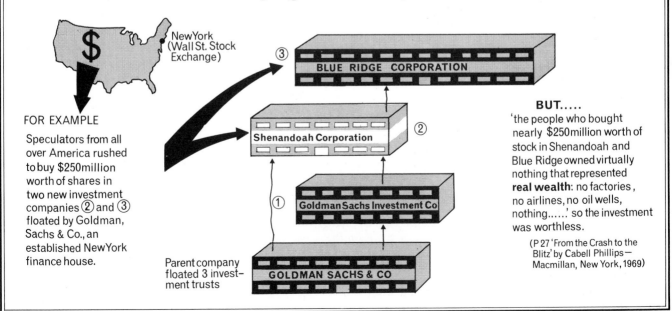

New York (Wall St. Stock Exchange)

③ BLUE RIDGE CORPORATION

Shenandoah Corporation ②

FOR EXAMPLE

Speculators from all over America rushed to buy $250million worth of shares in two new investment companies ② and ③ floated by Goldman, Sachs & Co., an established New York finance house.

① Goldman Sachs Investment Co

Parent company floated 3 investment trusts

GOLDMAN SACHS & CO

BUT.....
'the people who bought nearly $250million worth of stock in Shenandoah and Blue Ridge owned virtually nothing that represented **real wealth**: no factories, no airlines, no oil wells, nothing.....' so the investment was worthless.

(P 27 'From the Crash to the Blitz' by Cabell Phillips—Macmillan, New York, 1969)

24: The Depression: (i) The plight of the people

Brother, can you spare a dime?

In the year of the Wall Street Crash Herbert C. Hoover, a Republican, became President of the USA. He was sure that the Depression would last, at the most, a few months. But his assessment was to prove entirely wrong. After 1929 America experienced the worst trade recession in her history. Unemployment rocketed in the cities where many people could neither afford to buy food nor pay their rents. They had to beg, seek public charity and build their own emergency accomodation. The most desperate built shanties in settlements called 'Hoovervilles'; from a shack made of packing-cases and corrugated iron, a family would search the junkyards for a derelict car that might still have some old seats or an undrained oil sump. If they were lucky they would then be warm and comfortable for that night. Other unemployed Americans refused to become scavengers. They sold apples on the sidewalks or stood in breadlines organized by city charities—for America had no dole, no social security. And if they met a wartime buddy they might ask him for the price of a cup of coffee: 'Brother, can you spare a dime?' This was the title of a song written by Yip Harburg at the end of 1929 and later recorded by Bing Crosby. More than any other song of the period, it spelt out the loss of self-respect sensed by millions of frustrated Americans who believed that the Depression, whatever its cause, was no fault of theirs:

> Once in khaki suits,
> Gee, we looked swell,
> Full of Yankee Doodle-de-dum.
> Half a million boots went sloggin' through Hell,
> I was the kid with the drum.
> Say, don't you remember, they called me Al,
> It was Al all the time,
> Say, don't you remember I'm your pal,
> Brother, can you spare a dime?*

25,000 World War I veterans marched on the capital during 1932 to demand the bonuses they had earned during 1917–18. Calling themselves the BEF (*Bonus Expeditionary Force*), they made camp in Washington DC. President Hoover promptly called out the police who, after bitter hand-to-hand fighting, managed to disperse the marchers. For many this was a decisive moment. After defeat in the capital and with the prospect of a bitter winter ahead, thousands of city dwellers migrated to the countryside in search of work on the farms.

*Quoted in *Hard Times* by Studs Terkel, p. 19 (Allen Lane, The Penguin Press, 1970).

Migration

They could not have chosen a worse moment. Homesteaders had faced hard times since 1918; but during the early Thirties conditions in several Plains states had become intolerable. Unwise farming methods, especially in the Tennessee Valley, had led to large-scale erosion. A visiting British biologist, Julian Huxley, compared conditions in the Valley with 'cultivation of the type normally associated with primitive African tribes'.** Persistent drought led to the creation of a giant 'dustbowl' and the homesteaders simply piled their belongings on their farm trucks and drove off in search of the 'promised land'—California. At the same time, Negroes were leaving the plantations in the Deep South and heading north to seek jobs in the cities—only to find they were replacing the jobless whites who had migrated to the countryside. Throughout the land about a million people were wandering aimlessly; about 25% were under 21 and many were young girls. They were the 'free-riders' seeking something worthwhile in a fresh corner of the USA; their transport was by hitch-hiking or—more usually—by stealing a ride on the freight trains.

Survival

More than 12 million Americans were jobless by Christmas 1932—about 20% of the US work force. Even more were on short time. It was no exaggeration to say that about half the American people felt deprived by the winter of 1932–33. Yet they rarely resorted to violence though they did like to hear about it. There was no shortage of lurid description in the papers, on the radio and in the cinema newsreels. Congress repealed Prohibition in 1933 and the gangsters, deprived of their most lucrative source of income, fought among themselves to control what was left. Kidnapping, sparked off by the tragic Lindbergh case in 1932 when the kidnapper killed Colonel Lindbergh's baby son, was rife throughout 1933. But one crime was foiled. In February 1933 the President-elect, Franklin D. Roosevelt (a Democrat) came ashore at Miami at the end of a holiday cruise. Guiseppe Zangara, an unemployed bricklayer from New Jersey, fired six shots at him. He killed the man sitting next to Roosevelt—but missed his target. Roosevelt went on to become the President who restored hope to the American people.

**Quoted in *The New Deal* by John Major, pp. 32–33 (Longmans, 1968).

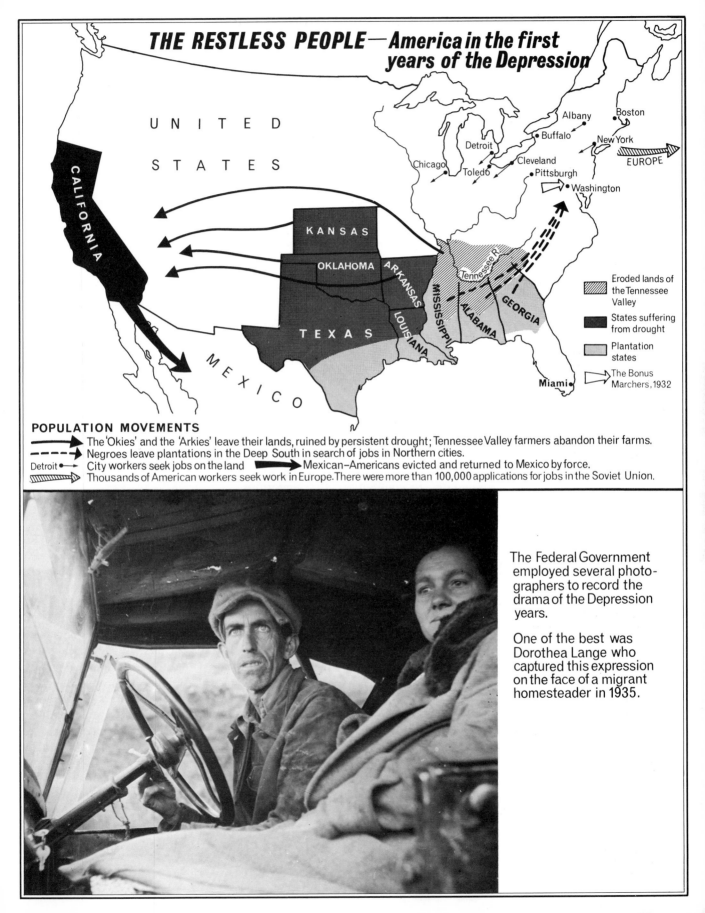

THE RESTLESS PEOPLE— *America in the first years of the Depression*

UNITED STATES

CALIFORNIA

KANSAS

OKLAHOMA

ARKANSAS

TEXAS

LOUISIANA

MISSISSIPPI

ALABAMA

GEORGIA

Tennessee R.

MEXICO

Albany • Boston
• Buffalo
Detroit • New York
Chicago • Cleveland EUROPE
Toledo • Pittsburgh
• Washington
Miami •

Eroded lands of
the Tennessee
Valley

States suffering
from drought

Plantation
states

The Bonus
Marchers, 1932

POPULATION MOVEMENTS

The 'Okies' and the 'Arkies' leave their lands, ruined by persistent drought; Tennessee Valley farmers abandon their farms.

Negroes leave plantations in the Deep South in search of jobs in Northern cities.

Detroit • City workers seek jobs on the land   Mexican–Americans evicted and returned to Mexico by force.

Thousands of American workers seek work in Europe. There were more than 100,000 applications for jobs in the Soviet Union.

The Federal Government employed several photographers to record the drama of the Depression years.

One of the best was Dorothea Lange who captured this expression on the face of a migrant homesteader in 1935.

25: The Depression: (ii) Roosevelt's New Deal

The Hundred Days' March—May 1933

When, on 4 March 1933, Roosevelt took the oath as President of the USA, unemployment had topped the 12 million mark and the entire capitalist system was in danger. Overseas investors had already removed their gold deposits; Americans were now withdrawing theirs before all the banks failed. Roosevelt immediately mounted a rescue operation; he declared a banking 'holiday' and outlawed all trading in bullion. Then he went on the radio to give the first of his 'fireside chats' in which he urged Americans to return their assets to the banks. It worked. Gold deposits worth $300 million returned to the Federal Reserve and these saved the banks from failure. The entire operation had taken eight days. Without a pause, Roosevelt pushed through a mass of legislation to tackle the other problems bedevilling American society. The most important acts are described below; they provided the President's 'New Deal' for the American people.

The Agricultural Adjustment Act (AAA) 1933

The *Triple A* subsidized poor farmers by paying them not to produce crops! Roosevelt agreed that it was a 'new means to rescue agriculture'—but there seemed no alternative. The Federal Government promised to pay benefits to farmers if they in turn promised not to grow basic crops such as maize and cotton. In addition, it would buy surplus crops; or even resettle destitute farmers. The last idea caught the imagination of Mrs Eleanor Roosevelt, the President's wife and she helped to found the first resettlement centre at Arthurdale and gave the scheme publicity. Resettlement certainly helped families who were driven from the dust-bowl; but it aroused the politicians' hostility and in 1936 the Supreme Court ruled the *Triple A* to be unconstitutional. By then the problem of surpluses barely existed. Cynics gave the credit to years of drought; others said it was due to the *Triple A* benefits.

The Home Owners Loan Act 1933

Americans buying their house on mortgage knew that if they lost their jobs they were likely to lose their homes also. Roosevelt wanted to help people facing this sort of crisis and, through the Home Owners Loan Corporation, he offered loans to pay off existing mortgages. About a million loans reached Americans in the next three years and there is no doubt that about 20% of America's home buyers regarded the scheme as a lifesaver during the Thirties.

The National Industrial Recovery Act 1933

'The Law I have just signed was passed to put people back to work—to let them buy more of the products of the farms and the factories and to start our business going at a living rate again.' With these words Roosevelt introduced his revolutionary, if short-lived, concept of fair competition in industry. Business men were now supposed to reduce the working week to a minimum of 30–40 hours; and to pay a minimum of 11–15 dollars. Moreover, they would allow their workers to join trade unions and engage in collective bargaining. They were asking to display the National Recovery Administration (*NRA*) emblem—the Blue Eagle—and join in a national publicity campaign. The idea caught the public's enthusiasm but rarely impressed big business. In January 1936 the Supreme Court declared *NRA* unconstitutional.

The Federal Emergency Relief Act 1933

This act provided a nation-wide programme of public works for the unemployed. There were two main agencies: the Civil Works Administration (*CWA*) and the Public Works Administration (*PWA*).* Their aim, as Roosevelt said, was to 'preserve not only the bodies of the unemployed from destitution but also their self-respect...' Led by the energetic Harry Hopkins, the *WPA* paid out $9 billion in wages between 1935 and 1940. By then Hopkins had found jobs for 8 million people and the map opposite gives some idea of the kind of work they undertook.

Two views of the New Deal

Many Americans remained suspicious of the New Deal and it never received unqualified praise. However, according to Raymond Moley, one of Roosevelt's trusted lieutenants, the New Deal did restore 'confidence in the American people, confidence in their banks, in their industrial system and in their Government. Confidence was the buoyant spirit that brought back prosperity'.† But Moley denied that the New Deal solved America's problems. One of Harry Hopkins' helpers, Joe Marcus, claimed that big business went along with the New Deal in order to *defend* the existing American society against a possible socialist or even communist alternative. 'It was a very unusual Depression in the history of societies. It lasted so long and went so deep.'** And, of course, the New Deal did not *end* the Depression. Unemployment, successfully checked during 1934–6, crept up again after 1937. World War II, not the New Deal, would solve that particular problem.

*Later supplemented by the bigger W.P.A. (Works Progress Administration).
†*Hard Times* by Studs Terkel (Allen Lane, The Penguin Press, 1970) p. 250.
**Ibid. p. 269.

NEW DEAL AGENCIES and the ENVIRONMENT

1. Civilian Conservation Corps (C.C.C.)

★ **S.E. OREGON Game Reserve**

★ **Roosevelt's "Tree fighters"** —men of the C.C.C. who fought forest fires

★ **THE WAR AGAINST THE SAWFLY PEST THAT ATTACKED SPRUCE TREES**

★ **Shenandoah Mts. Nat. Park**

ARTHURDALE (W. VIRGINIA)

★ Restoration of American battlefields of the Revolutionary and Civil Wars

2½ million young men served in the C.C.C. 47 died in the "Tree Fighters." They thinned overgrown forests, created wild-life sanctuaries and stocked lakes and rivers with fish. Above all, they planted half the trees that have ever been planted in the history of the USA.

☆ C.C.C. activities
▨ Tennessee Valley Authority

2. Tennessee Valley Authority (T.V.A.)

The most spectacular New Deal Agency. It built dams and fertilizer plants. But above all it helped to electrify America—the Tennessee Valley farmers became <u>full</u> members of the <u>consumer</u> society.

THE NEW DEAL IN ACTION

The Works Progress Administration (W.P.A.) employed 20% of America's labour force

☆ **WPA also built or improved 2,500 hospitals, 5,000 schools, 1,000 airfields and 13,000 playgrounds.**

☆ **La Guardia Airport, New York**

☆ **San Francisco's Aquatic Park**

ST. LOUIS WATERFRONT ☆

KENTUCKY ☆ **W. VIRG.**

☆ **Excavations in New Mexico**

Excavations in Georgia ☆

MEXICO

Key West Florida ☆

"WPA workers built La Guardia Airport in New York and the elaborate municipal recreation centre in San Francisco's Aquatic Park; salvaged the riverfront in St. Louis; sealed thousands of abandoned coal mines in Kentucky and West Virginia to prevent the seepage of sulphuric acid into the creeks and rivers; excavated Indian mounds in Georgia and New Mexico; took over the entire municipal function of the bankrupt and desolated city of Key West, Florida."

('From the Crash to the Blitz' by Cabell Phillips, pp. 277-8)

Federal power increases

One of the most obvious features of the New Deal was the marked increase in the powers of the Federal government. Yet, in general, these powers were neither dictatorial nor unwelcome. For example, when the *1935 Social Security Act* promised old age pensions and other benefits to the needy it was heralding a new set of American attitudes. For the very first time government accepted its duty to improve the lives of ordinary Americans and to make them less vulnerable to industrial and commercial exploitation. This is why the Social Security Act was 'the most important legacy of the New Deal'; why the old and infirm, the unemployed and the destitute called Roosevelt 'the only President who has cared for people like us'. Americans looked to Washington for assistance, not to their state capitals; in fact, by 1936 barely any state in the Union could handle the task of unemployment relief, let alone all the other problems.

Law and order

The campaign against the criminal elements showed the advantage of increasing Federal powers. In a series of spectacular interstate robberies, gangsters such as John Dillinger, Pretty Boy Floyd and Baby Face Nelson openly defied the law enforcement agencies. Congress therefore defined, in 1934, a series of Federal offences: kidnapping, shipping stolen goods across a state line, interstate racketeering and so on. Government agents (the famous G-men) from the *Federal Bureau of Investigation* received arms and fast cars so they could pursue criminals on even terms. Led by Edgar J. Hoover of the Department of Justice, the G-men moved into action and, during 1934, cornered and killed Dillinger, Floyd, Nelson and many other 'public enemies'. Six hundred special agents were at work all over America by 1936 and they very soon reduced the heavy crime rate characteristic of the age.

Recognition of the American Negro

For the first time in their lives, and as a direct result of the government's employment and relief policies, Negroes could feel that they were truly citizens of the United States of America. Certainly Roosevelt wanted them to feel this; and he was helped by the achievements of several outstanding black Americans. Joe Louis, heavyweight champion of the world, was a household name on both sides of the Atlantic; Jesse Owens, winner of four Gold Medals at the 1936 Berlin Olympics, became the idol of America. And when prejudiced authorities barred the distinguished contralto, Marian Anderson, from a Washington concert hall, Secretary Ickes arranged for her to perform from the steps of the Lincoln Memorial.

Recognition of the trade unions

Another result of New Deal legislation was the growth of trade union membership in America. The *1935 Wagner Act* allowed unions to seek recognition—a complete contrast to the attitude of previous governments, many of whom had tried to smash the labour movement in America. Unfortunately, the long-overdue growth of the unions was marred by violence and, as the map opposite shows, men would die before the labour leader John L. Lewis won general recognition for his *Committee for Industrial Organization*.

Roosevelt's rivals

Two popular agitators challenged the President. One was Huey Long, virtual dictator of Louisiana. At first he supported the President but turned against him when the Federal government refused to let Huey Long administer Federal funds. So Huey Long promised everyone a dream-world-*Share-the-Wealth*-where he would abolish private fortunes and give everybody a car, a radio and a good education. This appealed to the poor whites in Louisiana and soon Long claimed millions of followers. So did Father Coughlin, a radio demagogue who formed the *National Union for Social Justice*. Huey Long decided to ally himself with Coughlin and then run for President. But in 1935 an assassin shot Huey Long; and when Roosevelt entered his second term of office in 1936 Father Coughlin's political influence rapidly declined.

Would democracy survive?

More had been done to benefit Americans in the years 1933–39 than had been accomplished under any other President. Yet Roosevelt had never had to use methods favoured by the dictators Mussolini, Stalin and Hitler. In 1940, when war had already returned to Europe, Roosevelt asked the American people: *Is the book of democracy now to be closed and placed away on the dusty shelves of time? We Americans of today—all of us—we are characters in the living book of democracy . . . It falls upon us now to say whether the chapters that are to come will tell a story of retreat or a story of continuous advance.**

*Quoted on the last page of William Leuchtenburg's *Franklin D. Roosevelt and the New Deal* (Harper & Row 1963).

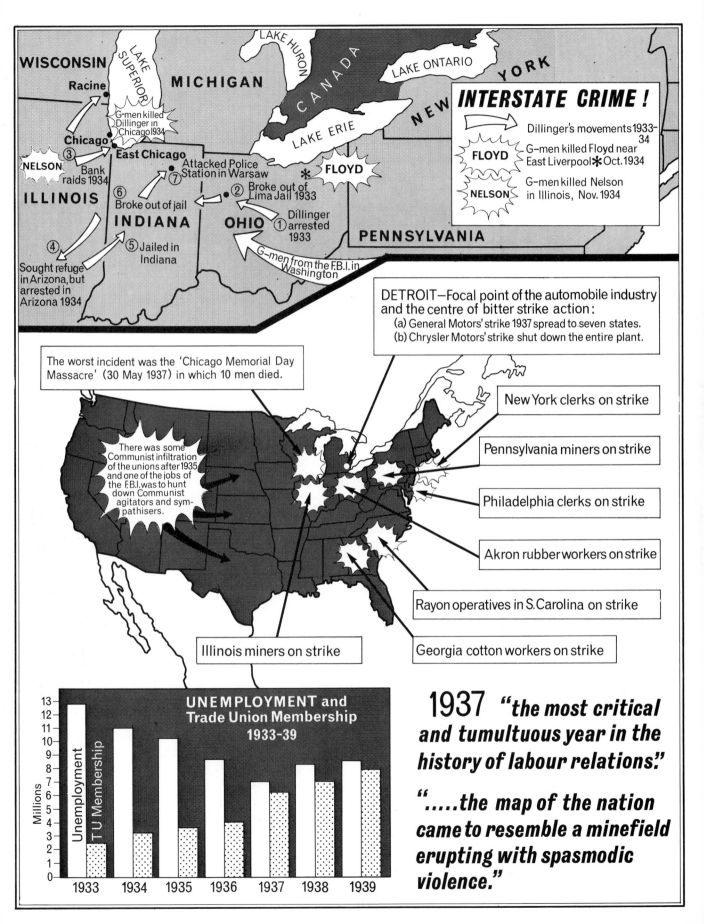

WISCONSIN

Racine

G-men killed Dillinger in Chicago 1934

Chicago

③

NELSON

Bank raids 1934

East Chicago

Attacked Police Station in Warsaw ⑦

ILLINOIS

⑥ Broke out of jail

INDIANA

④

⑤ Jailed in Indiana

Sought refuge in Arizona, but arrested in Arizona 1934

MICHIGAN

LAKE SUPERIOR

LAKE HURON

CANADA

LAKE ONTARIO

LAKE ERIE

NEW YORK

* **FLOYD**

② Broke out of Lima Jail 1933

OHIO ① Dillinger arrested 1933

G-men from the F.B.I. in Washington

PENNSYLVANIA

INTERSTATE CRIME!

→ Dillinger's movements 1933-34

FLOYD G-men killed Floyd near East Liverpool ✱ Oct. 1934

NELSON G-men killed Nelson in Illinois, Nov. 1934

DETROIT—Focal point of the automobile industry and the centre of bitter strike action:
(a) General Motors' strike 1937 spread to seven states.
(b) Chrysler Motors' strike shut down the entire plant.

The worst incident was the 'Chicago Memorial Day Massacre' (30 May 1937) in which 10 men died.

There was some Communist infiltration of the unions after 1935 and one of the jobs of the F.B.I. was to hunt down Communist agitators and sympathisers.

New York clerks on strike

Pennsylvania miners on strike

Philadelphia clerks on strike

Akron rubber workers on strike

Rayon operatives in S. Carolina on strike

Georgia cotton workers on strike

Illinois miners on strike

UNEMPLOYMENT and Trade Union Membership 1933-39

Unemployment

T U Membership

Millions

13 12 11 10 9 8 7 6 5 4 3 2 1 0

1933 1934 1935 1936 1937 1938 1939

1937 *"the most critical and tumultuous year in the history of labour relations."*

"....the map of the nation came to resemble a minefield erupting with spasmodic violence."

27: 'A world of disorder': America and Europe to 1941

The Neutrality Acts

Though most Americans had a hazy idea of the dangers building up in Europe after 1933, public opinion opposed any involvement in Europe's political problems. A few Americans joined the *Abraham Lincoln Brigade* and went to fight against Franco in the Spanish Civil War. But these were exceptions. Congress reflected most people's views when it passed the 1935 Neutrality Act compelling the President to declare an arms embargo on any nation involved in war. Congress went even further in 1937 when it forbade direct commerce with a belligerent nation. Roosevelt was equally anxious to minimize the risk of involvement in war; but, as he warned his people, 'we cannot have complete protection in a world of disorder in which confidence and security have broken down'.

Hitler's War

On 1 September 1939 Hitler invaded Poland; two days later Britain and France declared war on Germany and before long a flood of orders for war material arrived from the two allied nations. Naturally, these helped to vitalize America's flagging industrial machine and top priority went to the production of fighters, bombers and Pratt & Whitney aero engines. Unfortunately, America lacked the resources for private companies to produce these goods quickly; moreover, there was the difficulty of the 1935 arms embargo. The Americans therefore rationalized their position; on 4 November 1939 they permitted belligerents to buy arms on a 'cash and carry' basis. British and French money poured into the USA to finance new aircraft and munitions plants. But before much of the new equipment could reach the Western Front, Hitler's Panzers swept through France and Belgium, forcing the British army to make good its escape from the Dunkirk beaches during May–June 1940. With France on the verge of surrender, Britain secretly promised the Americans that she would take over all of her ally's contracts in the USA; and, as Britain's position was now desperate, she would accept any weapons—even *obsolete* guns—that the Americans cared to send.

Lend-Lease

Roosevelt responded by trading 50 World War I destroyers for British-owned bases in the Atlantic. Then he went further. America, he said, must become the 'arsenal of democracy'; the Nazis must not reach the Western Hemisphere. Therefore, on 11 March 1941, he signed the Lend-Lease Act, one of the most important pieces of legislation in American history. It authorized the President to send any 'defence article' to any country if such a move would *promote the defence of the United States*. Americans would never have agreed to Lend-Lease if they had not feared Germany in 1941 or if they had not been convinced that, for the first time in the history of the United States, they were 'confronted with an overwhelming army, including an overwhelming air force, and with the possibility of getting control of the Atlantic'.[*] Britain secured benefits from Lend-Lease almost immediately. During the Spring of 1941 the first convoy of food-ships arrived from America and helped to make up for the losses inflicted by U-boat attack. Soon the British people were eating American food: dried milk, dried eggs, dried peas and beans, vitamin tablets, canned fish and frozen pork. But few modern weapons appeared before the end of 1941—simply because the infant US munitions industry still needed time to tool up for the mass-production of *Maryland* bombers and *General Grant* tanks.

Gains for America

The Federal Government invested billions of dollars not only in Lend-Lease but also in re-equipping the American armed services. Almost every state in the Union benefited from a nation-wide industrial development programme. Ford built a new bomber plant at Willow Run; Kaiser constructed new shipyards in Richmond, California; Chrysler erected its Tank Arsenal in Detroit. And it was not just the industrial worker who benefited from this unprecedented production drive. America's farmers suddenly found their products in great demand. Poultry farmers were to supply an additional 300 million eggs annually; bean-growers were urged to boost their acreage by 35%; dairy farmers were to provide 33% more milk. In September 1941 Secretary Wickard[†] told them that 'for the first time in the history of agriculture in this country goals for all essential farm commodities have been established'. Farmers, he said, were part of a 'Food for Freedom' campaign. Not all were convinced—they remembered the dangers of over-production. But Congress soon allayed their fears by passing legislation to guarantee food prices; consequently, during 1941, 'every farm became a battle station in the defence of the United States against a Hitler victory'.[**] And of course America was still neutral!

[*]An American view of the German menace, expressed by the then Secretary of War, Henry L. Stimson.
[†]Secretary of Agriculture.
[**]See p. 102 Edward R. Stettinius, Jr. *Lend-Lease* (The Macmillan Company, New York, 1944).

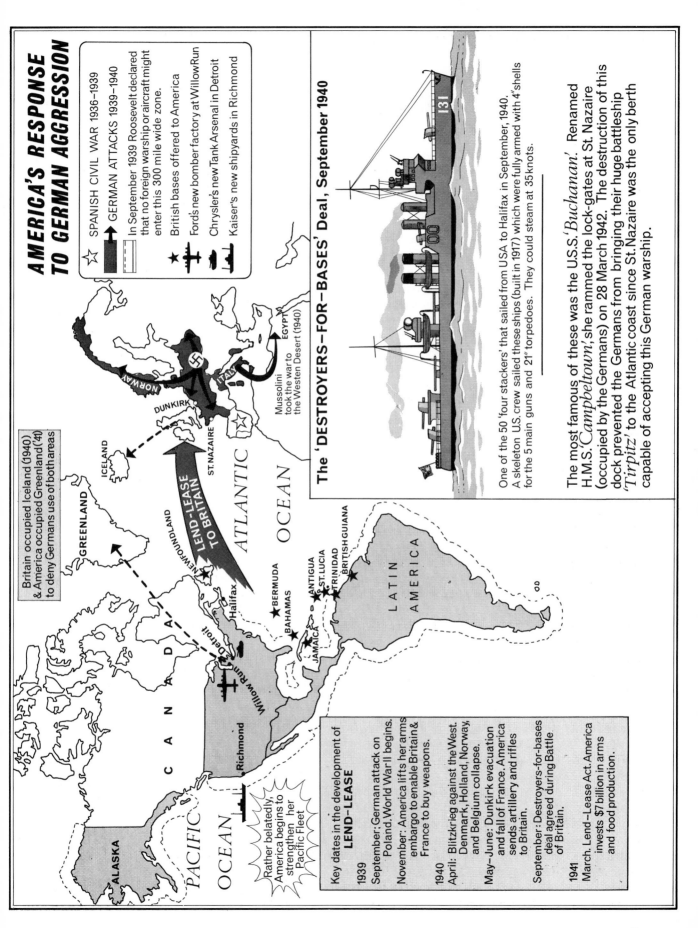

AMERICA'S RESPONSE TO GERMAN AGGRESSION

☆ SPANISH CIVIL WAR 1936–1939
◼▶ GERMAN ATTACKS 1939–1940

In September 1939 Roosevelt declared that no foreign warship or aircraft might enter this 300 mile wide zone.

◻ British bases offered to America
★ Ford's new bomber factory at Willow Run
✈ Chrysler's new Tank Arsenal in Detroit
⬡ Kaiser's new shipyards in Richmond

Britain occupied Iceland (1940) & America occupied Greenland (41) to deny Germans use of both areas

NORWAY

DUNKIRK

ITALY

ST. NAZAIRE

Mussolini took the war to the Westen Desert (1940)

EGYPT

ICELAND

GREENLAND

NEWFOUNDLAND

LEND–LEASE TO BRITAIN

ATLANTIC OCEAN

C A N A D A

Willow Run   Detroit

Halifax

BERMUDA

BAHAMAS

JAMAICA

ANTIGUA
ST.LUCIA
TRINIDAD
BRITISH GUIANA

L A T I N   A M E R I C A

Richmond

PACIFIC OCEAN

ALASKA

Rather belatedly, America begins to strengthen her Pacific Fleet

The 'DESTROYERS–FOR–BASES' Deal, September 1940

One of the 50 'four stackers' that sailed from USA to Halifax in September, 1940. A skeleton U.S. crew sailed these ships (built in 1917) which were fully armed with 4" shells for the 5 main guns and 21" torpedoes. They could steam at 35 knots.

The most famous of these was the U.S.S. 'Buchanan.' Renamed H.M.S. 'Campbeltown', she rammed the lock-gates at St. Nazaire (occupied by the Germans) on 28 March 1942. The destruction of this dock prevented the Germans from bringing their huge battleship 'Tirpitz' to the Atlantic coast since St. Nazaire was the only berth capable of accepting this German warship.

Key dates in the development of **LEND–LEASE**

1939

September: German attack on Poland. World War II begins.

November: America lifts her arms embargo to enable Britain & France to buy weapons.

1940

April: Blitzkrieg against the West. Denmark, Holland, Norway, and Belgium collapse.

May–June: Dunkirk evacuation and fall of France. America sends artillery and rifles to Britain.

September: Destroyers-for-bases deal agreed during Battle of Britain.

1941

March. Lend–Lease Act. America invests $7 billion in arms and food production.

61

28: American aid to China and the USSR

In the name of freedom and in the spirit of hostility towards all aggressor nations, Roosevelt offered aid to the Chinese and Russian peoples. There is no doubt about his generosity, but it is likely that he may have pinned extravagent hopes on the long-term effects that this aid would have.

The American view of China

After more than a century of commerce and missionary work in China, Americans felt that they had a fair idea of the country. They saw the Chinese as simple folk, struggling to free themselves from poverty and paganism. They were quite impressed by the Chinese leader, Chiang Kai-shek, especially after he announced his conversion to Methodism in 1931. But Chiang's failure to reduce poverty and introduce the land reform so desperately needed by the depressed Chinese peasantry completely escaped American attention. In fact, Americans reinforced their own myths about China in several films* which, though they stressed the hardship of peasant life, failed to demonstrate the inadequacies of Chiang Kai-shek's government.

Japanese aggression

There was an upsurge of American sympathy for China after Japan occupied Manchuria in 1931. Six years later Japan launched a full-scale assault upon China—Japanese planes sank the US gunboat *Panay* during one raid on the Yangtze Kiang—and captured Peking. Chiang fell back to Chungking and, in 1938, appealed for foreign aid. Britain and Russia—as well as America—sent him supplies, most of which had to reach him along the tortuous Burma Road. The surface and gradients of this mountain highway were usually too much for unskilled Chinese truck-drivers and a great deal of valuable war material was lost.

The Flying Tigers

Those trucks which did reach Chungking suffered from constant Japanese air attack and before long the *Zeros* had destroyed Chiang's collection of obsolete Russian fighters. He therefore decided to buy new planes and recruit fresh pilots** in the USA. Inspired by the persuasive tongue of Colonel Chennault, a retired US officer who had been air adviser to Chiang since 1937, about 250 pilots and ground crew signed on to fight in China. They sailed to Rangoon where Chennault turned his fliers into three pursuit squadrons called the *Flying Tigers*. Chiang referred to them as his *American Volunteer Group* and by December 1941 they were ready for action.

Barbarossa

On 22 June 1941 Hitler launched *Operation Barbarossa* against the Soviet Union. Within five weeks Harry Hopkins had visited Stalin in Moscow and returned to tell Roosevelt that the Russians needed every gun, every scrap of food that the USA could spare. Roosevelt immediately diverted a few light tanks and P.40 fighters for use in Russia, but his aid was limited by the heavy demands now being made on US arms production as well as by the sheer distances involved in supplying the Soviet Union. Aid to Russia was either by the long Pacific run, through the ill-developed Persian Gulf route or—most dangerous of all—across the Barents Sea to Murmansk and Archangel. However, despite the difficulties, 28 US freighters reached Russia during October–November 1941.

Moving closer to war

Throughout 1941 America was looming large as an implacable enemy of the aggressor nations. The President's hostility to Germany in particular was undisguised. In his message to Congress (January 1941) Roosevelt talked of creating a new world founded upon four essential freedoms, denied to the people of German occupied Europe. He listed the freedom of speech and expression, the freedom of every person to worship God in his own way, the freedom from want and the freedom from fear. Inevitably, there were some ugly incidents in the Atlantic. A U-boat torpedoed the US freighter *Robin Moor*; a US destroyer depth-charged a U-boat. Before long Roosevelt was asking for a meeting with Winston Churchill and in August the two leaders met on board ship in Placentia Bay. There they issued a Joint Declaration—the *Atlantic Charter*—which spoke of the destruction of Nazi tyranny and a search for a 'wider and more permanent system of general security'. In October the USS *Kearney* depth-charged a U-boat which retaliated by firing a torpedo into the side of the American destroyer. On 13 November Congress repealed the *Neutrality Acts* and Roosevelt ordered American ships to shoot on sight when they encountered a U-boat. But while the President concentrated his attention on the Atlantic, the Japanese Admiral Yamamoto was submitting to his government a plan for the destruction of the American Pacific Fleet: there would be a surprise carrier-borne air strike on the huge American base at Pearl Harbor.

*Best known is M.G.M.'s *The Good Earth* (1937) starring Paul Muni.
**A few had already joined the RAF, fought in the Battle of Britain 1940, and formed the nucleus of the famous No. 17 'Eagle Squadron'.

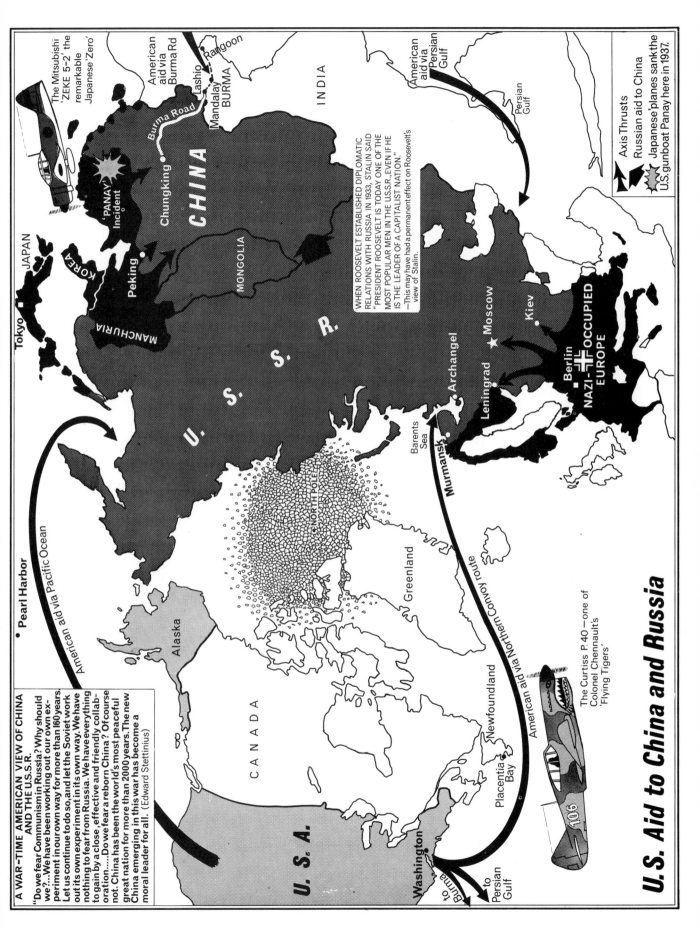

U.S. Aid to China and Russia

The Mitsubishi 'ZEKE 5-2' the remarkable Japanese 'Zero'

American aid via Burma Rd

Rangoon

Lashio

Mandalay BURMA

Burma Road

BURMA

American aid via Persian Gulf

Persian Gulf

INDIA

CHINA

Chungking

'PANAY' Incident

Peking

KOREA

MANCHURIA

Tokyo

JAPAN

MONGOLIA

U. S. S. R.

WHEN ROOSEVELT ESTABLISHED DIPLOMATIC RELATIONS WITH RUSSIA IN 1933, STALIN SAID "PRESIDENT ROOSEVELT IS TODAY ONE OF THE MOST POPULAR MEN IN THE U.S.S.R., EVEN IF HE IS THE LEADER OF A CAPITALIST NATION."
—This may have had a permanent effect on Roosevelt's view of Stalin.

Moscow

Kiev

Berlin

NAZI-OCCUPIED EUROPE

Leningrad

Archangel

Barents Sea

Murmansk

Pearl Harbor

American aid via Pacific Ocean

NORTH POLE

Alaska

Greenland

CANADA

U. S. A.

Washington

Placentia Bay

Newfoundland

American aid via Northern Convoy route

American aid via Persian Gulf

to Persian Gulf

to Burma

The Curtiss P.40 —one of Colonel Chennault's 'Flying Tigers'

106

Axis Thrusts

Russian aid to China

Japanese planes sank the U.S. gunboat Panay here in 1937.

63

Further Reading

Theme 4 – The Preservation of Democracy in America

Spread

22. The quest for peace and stability

America in the Twentieth Century, D.K. Adams, CUP, 1964
USA—the Twenties to Viet Nam, Daniel Snowman, Batsford, 1968

23. The Roaring Twenties—and the Crash of '29

From the Crash to the Blitz, Cabell Williams, Macmillan, New York, 1969

24. The Depression (i) the plight of the people

Hard Times, Studs Terkel, Allen Lane, The Penguin Press, 1970
The Grapes of Wrath, John Steinbeck, Penguin, 1971

25. The Depression (ii) Roosevelt's New Deal

Franklin Roosevelt, C.P. Hill, OUP, 1966

26. Democracy preserved

From the Crash to the Blitz, Cabell Williams, Macmillan, New York, 1969

27. 'A world of disorder'

Lend-Lease—Weapon for Victory, Edward R. Stettinius Jr., Macmillan, 1944
American Aid to France, History June, 1971

28. American aid to China and the USSR

Lend-Lease—Weapon for Victory, Edward R. Stettinius Jr., Macmillan, 1944
The Reluctant Belligerent, Robert Divine, John Wiley, 1965

THEME 5

World War II

The Japanese attack upon Pearl Harbor, closely followed by Hitler's declaration of war, made the United States an immediate if reluctant ally of Britain and the USSR. A unique set of advantages enabled the Americans to make the decisive contribution to the allied victory. By invading the Soviet Union, the Germans had committed the majority and the best of their armed services to a war of attrition on the Russian front. Then, by their rapid advance through the Pacific and SE Asia, the Japanese had over-extended their supply lines and created a defence perimeter that they simply couldn't hold. In contrast, the British had fended off all enemy attacks and now provided the Americans with an ideally located base for the strategic bombing of Germany and, ultimately, for the invasion of Western Europe.

One of the most promising features of World War II was the alliance between the Russian and American peoples. The large quantities of Lend-Lease material sent to Russia and the apparent *bonhomie* existing between Roosevelt and Stalin at the Teheran and Yalta Conferences seemed to augur well for the future. Yet there was little genuine co-operation between the two peoples. Stalin's persistent calls for a Second Front in Europe revealed little sympathetic understanding of the immense logistic problems facing Britain and America before they could mount the D-Day landings in 1944. His reluctance to allow Allied planes to use Soviet bases frustrated US Air Force generals. His inflexibility over the Polish problem and his un-willingness to attack Japan until the war had virtually ended did nothing to improve relations between Russia and the United States.

In fact, once the Germans surrendered in May 1945, President Truman decided it was time to cut off aid to Russia; and in June 1945—just a few days before he became Secretary of State—James F. Byrnes confided that the atomic bomb 'would make Russia more manageable in Europe'.* This sort of attitude hardened Russia's suspicion of America and, in an atmosphere of mutual distrust, the Cold War was born.

*Quoted in *America, Russia and the Cold War* by Walter La Feber (John Wiley, 1967) p. 21.

29: Pearl Harbor

The Japanese plan

Yamamoto was proposing the most audacious and ambitious plan in the history of modern warfare. He argued that, given a series of carefully synchronized land, sea and air attacks, Japan had an excellent chance of gaining control in the Pacific and Far East. The object would be the creation of a vast defence perimeter stretching from the Kuriles to the Dutch East Indies. Within this perimeter Japan would find all the oil, rubber, tin and rice she needed. And, as the Americans were already terminating their commercial treaties with Japan as well as blocking her financial assets in the USA, the matter was urgent. Japan must act swiftly and brutally. If she could eliminate the American fleet at Pearl Harbor there would be nothing left to hinder her attacks. Therefore Yamamoto made a promise to Prime Minister Tojo: '. . . in the first six months to a year of war with the United States and England I will run wild, and I will show you an uninterrupted succession of victories'.

The Hawaiian Operation

On 25 November 1941 a Japanese task force commanded by Admiral Nagumo began its mission to destroy the US fleet. Battering its way through heavy seas, it arrived unnoticed at a point 200 miles north of the Hawaiian Islands where, on 7 December 1941, Nagumo released his first wave of attack aircraft. Off Pearl Harbor, the US destroyer *Ward* was already in action, depth-charging an unidentified submarine. At the local radar post two perplexed American signallers watched a mass of blips appearing on their screens. They reported the sighting to the duty officer, who told them not to worry. An hour later 214 Japanese planes swept down to attack the unsuspecting Americans. When a second wave of 170 planes arrived they saw below them a scene of utter devastation. Billowing smoke rose from hundreds of wrecked American aircraft, from sinking warships and battered shore installations. In all, the Japanese lost 29 planes; and for that price they put every battleship in Pearl Harbor out of action. Fortunately for the Americans, none of their big carriers was there that day. The *Enterprise* had gone to Wake Island; the *Lexington* was at Midway; while the *Saratoga* was leaving Puget Sound en route for Pearl Harbor. Their survival was to be of crucial importance in the Pacific war.

A global war

When the Americans had threatened to end their commercial agreements with Japan, their ambassador in Tokyo, Joseph C. Grew, had sent a clear warning to Washington that 'if we once start sanctions against Japan, we must see them through to the end and the end may be conceivably war. If we cut off supplies of oil. . . she will, in all probability, send her fleet down to take the Dutch East Indies.' * Moreover, American intelligence men had intercepted messages from Japanese agents in Hawaii who were showing a marked interest in the warships anchored off Ford Island. Despite these hints of danger, Roosevelt referred to the attack upon Pearl Harbor as an 'unexpected thing' and described Sunday 7 December 1941 as 'a day which will live in infamy'. Congress declared war on Japan on 8 December; Britain had already done so. A few days later Germany and Italy declared war on America. So now the conflict was global: Britain, America and the Soviet Union were allied in their struggle against Germany and Italy. But, in the Pacific, Russia remained neutral until *after* the first atomic bomb fell on Hiroshima. Only then did Stalin declare war on Japan. In 1941 America's immediate task was to stop the Japanese 'Greater Eastern Co-Prosperity Sphere' from taking shape in the Pacific; but the sheer *speed* of Japan's attacks appeared to make this task impossible.

The epic fight on Wake

There was a glimmer of hope when the American defence of Wake Island demonstrated the all-important nature of air power in the Pacific. The *Enterprise* had delivered 12 *Wildcat* fighters to reinforce the 400 marines based on the island. On 8 December Japanese bombers strafed the airstrip and destroyed seven of the fighters. But the surviving *Wildcats* fought back next day and every day until a huge Japanese assault overwhelmed them on 23 December. They had inflicted very heavy casualties on the Japanese who, after the war, agreed that 'Our humiliating defeat during the initial landing operation (and this was the only such defeat early in the war) and the valuable lessons obtained at such high price appeared to have been quickly forgotten. Japan was much too jubilant at the news of victory which rolled in from all corners of the Pacific to heed the bitter lesson of Wake Island'.** But the Americans *did* heed the lesson: Roosevelt immediately ordered the mass production of aircraft for the Pacific theatre.

*Quoted in J. P. Duroselle, *From Wilson to Roosevelt: foreign policy of the United States* (Chatto & Windus, 1964) p. 300.
**See page 119 *Zero!* by Okumiya and Horikoshi (Corgi Edition, 1958).

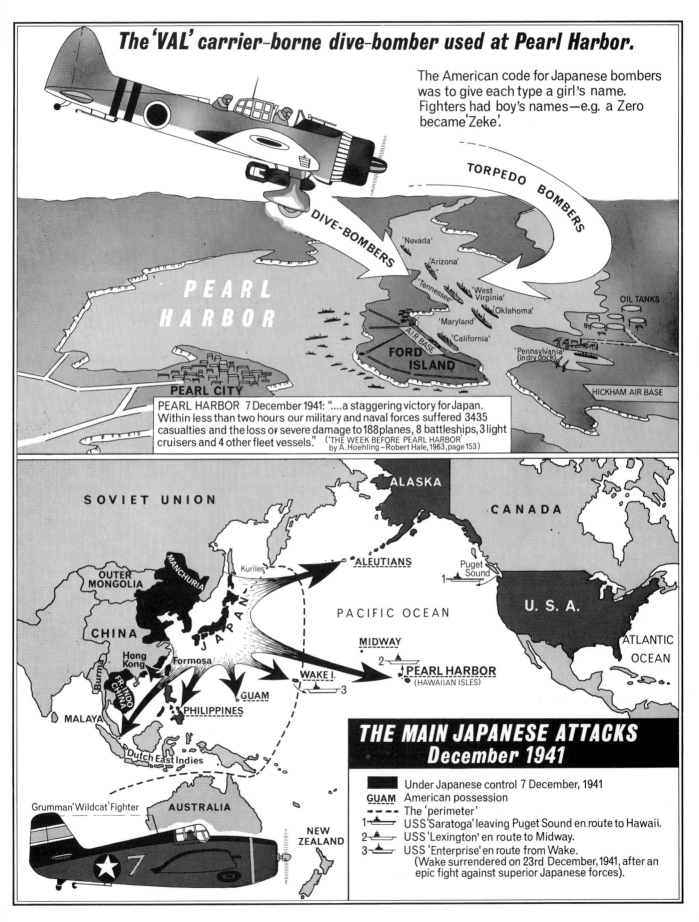

The 'VAL' carrier-borne dive-bomber used at Pearl Harbor.

The American code for Japanese bombers was to give each type a girl's name. Fighters had boy's names—e.g. a Zero became 'Zeke'.

TORPEDO BOMBERS

DIVE-BOMBERS

PEARL HARBOR

PEARL CITY

'Nevada'
'Arizona'
'Tennessee'
'West Virginia'
'Oklahoma'
'Maryland'
'California'
'Pennsylvania' (in dry dock)

AIR BASE

FORD ISLAND

OIL TANKS

HICKHAM AIR BASE

PEARL HARBOR 7 December 1941: "....a staggering victory for Japan. Within less than two hours our military and naval forces suffered 3435 casualties and the loss or severe damage to 188 planes, 8 battleships, 3 light cruisers and 4 other fleet vessels." ('THE WEEK BEFORE PEARL HARBOR' by A. Hoehling – Robert Hale, 1963, page 153)

SOVIET UNION

ALASKA

CANADA

OUTER MONGOLIA

MANCHURIA

Kuriles

ALEUTIANS

Puget Sound

1

U.S.A.

CHINA

JAPAN

PACIFIC OCEAN

MIDWAY

ATLANTIC OCEAN

Hong Kong

Formosa

2

PEARL HARBOR (HAWAIIAN ISLES)

Burma

FR. INDO CHINA

WAKE I.

3

GUAM

MALAYA

PHILIPPINES

Dutch East Indies

THE MAIN JAPANESE ATTACKS
December 1941

Grumman 'Wildcat' Fighter

AUSTRALIA

NEW ZEALAND

Under Japanese control 7 December, 1941
GUAM   American possession
- - -   The 'perimeter'
1   USS 'Saratoga' leaving Puget Sound en route to Hawaii.
2   USS 'Lexington' en route to Midway.
3   USS 'Enterprise' en route from Wake.
    (Wake surrendered on 23rd December, 1941, after an epic fight against superior Japanese forces).

30: Attrition in the Pacific

Coral Sea and Midway 1942

By the spring of 1942 the Japanese had ejected the Dutch from the East Indies, driven the British from Hong Kong, Malaya and Burma and forced the Americans to surrender most of their possessions in the Pacific. In fact, with Japanese bombers operating from the Aleutians, there was a risk that US cities might come under attack.* Then the Japanese suffered their first setback at the Battle of the Coral Sea (May 1942). This was the first 'carrier versus carrier' engagement in which the losses on both sides were caused by naval aircraft. The Americans lost their carrier *Lexington* but managed to prevent a Japanese occupation of Port Moresby. Next month saw the decisive Battle of Midway. In this attempt to capture Midway Island the Japanese lost half of their carriers and most of their experienced torpedo and dive-bomber crews. America's loss was the carrier *Yorktown*.

The strategy

Destuction of enemy power in the Pacific was now a possibility. But it would depend upon the recapture of the Philippines—his strongest and most valued base—and ultimately on an invasion of Japan. This meant the reconquest of literally hundreds of Japanese-occupied islands stretching across 4000 miles of ocean. It was bound to take years. The planners in Washington decided that General MacArthur would wrest New Guinea and the Solomons from the enemy; Admiral Nimitz would assemble task forces at Pearl Harbor and carry out a systematic attack on the islands of the Central and Northern Pacific. When both commands were within striking distance of the Philippines, General MacArthur would have the chance to make his promise 'We shall return' come true.

The tactics

(a) *in the South Pacific*: The American assault on the Solomons began badly and it was soon clear that the Japanese had no intention of abandoning their bases on Guadalcanal. A series of bitter naval engagements produced no decisive results and at the Battle of Santa Cruz (October 1942), the Americans came off worse when the Japanese sank the carrier *Hornet* and badly damaged the *Enterprise*. Fighting for Guadalcanal continued throughout 1943 and eventually the Americans decided to bypass the next big Japanese base at Rabaul and leapfrog along the northern coast of New Guinea into the Pacific. MacArthur reached Morotai during 1944 and began his preparations for the invasion of the Philippines.

(b) *in the North Pacific*: Both the Japanese and the Americans appreciated the strategic value of the island chain between Kamchatka and Alaska. Japanese units captured Attu and Kiska during 1942. American forces, helped by Canadian troops, counter-attacked during 1943. After brief but bitter fighting the Japanese slipped away to leave the Aleutians under US control again.

(c) *in the Central Pacific*: The task forces from Pearl Harbor began their efforts to drive the Japanese from the Central Pacific in November 1943. One of the first objectives was Tarawa Atoll, a tiny ring of coral defended by 4,836 Japanese and Korean troops. It took three days to capture Tarawa and the attack cost the Marines more than 3000 casualties; they had killed 4,690 of the enemy in the process. Such was the fight for Tarawa—3000 miles away from Japan! Clearly, an island-by-island struggle across the Pacific with this sort of casualty rate was unacceptable. Instead, the Americans adopted a policy of 'atoll hopping'; they would not send in valuable Marine contingents to capture unimportant islands. They therefore struck at specific islands in the Marshall group. *Operation Flintlock* moved in against Kwajalein Atoll with great success; *Operation Catchpole* led to the capture of Eniwetok. Kwajalein and Eniwetok gave the Americans new bases for dealing with enemy counter-attacks and almost immediately they fought and won a carrier battle in the Philippine Sea—sometimes called 'The Great Marianas Turkey Shoot'. Another gain from 'atoll-hopping' was that it isolated thousands of Japanese fighting men on remote Pacific islands. The Americans could afford to ignore them and they moved on to capture Saipan, Tinian and Guam—bases from which heavy bombers could carry out raids on Japan.

The assault on the Philippines 1944

The Philippines—the richest prize in the Pacific—was the next target. American troops landed on Leyte on 20 October 1944. As they hit the beaches a Japanese naval force steamed in to destroy the US transports. For three days a furious battle raged in the waters of Leyte Gulf and when it was over the Japanese Navy and Naval Air Force had virtually ceased to exist. Within two months the Americans controlled Leyte and were ready to take the next step in their unrelenting advance across the Pacific Ocean.

---

*The first Japanese bombers over the Aleutians were Vals from the carrier *Junyo*. They attacked Dutch Harbor on 4 June 1942.

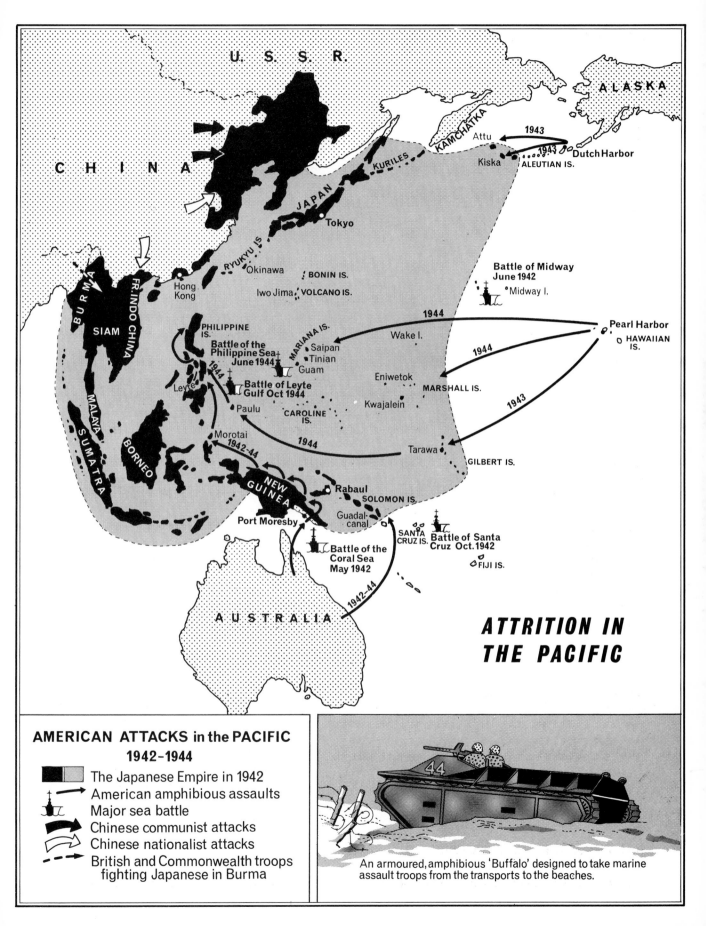

U. S. S. R.

ALASKA

CHINA

KAMCHATKA

1943
Attu
1943
Kiska
Dutch Harbor
ALEUTIAN IS.

KURILES

JAPAN

Tokyo

RYUKYU IS

Okinawa

BONIN IS.

**Battle of Midway
June 1942**
Midway I.

BURMA

Hong Kong

Iwo Jima

VOLCANO IS.

SIAM

FR. INDO CHINA

PHILIPPINE IS.

**Battle of the
Philippine Sea
June 1944**

MARIANA IS.

Saipan
Tinian
Guam

Wake I.

1944

1944

Pearl Harbor

HAWAIIAN IS.

Leyte

1944

**Battle of Leyte
Gulf Oct 1944**

Eniwetok

MARSHALL IS.

MALAYA

Paulu

**CAROLINE
IS.**

Kwajalein

1943

SUMATRA

BORNEO

Morotai

1942-44

1944

Tarawa

GILBERT IS.

NEW
GUINEA

Rabaul

SOLOMON IS.

Port Moresby

Guadal-
canal

SANTA
CRUZ IS.

**Battle of Santa
Cruz Oct. 1942**

**Battle of the
Coral Sea
May 1942**

FIJI IS.

1942-44

AUSTRALIA

ATTRITION IN
THE PACIFIC

An armoured, amphibious 'Buffalo' designed to take marine
assault troops from the transports to the beaches.

69

31: The air war against Germany

The USAAF in England

Despite the massive American commitment in the Pacific, President Roosevelt agreed that the defeat of Hitler's Germany should have absolute priority over all other war aims. However, in 1942 the only form of attack that Britain and the USA could undertake was the bombing of targets in Occupied Europe. Accordingly, the President charged the 8th United States Army Air Force with the task of taking the war to the enemy. Advance units arrived in England during January 1942 to co-operate with the Air Ministry in the construction of bases for the American Flying Fortress and Liberator bombers. Eventually the Americans had 66 airfields from which to conduct their hazardous daylight missions.

The early raids

In August 1942 the USAAF flew its first mission from an East Anglian base. Twelve B.17 Fortresses attacked marshalling yards at Rouen and all returned safely. Soon the aircrews built up experience of daylight raids over Occupied France and in January 1943 they attacked the U-boat pens at Wilhelmshaven. They lost three of their 'ships' on this mission but they expected modest losses and continued to raid Northern Germany throughout February and March. Their success forced the Luftwaffe chiefs to revise their ideas on the defence of the German Reich.

The summer of 1943

American designers had equipped each bomber with thirteen heavy machine-guns in the hope that a barrage of lead would deter enemy fighters. But the Germans, with recent memories of their daylight operations during the *Battle of Britain (1940)*, knew that all bombers were vulnerable to persistent fighter attack. They therefore concentrated on the production of heavily armoured fighters such as the FW 190 which could break up bomber groups. In England, the US General Eaker appreciated that German fighters in large numbers might break through a machine-gun barrage and inflict casualties on his tightly bunched formations. His answer was to attack the factories which produced the German fighters. The clash between the 'combat boxes' of US bombers and the swarms of German fighters led to some of the most horrifying battles in history. Literally thousands of men—American and German—were in combat thousands of feet above the earth. Throughout July and August 1943 the Americans showered enemy aircraft plants with high explosive and lost scores of bombers on every raid. The climax came on 17 August 1943 when two separate bom-

ber armadas attacked factories at Schweinfurt and Regensburg. Hundreds of German fighters hurled themselves at the cumbersome bomber groups. Sixty bombers fell flaming to the ground. Scores limped home with burning engines, splintered gun turrets and tattered tail fins. Very lights, indicating wounded crewmen on board, trailed from most cockpits as the 'ships' circled their bases in Norfolk and Suffolk. The 8th Air Force had almost had enough. But fresh crews and brand-new B.17s arrived from the States and during October they tried another week of daylight raids. They lost 148 bombers. There seemed no answer to the German defences.

The destruction of the German fighter arm

Fortunately, Anglo-American technology evolved the P-51 Mustang fighter, capable of accompanying the bombers on their longest missions. With hundreds of Mustangs as escorts—pilots called the job a 'ramrod'—few German fighters could approach the bomber groups. During 1944 huge formations of silver bombers, escorted by the new fighters, left East Anglia to fight decisive air battles over Germany's aircraft factories. By March the German fighter losses exceeded the combined American fighter and bomber losses. And it was not enough for the Germans to replace their crashed fighters—they could do this easily enough. What they could not do was to replace their dead *pilots*. A German historian has admitted that 'despite the output of machines, which mounted from month to month, the fighter defence of the Reich was finally a mere shadow of its former self'.* By the end of May—just a week before D-Day—the Germans could put a mere 280 planes into the air. The Americans flaunted a thousand long-range fighters and were now masters of Germany's air space. Because of this they could pick their targets—and chose to obliterate Germany's oil industry. By September Germany's oil supplies were insufficient for the adequate defence of the Reich; the attacks, as the German Minister Speer admitted after the war, caused 'the breakdown of the German armaments industry'. So a harsh conclusion can be drawn from the US air offensive 1942–4: the years of bombing were not in themselves decisive. The USAAF's achievement was the destruction of the German fighter arm. Only then were the Americans free to destroy the vital target—Germany's sources of oil supplies.

*Cajus Bekker in his *Luftwaffe Diaries* (Corgi Edition, 1969) p. 450.

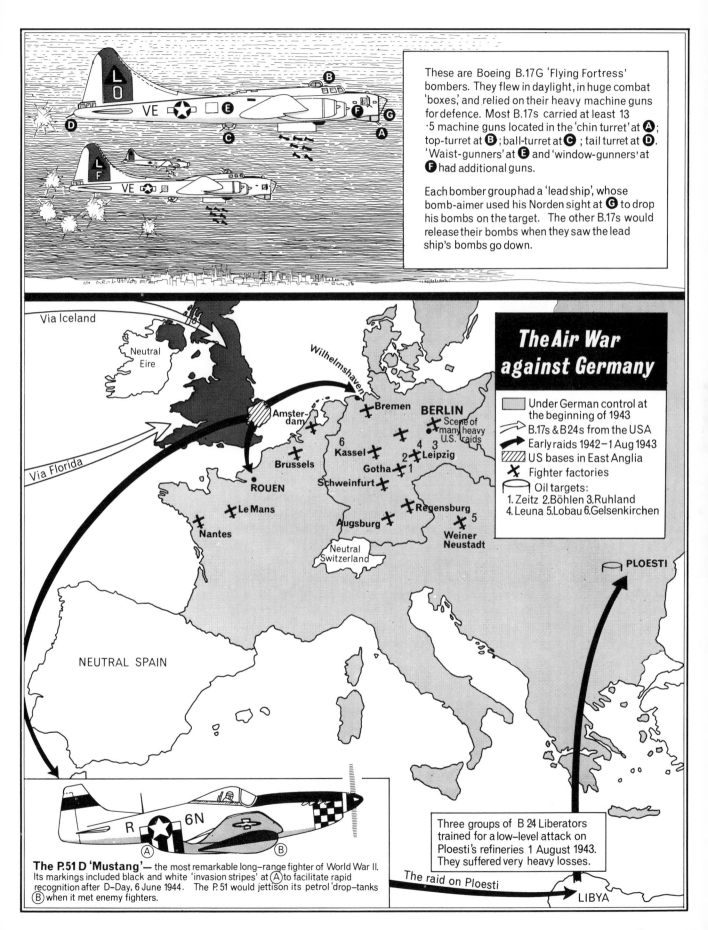

These are Boeing B.17G 'Flying Fortress' bombers. They flew in daylight, in huge combat 'boxes', and relied on their heavy machine guns for defence. Most B.17s carried at least 13 ·5 machine guns located in the 'chin turret' at **A**; top-turret at **B**; ball-turret at **C**; tail turret at **D**. 'Waist-gunners' at **E** and 'window-gunners' at **F** had additional guns.

Each bomber group had a 'lead ship', whose bomb-aimer used his Norden sight at **G** to drop his bombs on the target. The other B.17s would release their bombs when they saw the lead ship's bombs go down.

The Air War against Germany

| Under German control at the beginning of 1943 |
| B.17s & B24s from the USA |
| Early raids 1942–1 Aug 1943 |
| US bases in East Anglia |
| Fighter factories |
| Oil targets: 1. Zeitz 2.Böhlen 3.Ruhland 4. Leuna 5.Lobau 6.Gelsenkirchen |

Via Iceland

Neutral Eire

Via Florida

Wilhelmshaven

Amsterdam

Bremen

BERLIN — Scene of many heavy U.S. raids

6 Kassel

4 3

2 Leipzig

Brussels

Gotha 1

ROUEN

Schweinfurt

Le Mans

Regensburg

Augsburg 5

Nantes

Neutral Switzerland

Weiner Neustadt

NEUTRAL SPAIN

PLOESTI

The P.51 D 'Mustang'— the most remarkable long-range fighter of World War II. Its markings included black and white 'invasion stripes' at (A) to facilitate rapid recognition after D-Day, 6 June 1944. The P.51 would jettison its petrol 'drop-tanks' (B) when it met enemy fighters.

Three groups of B 24 Liberators trained for a low–level attack on Ploesti's refineries 1 August 1943. They suffered very heavy losses.

The raid on Ploesti

LIBYA

32 : The Second Front

North Africa and Italy

'Are you going to let us do all the work while you look on? Are you never going to start fighting? You will not find it too bad once you start!' Stalin flung these undeserved taunts at Churchill when the British Prime Minister visited Moscow in 1942. Churchill told him that a full-scale invasion of Western Europe was out of the question for the time being but he would try to relieve pressure on the Red Army by an Anglo-American attack in the Mediterranean. *Operation Torch*, commanded by General Eisenhower, began in November and when the last of the Afrika Korps surrendered in May 1943 the Allies pushed on into Sicily and Italy. Fierce fighting delayed their arrival in Rome until 4 June 1944; two days later General Eisenhower, now Supreme Allied Commander, announced the invasion of France.

D-Day 6 June 1944

Shortly after midnight, in what has been called 'the most crucial single event of the Second World War', the first invaders landed on the soil of Normandy. Not all the attacks went according to plan. Both of the American airborne divisions parachuted miles away from their dropping zones; while off Omaha beach most of the Duplex-Drive amphibious Shermans and small landing craft foundered in the heavy seas. German guns raked the survivors as they waded ashore and by the end of the day one thousand Americans had died on Omaha beach. Later Eisenhower wrote in his official report: 'the comparatively light casualties which we sustained on all beaches except Omaha were in large measure due to the success of the novel mechanical contrivances which we employed and to the staggering moral and material effect of the mass of armour in the leading waves of the assault.'*

Normandy breakout

For weeks the Allies were trapped in the tall hedgerows of the Normandy *bocage*, a natural cover for the German 88mm. guns. But after fierce battles, massive air bombardments and the use of the ingenious Rhino, they forced their way out, caught and killed thousands of Germans in the Falaise Gap and began the 'Great Swan' to the Siegfried Line. Before long, Eisenhower faced a serious fuel shortage: 'fuel was more vital than ammunition. Approximately a million gallons of gasoline were needed at the front every day to enable the armoured columns to maintain the headlong rate of their advance'.** Huge supply trucks—the famous Red Ball Express—thundered night and day to bring petrol from Cherbourg but their efforts proved inadequate. Eisenhower needed the nearby port of Antwerp before continuing his sweep into Germany but it was not until 28 November that the first of his supply ships managed to nose its way through the mine-free channels of the River Scheldt.

The Battle of the Bulge: the Ardennes 1944–5

'I have made a momentuous decision. I am taking the offensive'. Adolf Hitler stabbed his finger at the map. 'Here—out of the Ardennes, across the Meuse and on to Antwerp.' It was a daring plan and destined to become the Führer's final blitzkrieg. His aim was to split the Allies in two and thus repeat his successes of 1940. Already he had battered Antwerp with his deadly V-1 and V-2 missiles and now, on 16 December 1944, he sent in a quarter of a million men and the pick of his Panzers. The pitched battle that followed was the biggest ever fought by US troops. It was on the same grand scale as Stalingrad, involving over a million men and, in its early stages, saw the surrender of thousands of bewildered GIs. The Battle of the Bulge featured the 101st Airborne's epic defence of Bastogne and the atrocities against 86 US soldiers captured by *Obersturmbannführer* Peiper's SS Battle Group. It saw the daring efforts of Otto Skorzeny's air and ground commandos who spread panic and confusion behind the American lines. Skorzeny's men spoke American, wore American uniforms, drove American jeeps—and often died in front of American firing squads. Von Rundstedt, the German commander, freely admitted that the battle was a gamble—and within a month it had failed. In January 1945 the defeated Wehrmacht fell back towards the Rhine, leaving in the snow of the Ardennes 100,000 dead, wounded or captured comrades as well as their latest tanks and precious reserves of fighter-bombers. They were all irreplaceable. The Americans lost as many tanks and planes—and suffered 81,000 casualties. But they could bring up infantry replacements within a few hours; and provide brand-new Shermans within a week. America's greatest asset in World War II, apart from the valour and competence of her fighting men, was her ability to produce war material more quickly and in greater quantities than could any other nation in the world.

Report by the Supreme Commander to the Combined Chiefs of Staff (HMSO, 1946) p. 30.
**Ibid. p. 75.

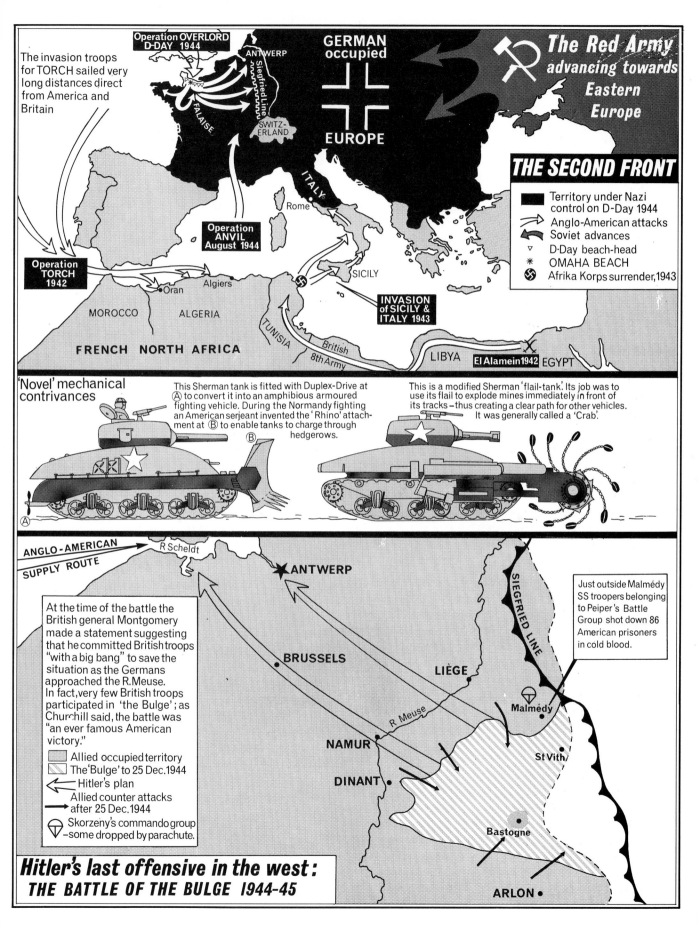

The invasion troops for TORCH sailed very long distances direct from America and Britain

Operation OVERLORD D-DAY 1944

ANTWERP

Siegfried Line

FALAISE

SWITZ-ERLAND

Operation ANVIL August 1944

Operation TORCH 1942

ITALY

Rome

GERMAN occupied

EUROPE

The Red Army advancing towards Eastern Europe

THE SECOND FRONT

- ■ Territory under Nazi control on D-Day 1944
- ➔ Anglo-American attacks
- ➔ Soviet advances
- ▽ D-Day beach-head
- ＊ OMAHA BEACH
- ⌗ Afrika Korps surrender, 1943

Oran Algiers

MOROCCO   ALGERIA

SICILY

INVASION of SICILY & ITALY 1943

TUNISIA

FRENCH NORTH AFRICA

British 8th Army

LIBYA   **El Alamein 1942** EGYPT

'Novel' mechanical contrivances

This Sherman tank is fitted with Duplex-Drive at Ⓐ to convert it into an amphibious armoured fighting vehicle. During the Normandy fighting an American serjeant invented the 'Rhino' attachment at Ⓑ to enable tanks to charge through hedgerows.

Ⓐ   Ⓑ

This is a modified Sherman 'flail-tank'. Its job was to use its flail to explode mines immediately in front of its tracks – thus creating a clear path for other vehicles. It was generally called a 'Crab'.

ANGLO-AMERICAN SUPPLY ROUTE   R Scheldt   ★ANTWERP

SIEGFRIED LINE

Just outside Malmédy SS troopers belonging to Peiper's Battle Group shot down 86 American prisoners in cold blood.

At the time of the battle the British general Montgomery made a statement suggesting that he committed British troops "with a big bang" to save the situation as the Germans approached the R.Meuse.
In fact, very few British troops participated in 'the Bulge'; as Churchill said, the battle was "an ever famous American victory."

- ▨ Allied occupied territory
- ▨ The 'Bulge' to 25 Dec.1944
- ← Hitler's plan
- ➔ Allied counter attacks after 25 Dec.1944
- ▽ Skorzeny's commando group –some dropped by parachute.

● BRUSSELS

LIÈGE

Malmédy

R Meuse

St Vith

NAMUR

DINANT ●

Bastogne

Hitler's last offensive in the west:
THE BATTLE OF THE BULGE 1944-45

ARLON ●

33: The American people at war

In World War II 90% of the American people were lucky enough not to hear the sound of guns fired in anger. For them the war was something which gave everyone a job and a good living wage

Conversion to a wartime economy

But there was no doubt that the people entered whole-heartedly into the 'Battle of Production'. In January 1942 President Roosevelt created the War Production Board (WPB) and gave to Donald M. Nelson the job of providing enough weapons for Americans and their allies to win the war. With a year's experience of Lend-Lease* behind them, the factories achieved some remarkable results. By May 1942 Nelson was stating that American industry 'was executing programmes which sounded utterly fantastic no more than six months ago'. By the beginning of 1943 the USA was out-producing the *combined* war production of all the enemy nations. Inevitably, there was some waste and inefficiency. For example, the government spared no effort to persuade motorists to part with their spare tyres once the Japanese had overrun America's main source of natural rubber in Malaya. Cartoon films by Walt Disney and AAP (still sometimes seen on British television) rammed home the message to cinema audiences and millions of Americans responded. Spare tyres soon choked the storage depots—but they were rarely put to good use.

Rationing

Americans accepted rationing and other restrictions in a patriotic spirit but rebelled against government inefficiency, especially over the distribution of foodstuffs. Coffee rationing began in 1942 but was so ineffective that the government abandoned it the following year. Sugar rationing also began in 1942, though the shortage could have been made good by more vigorous government action despite the fact that sugar was used in the manufacture of synthetic rubber and explosives. Butter rationing *was* essential, partly because government price control did not encourage dairy farmers to produce large quantities of this commodity. Cream, however remained unrationed. Americans who could spare cash to buy cream as well as the time to churn it could make as much butter as they wanted. Petrol rationing was very unpopular in such a highly motorized society especially as there was usually a surplus of low-octane gasoline in the oil-producing states. Understandably, the government failed to placate car owners in these areas when it told them that petrol rationing at least saved them from wearing out their tyres!

Population movements

Clearly the war brought a great deal of inconvenience to most Americans. About 15 million men entered the armed services but of these approximately 6 million remained in the United States, usually in bases far removed from their home towns. Their wives often moved house to be near them and this movement helped to accentuate the accommodation difficulties being felt in many urban areas. At the time, about 5 million people drifted from the farms to the cities, despite the fact that wartime agriculture enjoyed a permanent boom. And, as in World War I, thousands of Negroes migrated from the Deep South to find work in the expanding industry of the Northern and Far Western states. Here they met varying degrees of racial hostility, frequently prompted by the overcrowding that characterized the cities during World War II. Yet the American Negroes managed to advance both socially and economically during what was in fact a period of major social upheaval. One, Benjamin O. Davis, rose to the rank of Brigadier-General**. But none fought or worked in the same squads as enlisted white men, for the US Army delayed operating a policy of 'integration' until after the war. It would be fair comment to say that the contribution of the Negro in the munition plants, in the combat teams and engineer units was a major factor in the ultimate victory of America in World War II.

Higher wages

Between 1943 and 1944 unemployment disappeared in the USA. Industrial production had already increased by 100% in the year *before* Pearl Harbor; when it became even more dramatic the civilian war-workers enjoyed major pay increases. Inevitably, this led to increased consumer spending and a tendency towards inflation. Fortunately, the government managed to siphon off the surplus cash in all sorts of ways: one of the tasks assigned to Major Glenn Miller's Air Force Band was to persuade G.I.s serving overseas to invest some of their generous pay in War Bonds. Due to savings such as these, to increased taxes and to a fairly successful system of price controls, the Federal government prevented the worst features of inflation from appearing in wartime America.

---

*Of course, Lend-Lease continued in ever-mounting quantities to all of America's allies throughout the war.
**He commanded the 332nd Fighter Group, the only one composed solely of Negro fighter pilots.

An example of United States industrial supremacy

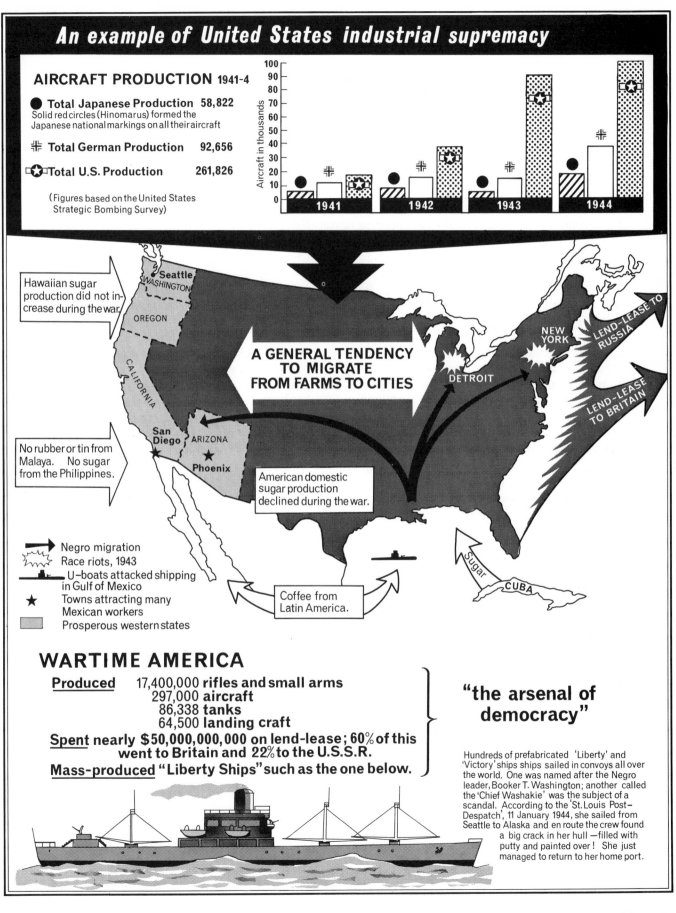

AIRCRAFT PRODUCTION 1941-4

● **Total Japanese Production** 58,822
Solid red circles (Hinomarus) formed the
Japanese national markings on all their aircraft

✠ **Total German Production** 92,656

✪ **Total U.S. Production** 261,826

(Figures based on the United States
Strategic Bombing Survey)

Aircraft in thousands — 1941, 1942, 1943, 1944

Hawaiian sugar
production did not in-
crease during the war.

Seattle
WASHINGTON
OREGON
CALIFORNIA

A GENERAL TENDENCY
TO MIGRATE
FROM FARMS TO CITIES

DETROIT
NEW YORK
LEND-LEASE TO RUSSIA
LEND-LEASE TO BRITAIN

No rubber or tin from
Malaya.   No sugar
from the Philippines.

San Diego
ARIZONA
Phoenix

American domestic
sugar production
declined during the war.

→ Negro migration
Race riots, 1943
U–boats attacked shipping
in Gulf of Mexico
★ Towns attracting many
Mexican workers
Prosperous western states

Coffee from
Latin America.

Sugar
CUBA

WARTIME AMERICA

Produced   17,400,000 **rifles and small arms**
                   297,000 **aircraft**
                    86,338 **tanks**
                    64,500 **landing craft**

Spent nearly $50,000,000,000 on lend-lease; 60% of this
went to Britain and 22% to the U.S.S.R.

Mass-produced "Liberty Ships" such as the one below.

"the arsenal of democracy"

Hundreds of prefabricated 'Liberty' and
'Victory' ships ships sailed in convoys all over
the world. One was named after the Negro
leader, Booker T. Washington; another called
the 'Chief Washakie' was the subject of a
scandal. According to the 'St. Louis Post–
Despatch', 11 January 1944, she sailed from
Seattle to Alaska and en route the crew found
a big crack in her hull —filled with
putty and painted over! She just
managed to return to her home port.

34: Victory in Europe, 1945

Diplomacy by friendship

President Roosevelt regularly conferred with the Allied leaders about the progress of the war and the plans for a peaceful and united world. He had met Prime Minister Churchill in North America on several occasions and during 1943 he made trips to Casablanca, Cairo and Teheran. But it was at Yalta, in the Russian Crimea, that he made his major attempt to secure lasting friendship with the Soviet Union so that the war and the peace might be won on the basis of mutual trust between the Russian and American peoples. Roosevelt believed that the American people had 'learned to be citizens of the world, members of the human community. We have learned the simple truth—"the only way to have a friend is to be one".' At Yalta Roosevelt appeared to have made a friend in Marshal Stalin. The Russian leader said he was willing, at a later date, to enter the war against Japan; he would consider joining a United Nations Organization; he would help the Polish people to establish a government of their own choice. For his part, Roosevelt agreed that Germany must pay for all the suffering she had caused and that the Allies must occupy the zones suggested by the European Advisory Commission in January 1945.

The death of the President

Roosevelt was a very sick man when he returned from the Crimea. Pressure of work and the burden of his disability—he had been a polio victim in 1921—forced him to seek recuperation at Warm Springs in Georgia. He was well aware that Stalin was already breaking his promises to the Polish people and that this was one of many problems beginning to blight the idea of Soviet-American friendship. However, he hoped to minimize these problems at least until the first meeting of the United Nations Conference scheduled to meet in San Francisco on 25 April 1945. On 12 April the President complained of a 'terrific headache'. He died that afternoon. Harry S. Truman, America's Vice-President, took over the prosecution of the war.

The defeat of Nazi Germany 1945

Throughout February and March 1945 the Western Allies and the Soviets made massive inroads into Hitler's Third Reich. British and US armies prepared for the crossing of the River Rhine where, at Remagen, the Americans were able to capture the Ludendorff railway bridge intact. Once across, there were arguments over the next objective. Montgomery wanted to press on to the Elbe and then drive his armour straight for Berlin. Eisenhower believed that Berlin had no military significance and preferred a steady advance on a broad front as a safer alternative. Consequently, it was the Russians who laid siege to Berlin where, on 30 April 1945, Adolf Hitler committed suicide. Already the 1st US Army had split Germany in half by linking up with Marshal Konev's 5th Guards Army at Torgau; while on 2 May the British 6th Airborne rushed into Wismar to stop Soviet troops from entering Schleswig-Holstein. 'So far as I was concerned,' said Montgomery, 'the oncoming Russians were more dangerous than the stricken Germans.' In fact, there was very little room in which the surviving German forces could deploy for battle and their new Führer, Admiral Dönitz, was realistic enough to authorize their surrender on 7 May 1945. Two days later, after the Russians had insisted that another ceremonial surrender should take place in Berlin, the shooting war was over. In the words of General Eisenhower: 'With this final capitulation by the German leaders, the mission of the Allied Expeditionary Force placed under my supreme command on 14 February 1944 was accomplished'.

The Allied War leaders at Yalta. Roosevelt, in this shot specially posed for the cameras, shows signs of physical strain.

ROOSEVELT'S IMPORTANT CONFERENCES — he was the first U.S. President to leave his country in wartime.

Extent of German controlled territory at time of Yalta Conference.

RUSSIANS

ANGLO-AMERICANS

Quebec 1943 & 1944

ATLANTIC CHARTER 1941

UNITED STATES

Washington 1941, 1942 & 1943

San Francisco ☆

Warm Springs Georgia ☆

Casablanca 1943

Yalta 1945

CRIMEA

Teheran 1943

Cairo 1943

THE DESTRUCTION OF THE THIRD REICH — 1945

THE MAP SHOWS THE EXTENT TO WHICH THE ANGLO-AMERICAN ARMIES PENETRATED THE RUSSIAN ZONE OF GERMANY. THESE ARMIES WITHDREW INTO THEIR OWN ZONES WHEN HOSTILITIES WERE OVER.

American views of the Russians in 1945 are interesting:

GENERAL EISENHOWER: "In his generous instincts, in his love of laughter, in his devotion to a comrade, and in his healthy, direct outlook on the affairs of workaday life, the ordinary Russian seems to me to bear a marked similarity to what we call an 'average American'."

HARRY HOPKINS: "We find the Russians as individuals easy to deal with — They like the United States. They trust the United States more than they trust any other power in the world...."

German territory–1937 frontiers   Anglo-American advance, 1945   Red Army advance, 1945

SCHLESWIG HOLSTEIN

Northern sector of E. Prussia under Russian control

Wismar

Under U.S. Control

R ELBE

RUSSIAN

R ODER

BRITISH ZONE

BERLIN

R RHINE

ZONE

GERMAN TERRITORY EAST OF THE RIVERS ODER AND NEISSE TO BE UNDER POLISH CONTROL

• Warsaw

Torgau

R NEISSE

Remagen

Dresden

POLAND

FRENCH ZONE

AMERICAN ZONE

Prague

C Z E C H O S L O V A K I A

FRANCE

AUSTRIA

35: Assault from the air: the defeat of Japan, 1945

The raids begin

'I happened to be in the Ginza, the main thoroughfare of Tokyo, at the time. The warning was sounded at five minutes past twelve on Saturday 18 April 1942 ... Almost immediately, American bombers appeared over the city, flying so low that their distinguishing marks were clearly visible. They appeared to be unopposed.'*

This, the first attack upon the Japanese capital, was the work of General Doolittle's B.25 *Mitchell* bombers which had flown off the US carrier *Wasp*, 800 miles out to sea. Doolittle's raid was little more than a gesture of American defiance and there were no more raids upon Tokyo until November 1944. By then the Americans had not only captured new air bases in the Marianas but had also developed the huge, long-range B.29 *Superfortress* bomber. More than a hundred Superfortresses roared across the Pacific to attack the Musashina factory in Tokyo. A mere 24 planes found their target and the high-level bombing was largely inaccurate. This apparent failure did not deter the Americans. Despite enemy fighters and anti-aircraft fire, despite the appalling weather conditions prevailing at high altitudes over Japan, they flew scores of missions throughout the winter of 1944–5.

American air and sea superiority

In March 1945 they switched to night operations and dropped fearsome jelly-gasoline bombs on Tokyo, Nagoya and Osaka. On the night of the Tokyo firestorm, March 10/11, the B.29s caused the death of 80,000 Japanese in what is considered to be the worst air raid in history. In April, the Americans reverted to their daylight attacks. This was because they had captured the island of Iwo Jima which placed Japan within US fighter range. On 7 April the B.29s bombed Japan with more than a hundred P.51 *Mustangs* to protect them; and before long American and British Task Force carriers were launching air strikes against the main Japanese islands. Concerted efforts such as these meant that the Japanese people were suffering an unprecedented assault from incendiary and high-explosive bombs.

The condition of Japan in 1945

The continual bombardment meant that Japan was incapable of waging an offensive was in the Pacific; but she could still muster some formidable defences for use against a possible American invasion. Two million soldiers, 5000 *kamikaze* aircraft and 3000 suicide ships were standing by on Kyushu, Shikoku and Honshu, where the population had reconciled themselves to a fight to the finish. At the same time, American marines

and assault troops were steeling themselves for an invasion—it was expected, on the basis of previous experiences at Iwo Jima and Okinawa, that the fighting in Japan would cost them a million casualties. In fact, President Truman knew that the Japanese could be forced to surrender without a costly amphibious invasion. He could easily step up the air attacks; he could *threaten* to use new and terrible devices against the Japanese people; or, if his scientists at Alamagordo Air Base were successful in their bid to produce a nuclear weapon, he could drop atomic bombs on the enemy.

The atomic bombs

In July 1945 President Truman attended the Potsdam Conference, held in the suburbs of occupied Berlin. Here he met Churchill and Stalin and informed the Russian leader that America now possessed 'a weapon of unusually destructive force'.** On 26 July Truman and Churchill issued their Potsdam Ultimatum, threatening Japan with 'prompt and utter destruction' if she refused to surrender. Two days later the Japanese Prime Minister Suzuki announced that his government would *mokusatsu* (i.e. 'ignore' or 'refrain from commenting upon') the Potsdam Ultimatum. So, though there may have been other ways of ending World War II, President Truman chose to use atomic bombs. On 6 August 1945 the B.29 *Enola Gay* dropped an atomic bomb on Hiroshima and killed 70,000 people. On 8 August 1945 Stalin declared war on Japan. On 9 August 1945 the B.29 *Bockscar* dropped an atomic bomb on Nagasaki and killed 36,000 people. Russian troops invaded Manchuria and Korea on the same day.

Surrender

As the Japanese reeled under atomic and Soviet attack, hordes of carrier planes harried the islands of Kyushu and Honshu. Tokyo suffered a heavy raid from 'conventional' bombers on 13 August. It was this sheer destructive power of the Allied Air Forces that forced Emperor Hirohito to say in a recorded broadcast on 15 August: 'We have resolved to pave the way for all the generations to come by enduring the unendurable and suffering the insufferable'. The Japanese had surrendered.

*pp. 184–185 *Traveller from Tokyo* by John Morris (Penguin Books, 1946)
**Stalin might have known about the bomb already through his spy rings in Canada and the USA.

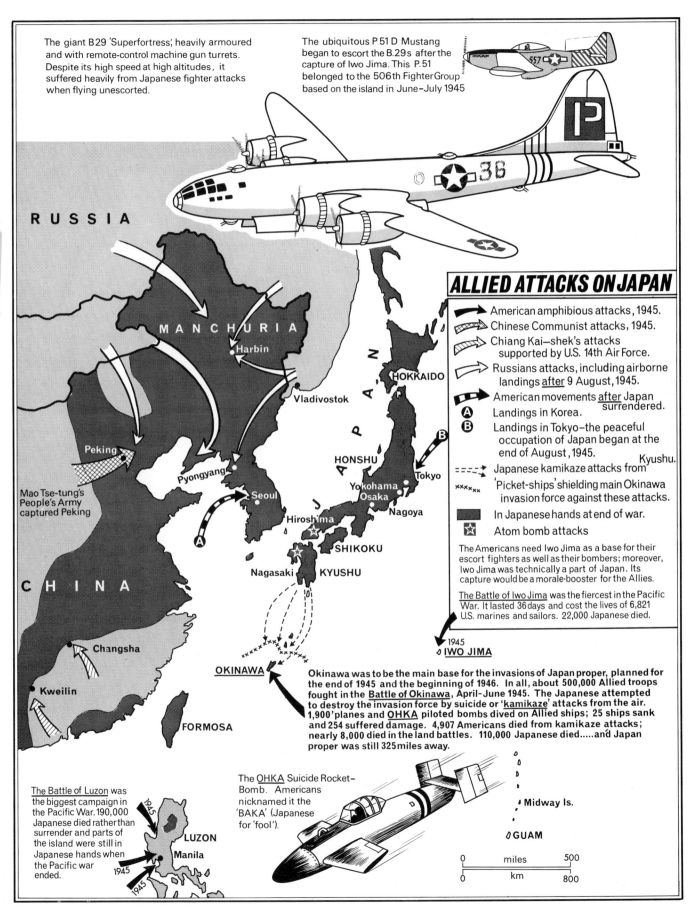

The giant B29 'Superfortress', heavily armoured and with remote-control machine gun turrets. Despite its high speed at high altitudes, it suffered heavily from Japanese fighter attacks when flying unescorted.

The ubiquitous P 51 D Mustang began to escort the B.29s after the capture of Iwo Jima. This P.51 belonged to the 506th Fighter Group based on the island in June–July 1945

RUSSIA

MANCHURIA

Harbin

Vladivostok

Peking

Mao Tse-tung's People's Army captured Peking

Pyongyang

Seoul

HOKKAIDO

HONSHU

Tokyo

Yokohama
Osaka

Nagoya

Hiroshima

SHIKOKU

Nagasaki   KYUSHU

CHINA

Changsha

Kweilin

FORMOSA

OKINAWA

ALLIED ATTACKS ON JAPAN

American amphibious attacks, 1945.

Chinese Communist attacks, 1945.

Chiang Kai–shek's attacks supported by U.S. 14th Air Force.

Russians attacks, including airborne landings after 9 August, 1945.

American movements after Japan surrendered.

Ⓐ Landings in Korea.

Ⓑ Landings in Tokyo–the peaceful occupation of Japan began at the end of August, 1945.

Japanese kamikaze attacks from Kyushu. 'Picket-ships' shielding main Okinawa invasion force against these attacks.

In Japanese hands at end of war.

Atom bomb attacks

The Americans need Iwo Jima as a base for their escort fighters as well as their bombers; moreover, Iwo Jima was technically a part of Japan. Its capture would be a morale-booster for the Allies.

The Battle of Iwo Jima was the fiercest in the Pacific War. It lasted 36 days and cost the lives of 6,821 U.S. marines and sailors. 22,000 Japanese died.

1945
◊ IWO JIMA

Okinawa was to be the main base for the invasions of Japan proper, planned for the end of 1945 and the beginning of 1946. In all, about 500,000 Allied troops fought in the Battle of Okinawa, April–June 1945. The Japanese attempted to destroy the invasion force by suicide or 'kamikaze' attacks from the air. 1,900 'planes and OHKA piloted bombs dived on Allied ships; 25 ships sank and 254 suffered damage. 4,907 Americans died from kamikaze attacks; nearly 8,000 died in the land battles. 110,000 Japanese died.....and Japan proper was still 325 miles away.

The Battle of Luzon was the biggest campaign in the Pacific War. 190,000 Japanese died rather than surrender and parts of the island were still in Japanese hands when the Pacific war ended.

1945

LUZON
Manila

1945

The OHKA Suicide Rocket-Bomb. Americans nicknamed it the 'BAKA' (Japanese for 'fool').

• Midway Is.

◊ GUAM

| 0 | miles | 500 |
| 0 | km | 800 |

Further Reading

Theme 5 – World War II

See *Purnell's History of the Second World War* for a detailed and well-illustrated account.

Spread

29. Pearl Harbor

The Week before Pearl Harbor, A. A. Hoehling, Robert Hale, 1963

Zero!, Okumiya and Horikoshi, Corgi, 1958

30. Attrition in the Pacific

Tarawa, Henry Shaw, Purnell Battle Book

31. The air war against Germany

Luftwaffe War Diaries, Cajus Bekker, Corgi, 1969

The Mighty Eighth, Roger Freemen, Doubleday, 1973

32. Second Front

Struggle for Europe, Chester Wilmot, Collins, 1952

Top Secret, Ralph Ingersoll, Partridge, 1946

A Walk in the Sun, Harry Brown, Panther, 1968 (war novel)

33. The American people at war

USA—the Twenties to Viet Nam, Daniel Snowman, Batsford, 1968

34. Victory in Europe

Report by the Supreme Commander to the Combined Chiefs of Staff *on the Operations in Europe 6 June 1944 to 8 May 1945*, HMSO, 1946

35. Assault from the air

B.29 Superfortress, Carl Berger, Purnell Weapon Book *American Diplomacy during the Second World War*, Gaddis Smith, John Wiley, 1966 (see Ch. 9 'The Bomb')

History of Modern Japan, Richard Storry, Penguin, 1961

THEME 6

America and the Cold War

The slender links binding Russia and America in their fight against Nazi Germany had shattered by the end of World War II. The Red Army's occupation of Eastern Europe, the refusal of Stalin to demobilize his armed forces, the fear that Soviet troops might erupt across the River Elbe, the appearance of Communist guerrillas in Northern Greece—all of these factors forced America to devise her rigid policy of 'containment' towards Communism. Possibly the United States exaggerated the extent of the communist threat during the early stages of the Cold War. Nevertheless, President Truman had to provide for the physical security of his country and he decided to protect the democratic institutions of his people and those of his allies by means of Marshall Aid, the extravagent support of Berlin during the 1948–9 blockade and by the creation of NATO.

There were radical changes in the nature of the Cold War. Russia's possession of the atomic bomb in 1949 made open warfare between America and the Soviet Union unacceptable and therefore unlikely except in the most dangerous crisis situation. The emergence of Communist China the same year presented America with a new challenge but the defeat of Chinese armies in Korea during 1951 gave the United States confidence in her ability to handle *conventional mass attack* from Communist foes in the Far East. Stalin's death in 1953 helped to reduce international tension though Berlin re-appeared as the focal point in the Cold War during the 1958–60 Khrushchev Crisis and again during the building of the Wall in 1961.

The following year saw the short-lived but terrifying Cuban missile crisis and—though it received little publicity—the beginning of Operation Sunrise by US 'advisers' in South Viet Nam. Before long the war in Viet Nam dominated America's domestic and foreign affairs; and the harder the Americans hit North Viet Nam the more aid arrived in Haiphong from Russia. When Nixon became President he began his policy of Vietnamization. But as soon as he had pulled the majority of US troops out of Viet Nam the North Vietnamese, armed with highly sophisticated Soviet armour and ground-to-air missiles, began a *conventional mass attack* against the South.

America withdrew from the war in 1973—the fighting ended in victory for the North Vietnamese in 1975—and attempted to concentrate on *détente* with Russia. Two major arms limitation treaties were signed (1972 and 1979) but the beginning of the 1980s saw a new American President condemning 'Soviet adventurism' and calling for increased spending on defence.

36: The coming of the Cold War, 1945–1947

The American dream

'Oh boy, oh boy, what long-time prosperity we will have.' Millions of Americans shared Bernard Baruch's optimism as World War II came to an end. They wanted to transfer control of the atomic bomb to a trustworthy international agency; they intended to disarm and bring home all American troops stationed in Germany and Asia; they were anxious to give dollar aid to all the war-weary nations; and above all they expected to see the cause of democracy and free enterprise flourish in all parts of the globe.

The dream crashes

On 14 June 1946 Bernard Baruch, US delegate to the United Nations Atomic Energy Commission, proposed a plan for the international control of nuclear weapons. But the Russians were secretly developing their own atomic bombs and they spurned the American plan. Soviet agents, including the British nuclear scientist Allan Nunn May, had been busily passing atomic secrets to Moscow since August 1945 and when an appalled US State Department discovered the extent of Communist espionage in North America it realized it had only a head start in a nuclear arms race. The State Department was equally concerned by the Red Army's reluctance to withdraw its troops from the 'liberated' countries of Eastern Europe and from Northern Iran. It was also suspicious of Russian intentions in Greece and Turkey; and there seemed no hope of ever penetrating Eastern Europe with dollar aid and American business methods. The cause of democracy and free enterprise suffered all sorts of setbacks in the first nine months after World War II ended.

The Iron Curtain

This was certainly the view of Winston Churchill as early as March 1946. No longer a member of the British government, he still commanded great respect in the United States. Speaking in Fulton, Missouri—with President Truman at his side—Churchill declared that he wished to place certain facts before the American people: '. . . an iron curtain had descended across the continent. Behind that line lie all the capitals of the ancient states of Central and Eastern Europe . . . all are subject in one form or another . . . to a very high and increasing measure of control from Moscow . . . Turkey and Persia are both profoundly alarmed . . . this is certainly not the liberated Europe we fought to build up. Nor is it one

which contains the essentials of permanent peace . . .' Stalin called the Fulton speech a 'call to war with the Soviet Union'. Prime Minister Attlee hastened to say that Churchill did not speak for the British government—but the damage was already done. Truman had applauded Churchill's words; a state of fear and distrust now existed between Russia and the USA.

The Truman Doctrine and the Marshall Plan 1947

In February 1947 Attlee's government informed the President that Britain could no longer afford to send aid to Greece and Turkey. Truman immediately drew up plans to help these countries whose geographical location barred Russia's access to the Mediterranean. On 12 March 1947 he outlined the *Truman Doctrine* to both Houses of Congress: '. . . I believe that it must be the policy of the United States to support free peoples who are resisting attempted subjugation by armed minorities or by outside pressures . . . Our way of life is based on the will of the majority, and is distinguished by free institutions, representative government, free elections . . . The second way of life is based upon the will of the minority forcibly imposed upon the majority.' The United States would offer economic aid for, as Secretary Marshall declared on 5 June 1947, America's enemies were *not* Communists but hunger, poverty, desperation and chaos. Any government—including Russia—who would assist in the rehabilitation of Europe—could have this American aid. This was the essence of the *Marshall Plan*. Britain and France welcomed it; but Stalin declined the offer. He spoke on behalf of Russia and every country where the Red Army based its troops.

The containment of communism

In July 1947 the US diplomat George Kennan enlarged upon the significance of America's new policies. He predicted that the United States must resign herself to 'a long-term, patient but firm and vigilant *containment* of Russian expansive tendencies'. Communists from all over Europe protested and banded themselves into the Communist Information Bureau (*Cominform*). The Cominform then painted the Truman Doctrine, Marshall Aid and the concept of containment as aggressive moves on the part of American imperialists. In contrast, it claims the Soviet Union stood for world peace. Russia and the USA were now poles apart. The *Cold War*—in Europe at least—had begun.

America's hopes of promoting the growth of democratic institutions in Eastern Europe are foiled.

America's hopes of sending dollar aid and businessmen to Eastern Europe are dashed against the Iron Curtain.

In 1947 delegates from France, Italy and the Iron Curtain countries met in Poland to found the COMINFORM.

Moscow

SOVIET UNION

Russia's long-standing ambition— to break out from the Black Sea into the Mediterranean Sea.

FINLAND

Berlin
SOVIET SECTOR
POLAND
Warsaw

FRANCE

Czechoslovakia
AUSTRIA
Budapest
HUNGARY
YUGOSLAVIA
Belgrade
RUMANIA
Bucharest
BULGARIA
Sofia
ALBANIA
ITALY

Caspian Sea

Black Sea

TURKEY

GREECE

Mediterranean Sea

IRAN (PERSIA)
Middle East Oil fields

Legend:
- ■ Territory either subservient to or occupied by Russia 1945–1946
- ➤ Communist pressure
- ➤ Soviet withdrawal from Iran 1946
- Я Large communist parties in France and Italy
- 〰 Russian frontier 1939
- 〜 Iron Curtain in Europe 1945–46

Before her economic crisis in the winter of 1946–1947, Britain had sent aid to Greece & Turkey. A major communist uprising existed in Northern Greece.

Suez Canal

AMERICA'S PLANS FOR AN 'OPEN WORLD' CRASH INTO STALIN'S 'IRON CURTAIN' DURING 1945–1946

According to the Americans, Marshall Aid was "our simple duty as neighbours to take a generous part in helping these great people to help themselves

San Francisco
In June 1945 delegates from 50 nations adopted the Charter of the United Nations.

New York
HQ.of U.N.

$ MARSHALL AID TO WESTERN EUROPE

According to the Communists, Marshall Aid was "a European branch of the general world plan of political expansion being realised by the U.S."

THE TWO SIDES IN THE COLD WAR

Sixteen countries received Marshall Aid: Britain, France, Belgium, Netherlands, Luxembourg, Austria, Italy, Greece, Turkey, Switzerland, Norway, Sweden, Denmark, Portugal, Iceland and the three Western Zones of Germany. It was a natural Russian assumption that these areas had opted to support the policies of the United States.

37 : Crisis in Europe: the German problem, 1945–1949

'Bring the boys back home!'

During World War II the United States had contemplated a hare-brained scheme called the Morgenthau Plan to turn the Germans into a nation of farmers. But once the war ended, the US occupation forces could see that the urgent task in Germany was not to seek vengeance but to feed millions of hungry Germans, many of whom were refugees from Soviet-occupied territories. Yet it was not easy to enlist official aid for this; in the States, people urged Congress to reduce the size of the armed forces and 'bring the boys back home'. Most US troops returned home during 1945; those left behind were soon bored with peacetime duties and some demonstrated against remaining in Germany during 1946.

Bizonia

Matters soon changed. At the 1945 Potsdam Conference Stalin had agreed to co-operate in the government of Germany as a single economic unit. But he had already given Walter Ulbricht, a Moscow-trained German, the task of converting the Russian zone into a Communist state. Moreover he had ordered the systematic plundering of German farms and factories. When one appreciates how much Russia had suffered at the hands of the Germans it is easy to excuse Stalin's actions; but he was obviously not trying to run Germany as a 'single economic unit'. And when the Americans realized that, if they were going to solve the problems of inflation, the black market and food shortages, they would have to act independently of the Russians, then their actions are equally easy to understand. On 6 September 1946 Secretary Burns arrived in Stuttgart to reverse previous American attitudes towards Germany: 'We are not withdrawing. We are staying here. . . .' On 1 January 1947 Britain and America merged their zones into 'Bizonia'; and in 1948 introduced the *Deutschemark*—a new German currency, designed to combat inflation. By June, Britain, France and the USA had agreed it was time to consider the establishment of a *West* German government.

The Berlin blockade 1948–9

This was also the moment that Stalin chose to try to drive the Allies from their sectors in Berlin. On 24 June 1948 the Russians announced that bridge repairs on the River Elbe had caused 'technical difficulties with communications'. Lorries, trains and barges bound for West Berlin found their routes into the Soviet zone blocked by Russian sentries. President Truman could have ordered his troops to force a way through; but instead he hoped to foil Stalin's move by the use of American air power. On 26 June he authorized General Clay,* US Military Governor in Germany, to airlift supplies along the three air corridors into Berlin. Two days later, 150 transport planes touched down on Tempelhof airfield and unloaded 400 tons of supplies. Stalin was unperturbed. He knew that the Americans would have to fly in 4000 tons a day if they were to save 2.25 million West Berliners from starvation. Truman believed his planes could do just this. And to show Stalin he was in earnest, he ordered two groups of B.29 atom bombers to East Anglia and concentrated US fighter aircraft on German bases. Any attempt by the Red Air Force to stop the airlift would mean war. In fact, the Russians never intercepted a single transport but simply watched the Allies conduct their spectacular airlift. Allied planes made 270,000 flights to Berlin and brought in almost 2.5 million tons of supplies. Seventy British and American fliers died in accidents.

1949: NATO and a divided Germany

Stalin had obviously miscalculated. The Berlin airlift was a major communist defeat on the new ideological battlefields of the Cold War. He gained nothing from focussing world attention on this American success and on 12 May 1949 he lifted the blockade. President Truman had already taken much weightier decisions: in April he fundamentally changed US foreign policy by creating the North Atlantic Treaty Organization—a defensive military alliance; moreover, he persuaded the West Germans to agree upon the 'Basic Law'—destined to be the constitution of a new Federal German Republic. Stalin's retort was the creation of the German Democratic Republic in the Russian occupied zone. In this way America and Russia recognized their failure to solve the German problem; instead, their mutual fears had led to a divided Germany and a divided Berlin. Both were to prove a source of constant crisis for the world in general and the United States in particular.

*General Lucius D. Clay had already drawn up contingency plans for an airlift in the event of a Russian blockade of Berlin.

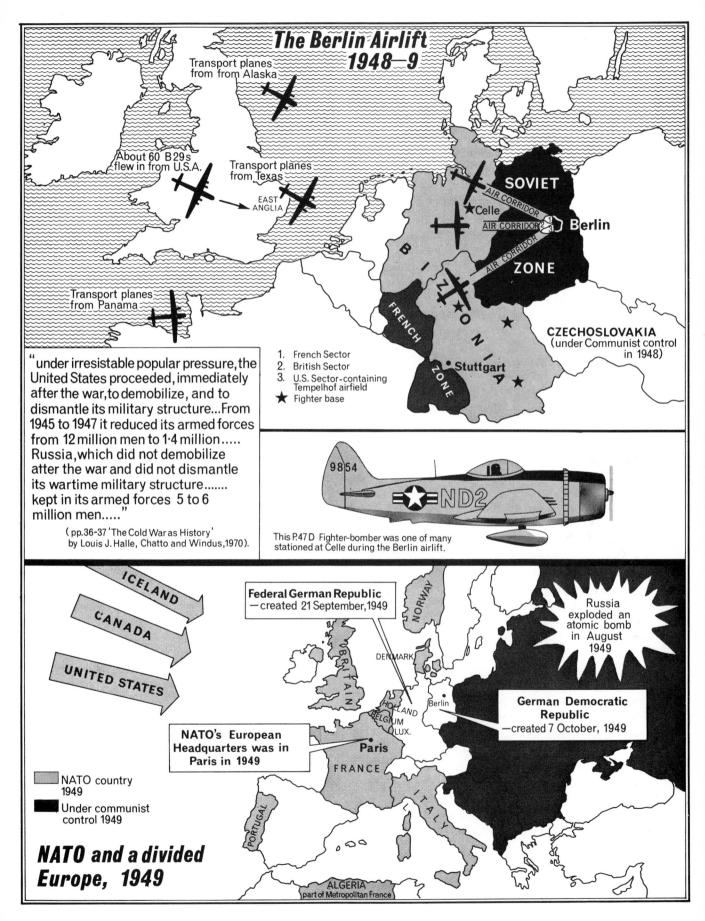

The Berlin Airlift 1948-9

Transport planes from from Alaska

About 60 B29s flew in from U.S.A.

Transport planes from Texas

EAST ANGLIA

Transport planes from Panama

SOVIET

★ Celle

AIR CORRIDOR

AIR CORRIDOR 2 1 3 — Berlin

B I Z O N I A

AIR CORRIDOR

ZONE

FRENCH ZONE

★ ★

• Stuttgart

★

CZECHOSLOVAKIA
(under Communist control in 1948)

1. French Sector
2. British Sector
3. U.S. Sector - containing Tempelhof airfield
★ Fighter base

"under irresistable popular pressure, the United States proceeded, immediately after the war, to demobilize, and to dismantle its military structure...From 1945 to 1947 it reduced its armed forces from 12 million men to 1·4 million..... Russia, which did not demobilize after the war and did not dismantle its wartime military structure....... kept in its armed forces 5 to 6 million men....."

(pp.36-37 'The Cold War as History' by Louis J. Halle, Chatto and Windus, 1970).

98 54   ND2

This P.47 D Fighter-bomber was one of many stationed at Celle during the Berlin airlift.

ICELAND

CANADA

UNITED STATES

Federal German Republic
—created 21 September, 1949

NORWAY

DENMARK

GT BRITAIN

HOLLAND
BELGIUM
LUX.

Berlin

Russia exploded an atomic bomb in August 1949

German Democratic Republic
—created 7 October, 1949

NATO's European Headquarters was in Paris in 1949

Paris

FRANCE

ITALY

NATO country 1949

Under communist control 1949

PORTUGAL

ALGERIA
part of Metropolitan France

NATO and a divided Europe, 1949

38: America and Asia, 1945–1950

Failure in China 1945

Throughout World War II America had always believed that it would be possible to unite the Chinese Communist and Nationalist parties and then bring their combined armies into action against the Japanese. But as early as 1944 a US Army Observation Section in Yenan (the Communist headquarters) had reported that the 'Communist governments are the first . . . in modern Chinese history to have positive and widespread support' and indicated that Chiang Kai-shek's Nationalists had little hope of beating Mao Tse-tung's People's Army. US Ambassador Hurley persuaded Mao to leave his Yenan headquarters (currently blockaded by Nationalist troops) and have talks with Chiang in Chungking during August 1945, but the two leaders failed to reach any agreement. In December President Truman showed where American sympathies lay by stating that he recognized Chiang's Nationalist Party as the legal government of China.

The Communist triumph in China 1946–50

Having failed to bring peace and unity to the Chinese people, the Americans gave Chiang every assistance. They flew his troops into Manchuria and Taiwan; they stockpiled surplus war material for his use; and they offered dollar aid in a futile effort to halt the inflation that was causing so much misery in Nationalist China. Soon it was clear that Chiang's cause was hopeless. Communist armies entered Central China; bands of guerillas operated more or less at will in the south. By September 1948 thousands of Nationalists were deserting to Mao— and taking their US manufactured vehicles and weapons with them. In April 1949 the Communist battle groups were across the Yangtze River and on 1 October Mao felt strong enough to declare the creation of the Central People's Government of China with himself as Chairman and Chou En-lai as Premier. By November the Communists had taken Chungking and the remnants of the Nationalist armies had fled to Taiwan. Many of America's allies recognized the Chinese People's Republic, but the United States—convinced that a new and deadly form of Communism now existed in China*—adopted a hostile and unrealistic attitude. America managed to prevent the admission of Communist China into the United Nations until as late as October 1971 and, until President Nixon's visit to Peking in 1972, persisted in supporting Chiang's Nationalists on Taiwan as the legal government of China.

*Especially after Mao visited Stalin in Moscow in December 1949.

Divided Korea

US troops did not land in Korea until September 1945, by which time the Russians were well-established in the North. Just as in Germany, the Soviet and US representatives failed to find a formula for reuniting Korea and eventually the UN approved an American plan to hold free elections in the south. On 15 August 1948 the pro-American Republic of Korea, led by Syngman Rhee, came into existence in the south; on 8 September 1948 the Communist Democratic Republic of Korea, led by Kim Il-sung, emerged north of the 38th Parallel. Despite this, the UN recognized the south as the legal government of Korea. In December 1948 the Russian occupation troops moved out of North Korea; in June 1949 the last of the Americans left the south—and the two halves of another divided country glared at one another across one of the flimsiest frontiers in the world.

The occupation of Japan—an American success

The US was not only responsible for the occupation of Japan but also for the repatriation of Japanese personnel in North Eastern Asia. American medical teams inoculated three million Japanese against Asian cholera and then the Seventh Fleet shipped the whole lot home—a remarkable feat of organization. In Japan itself the Americans and their Commonwealth allies met unexpected co-operation from police and local officials. The Emperor had 'quietly come down from the clouds' and admitted that he was not of divine origin. In his place General MacArthur, Supreme Commander of the Allied Powers, ruled the country from his Tokyo headquarters. He introduced a new constitution in 1946: Emperor Hirohito remained as a figurehead but the power of the state was now to be vested in the hands of the people. At the time, most Japanese were more concerned with food shortages than with constitutional change and were therefore delighted when MacArthur imported food from the USA. His benevolence and unusual dignity charmed the Japanese who progressively admired Americans and the American way of life. By 1948, when the Russians were making their bid to control Berlin and the Communists were thrusting across China, the Japanese were quite willing to be drawn inside America's Pacific defence perimeter. Japanese co-operation was to be of crucial importance when, in 1950, war broke out in nearby Korea.

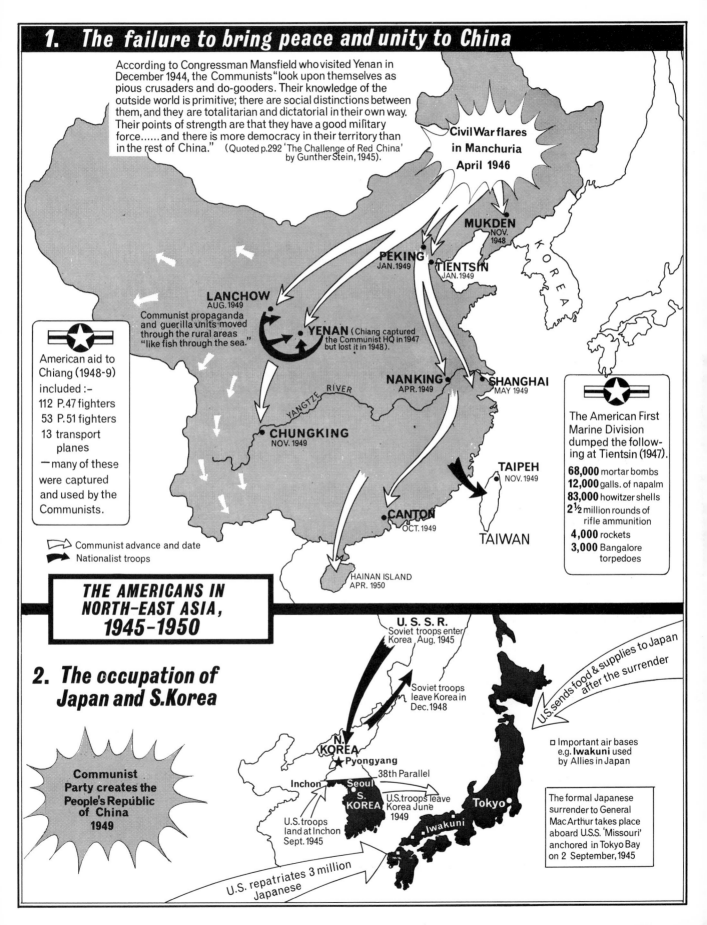

1. The failure to bring peace and unity to China

According to Congressman Mansfield who visited Yenan in December 1944, the Communists "look upon themselves as pious crusaders and do-gooders. Their knowledge of the outside world is primitive; there are social distinctions between them, and they are totalitarian and dictatorial in their own way. Their points of strength are that they have a good military force...... and there is more democracy in their territory than in the rest of China." (Quoted p.292 'The Challenge of Red China' by Gunther Stein, 1945).

Civil War flares in Manchuria April 1946

MUKDEN NOV. 1948

PEKING JAN. 1949

TIENTSIN JAN. 1949

LANCHOW AUG. 1949

Communist propaganda and guerilla units moved through the rural areas "like fish through the sea."

YENAN (Chiang captured the Communist HQ in 1947 but lost it in 1948).

American aid to Chiang (1948-9) included :–
112 P.47 fighters
53 P.51 fighters
13 transport planes
—many of these were captured and used by the Communists.

NANKING APR. 1949

SHANGHAI MAY 1949

YANGTZE RIVER

CHUNGKING NOV. 1949

TAIPEH NOV. 1949

The American First Marine Division dumped the following at Tientsin (1947).
68,000 mortar bombs
12,000 galls. of napalm
83,000 howitzer shells
2½ million rounds of rifle ammunition
4,000 rockets
3,000 Bangalore torpedoes

CANTON OCT. 1949

TAIWAN

⇨ Communist advance and date
➤ Nationalist troops

HAINAN ISLAND APR. 1950

THE AMERICANS IN NORTH-EAST ASIA, 1945-1950

2. The occupation of Japan and S.Korea

Communist Party creates the People's Republic of China 1949

U.S.S.R. Soviet troops enter Korea Aug. 1945

Soviet troops leave Korea in Dec.1948

U.S. sends food & supplies to Japan after the surrender

N. KOREA ★ Pyongyang

38th Parallel

Inchon

Seoul

S. KOREA

U.S.troops leave Korea June 1949

U.S. troops land at Inchon Sept. 1945

□ Important air bases e.g. **Iwakuni** used by Allies in Japan

Tokyo

Iwakuni

The formal Japanese surrender to General MacArthur takes place aboard U.S.S. 'Missouri' anchored in Tokyo Bay on 2 September, 1945

U.S. repatriates 3 million Japanese

39: War in Korea, 1950–1953

It was Saturday evening,* 24 June 1950, when Secretary Dean Acheson rang President Truman at his home in Independence, Missouri. 'Mr. President, I have very serious news. The North Koreans have invaded South Korea!'

Rising American fears 1949–50

Truman was not entirely surprised by the news. Subversion inside the United States and attack from international Communism were realities he knew he had to face. In January 1949, for example, the FBI had exposed the fact that there were disturbingly high numbers of Communist sympathizers inside the USA. In August the same year the USSR had exploded its first atomic bomb while, at the beginning of October, Mao Tse-tung's Communists had emerged victorious in China. Truman's own effort to secure international control of nuclear weapons had failed during January 1950 when the Soviet Union's delegation walked out of the UN, ostensibly in protest against the refusal to give Communist China a seat on the Security Council.

Aid to Korea

Such were the President's fears when he alerted the Security Council to the dangers of the Communist attack upon South Korea. The Council, meeting in New York, agreed (for the Russians were still absent) to 'furnish such assistance to the Republic of Korea as may be necessary to repel the armed attack and to restore international peace and security in the area'. Sixteen nations promised to send aid and, as America could offer the most, accepted that all UN forces should be placed under the command of General MacArthur.**

China intervenes

American troops arrived in Korea in the nick of time and managed to defend a perimeter around the port of Pusan; the rest of the country was in the hands of the North Koreans. On 15 September 1950 US 8th Army troops landed at Inchon, captured Seoul, crossed the 38th Parallel and pushed the North Koreans back to the Yalu River. There, without warning, two Chinese armies smashed into the over-confident, over-extended American forces. The UN front collapsed and, with the temperature at minus 30 degrees, chaos reigned in the hills of North Korea. Had it not been for her air power, America would have suffered an overwhelming defeat at the hands of the Chinese Communists. However, her fighter jets, supported by Australian and South African pilots flying Mustangs, blasted every Chinese soldier in sight; B.29s bombed targets in the rear of the Communists while helicopters evacuated hundreds of wounded. frost-bitten soldiers. The UN forces retreated south of the 38th Parallel and it was not until May 1951 that they were able to strike back. Then they inflicted crushing defeats—and more than 200,000 casualties—on the Chinese infantry forces. In spite of the fact that the Chinese were now in full retreat, the United Nations decided—quite wrongly, in the opinion of some authorities—to resist the temptation of a second, full-scale advance into North Korea. As a result, the ground forces settled down to a static war in the 'Main Line of Resistance'—a series of fortified hills straddling the middle of Korea.

Limited War

From July 1951 both sides limited the war to patrols, ambushes and bloodthirsty skirmishes, while peace talks went on first at Kaesong and then at Panmunjom. For two years the Americans and their UN allies endured heavy casualties in pointless, bitter battles on hills such as 'Pork Chop' and 'Luke the Gook's Castle' and in the 'Punchbowl'. Above the ground forces, air combats between the American Sabrejets and Russian-built Mig-15s resulted in consistent US victories: in September 1952, for example, the Sabrejets shot down 64 Migs for the loss of seven aircraft. By mid-1953 the Chinese had had enough. Apart from their recapture of Pork Chop, their final attacks were a dismal failure and on 27 July 1953 they signed the armistice which is still in force today. Neither side had won, but the Americans had effectively stopped the Communist conquest of Korea and had succeeded in their primary aim of containing the Communists.

*Sunday morning, Korean time.
**Truman relieved MacArthur on 11 April 1951 when the General wanted to carry the war into Manchuria.

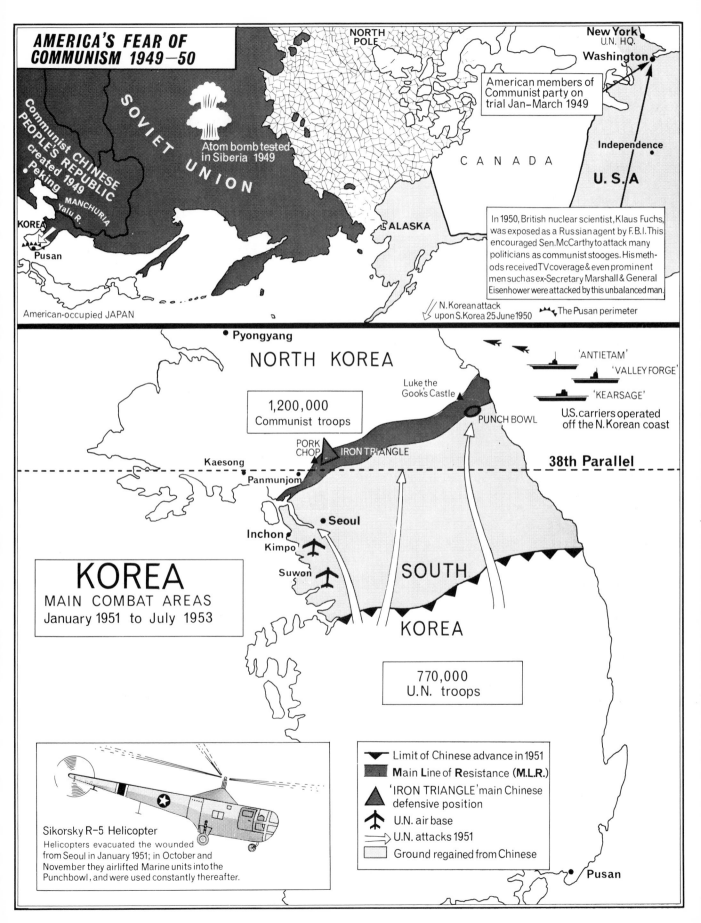

AMERICA'S FEAR OF COMMUNISM 1949–50

SOVIET UNION

Atom bomb tested in Siberia 1949

Communist CHINESE PEOPLE'S REPUBLIC created 1949

Peking

MANCHURIA

Yalu R.

KOREA

Pusan

American-occupied JAPAN

NORTH POLE

CANADA

ALASKA

NEW YORK
U.N. HQ.

Washington

Independence

U.S.A

American members of Communist party on trial Jan–March 1949

In 1950, British nuclear scientist, Klaus Fuchs, was exposed as a Russian agent by F.B.I. This encouraged Sen. McCarthy to attack many politicians as communist stooges. His methods received TV coverage & even prominent men such as ex-Secretary Marshall & General Eisenhower were attacked by this unbalanced man.

N.Korean attack upon S.Korea 25 June 1950   The Pusan perimeter

Pyongyang

NORTH KOREA

1,200,000 Communist troops

Luke the Gooks Castle

PUNCH BOWL

'ANTIETAM'

'VALLEY FORGE'

'KEARSAGE'

U.S. carriers operated off the N.Korean coast

PORK CHOP   IRON TRIANGLE

Kaesong

Panmunjom

38th Parallel

Seoul

Inchon

Kimpo

Suwon

SOUTH

KOREA

MAIN COMBAT AREAS
January 1951 to July 1953

KOREA

770,000 U.N. troops

Pusan

Limit of Chinese advance in 1951

Main **L**ine of **R**esistance (**M.L.R.**)

'IRON TRIANGLE' main Chinese defensive position

U.N. air base

U.N. attacks 1951

Ground regained from Chinese

Sikorsky R–5 Helicopter
Helicopters evacuated the wounded from Seoul in January 1951; in October and November they airlifted Marine units into the Punchbowl, and were used constantly thereafter.

40: The Eisenhower years, 1953–1961: (i) The arms race

By 1953 the Americans were rating Korea as the most unpopular war in their history. 130,000 casualties seemed an exessive price to pay for containing Communism in a remote corner of the globe. President Eisenhower, who had succeeded Truman in 1953, now had to promise America that he could reduce the size of the war-weary armed forces and yet at the same time deter the Russians from launching an attack upon the United States.

'The delicate balance of power'

Understandably, the President put his faith in air power. Curtis LeMay, chief of the Strategic Air Command (SAC), believed that 'Communism could best be handled from a height of 50,000 feet'; but as the Russians had already tested a hydrogen bomb in 1953 and—by 1955—possessed aircraft similar to SAC's B.52s, a far more sophisticated defence system was vital. Moreover, the Russians alarmed America by testing an Inter-continental Ballistic Missile (ICBM) during August 1957 and then, two months later, turned this alarm into panic by launching Sputnik I—the world's first artificial satellite. Eisenhower therefore tried to close the 'missile gap' by creating a fleet of submarines capable of delivering Polaris thermo-nuclear missiles to Soviet targets. This news was not entirely reassuring and many Americans echoed the words of Pete Seeger's song:

'. . . whether you're white, black, red or brown,
The question is this when you boil it down.
To be or not to be; that is the question.
And the answer to it all ain't military datum,
Like who gets there firstest with the mostest atoms,
But the people of the world must decide their fate—
We gotta stick together or disintegrate.
We hold these truths to be self-evident:
All men could be *cremated* equal . . .'

International crises

It was with this frightening thought that America conducted her foreign policy during the Fifties. John Foster Dulles, US Secretary of State, boasted of his 'brinkmanship' and of his hostility to Communist domination. But he did nothing when the Russians moved in to crush the 1956 Hungarian Revolt. Neither he nor the Russians intervened in the 1956 Suez Affair; and two years later the Russians remained passive when Eisenhower 'persuaded' the Arab states to accept US aid by flaunting the might of the US Sixth Fleet off their beaches.*

Khrushchev's crisis 1958–60

Chairman Khrushchev's approach to international affairs was, however, quite different. In fact, his flamboyant methods were quite beyond the experience of the US State Department. He announced in 1958 that it was time to settle the German problem; Berlin, he said, was a bone that stuck in the Russian gullet. He proposed to give the Americans six months to quit the city. After that, they would have to fight 'a big war', the flames of which would 'inevitably reach the American continent'. Two months before the deadline, Khrushchev proposed a summit meeting with Eisenhower—and then allowed the deadline to pass without incident. Next he cooled the international temperature by accepting an invitation to visit America and on 15 September 1959 a bemused world noted that the Khrushchevs were dining with the Eisenhowers in the White House. The two leaders agreed to attend a Paris Summit the following year—though it was difficult to see what Khrushchev could possibly gain from such a meeting. So it seemed suspiciously convenient that Khrushchev could announce in Paris on 5 May 1960 that Soviet ground-to-air missiles had shot down an American U-2 spy plane over Russia. Khrushchev accused Eisenhower of war-mongering and the Paris Summit collapsed. For more than a year the Berlin problem remained unsolved while, in Cuba and Indo-China, new problems had arisen to tax the President's skill in international affairs.

*US troops landed on the Lebanon beaches—the Marines waded ashore amidst crowds of bewildered holidaymakers.

The Deterrent !

U.S. AIR FORCE

The B.52 Stratofortress subsonic bomber. Eight engines; 600mph; carried 3 hydrogen bombs at 50,000 feet

Hungarian Uprising 1956

U.S. Intervention in the Lebanon 1958

Suez Crisis 1956

Khrushchev Crisis 1958–60

THE SOVIET BLOC
(Warsaw Pact, 1955, united the communist countries in a military alliance

TURKEY

• MOSCOW

Budapest•

•Berlin

North Pole

HOLY LOCH

Paris•

THULE

Greenland

Fairchild
S.T.Abr
Warren
OFFUT
Lowry
Cooke
Forbes TURNER
BROCKLEY
Groton

ATLANTIC OCEAN

RAMEY

POLARIS

"A new and flexible element will now be added to the strategic nuclear deterrent."
—Harold Macmillan, 1960.
The first Polaris nuclear submarine was the U.S.S. 'George Washington' launched by President Eisenhower on 9 June 1959. 5,400 tons; 380 feet long; cost $100m, it carried 16 Polaris thermo-nuclear missiles.

U2 incident, 1960
NATO, incl. W.Germany, Turkey & Greece by 1955
S.A.C. Bases
Missile Sites on U.S. Air Force bases
Polaris Base
U.S. Sixth Fleet

MISSILES

1957–1958 America built a number of I.C.B.Ms. (Intercontinental Ballistic Missiles) bases for her Atlas and Titan rockets. These had a range of 5,500 miles.

Polaris is an I.R.B.M. (Intermediate Range Ballistic Missile) with a range of 1,500 miles.

41: The Eisenhower years, 1953–1961: (ii) New problems appear

VIET NAM

The Geneva Conference, 1954

Before 1949 America had paid very little attention to this remote corner of South-East Asia. But once the Chinese threat appeared, the United States mistakenly assumed that the war France was fighting against the Viet Minh nationalists in Viet Nam was simply an extension of the struggle to contain communism. This grave error of judgement led the USA to send quantities of military aid to the French. Vice-President Richard Nixon, for example, was vehement in his support of the French army in Viet Nam: 'It is impossible to lay down arms until victory is won!' The French shared his view—until their defeat at the Battle of Dien Bien Phu (1954) led to their withdrawal from Indo-China. An international conference at Geneva ruled that free elections should be held in Viet Nam during 1956; meanwhile Priemier Ho Chi Minh would continue to rule the north while non-Communists would govern the land south of the 17th Parallel.

SEATO

John Foster Dulles was very suspicious of the likely outcome of this arrangement. He believed that Ho Chi Minh was a Communist and that elections would lead to a communist take-over in the whole of Viet Nam. He refused to endorse the Geneva agreements and worked, as he put it, to 'save all of South East Asia, if it can be saved' from the threat of Communism. He persuaded Britain and seven other countries to sign the South East Asia Collective Defence Treaty 'so that SEATO (South East Asia Treaty Organization) members could 'prevent and counter subversive activities directed from without against their territorial integrity.' (September 1955)

Ngo Dinh Diem

Next month the Catholic leader Ngo Dinh Diem proclaimed himself President of an anti-Communist 'Republic of South Viet Nam'. He refused to hold free elections and, because he claimed to oppose the spread of Communism, he received immediate US aid. But Diem misused this aid and utterly failed to create even the semblance of democratic institutions in the south. Though he claimed to be fighting the Viet Minh (now termed Viet Cong = Vietnamese Communist), he had neither the respect of the peasantry nor the support of his own soldiers. In November 1960 his crack paratrooper regiment tried to assassinate him—without success. Diem's misgovernment destroyed any confidence the people might have had in him and forced thousands to join the ranks of the Viet Cong. In fact, by the time President Eisenhower's administration ended in 1961, far more peasants were aiding the Viet Cong than were supporting Diem's government in Saigon; it meant that much of the countryside fell into the hands of Ho Chi Minh's supporters—ordinary men and women whom the Americans chose to identify as Communists.

CUBA

Communism in Cuba

In 1959 the young Cuban guerrilla leader Fidel Castro overthrew the corrupt and dictatorial rule of Fulgencio Batista. Castro had two specific aims: first, to establish a truly democratic form of government in Cuba and, secondly, to liberate his people from economic dependence upon the USA. At first he asked Eisenhower to finance his reform programme—Batista had fled from Cuba with all the government's funds! Regrettably, Eisenhower refused to offer unconditional aid and this forced Castro to adopt desperate measures. He nationalized the oil refineries belonging to Shell, Esso and Texaco; he commandeered the Havana Hilton for use as a hospital; and—most worrying of all—he showed keen interest in securing help from Communist countries. These moves convinced Eisenhower that there was a hostile Communist base 90 miles away from Florida. On 17 March 1960 he authorized his Central Intelligence Agency (CIA) to form all Cuban refugees into a liberation army. In May he cut off *all* aid; in July he wrecked Cuba's economy by refusing to buy sugar, Cuba's staple export. By the end of 1960 there were more than a thousand Cuban refugees reaching Florida every week; aid was flowing in to Cuba from Russia and her satellites; and in Nicaragua, Florida and Guatemala CIA training camps were preparing more than 2000 Cubans for an assault upon their homeland. It was in this atmosphere of increasing tension that John F. Kennedy became President of the United States in January 1961.

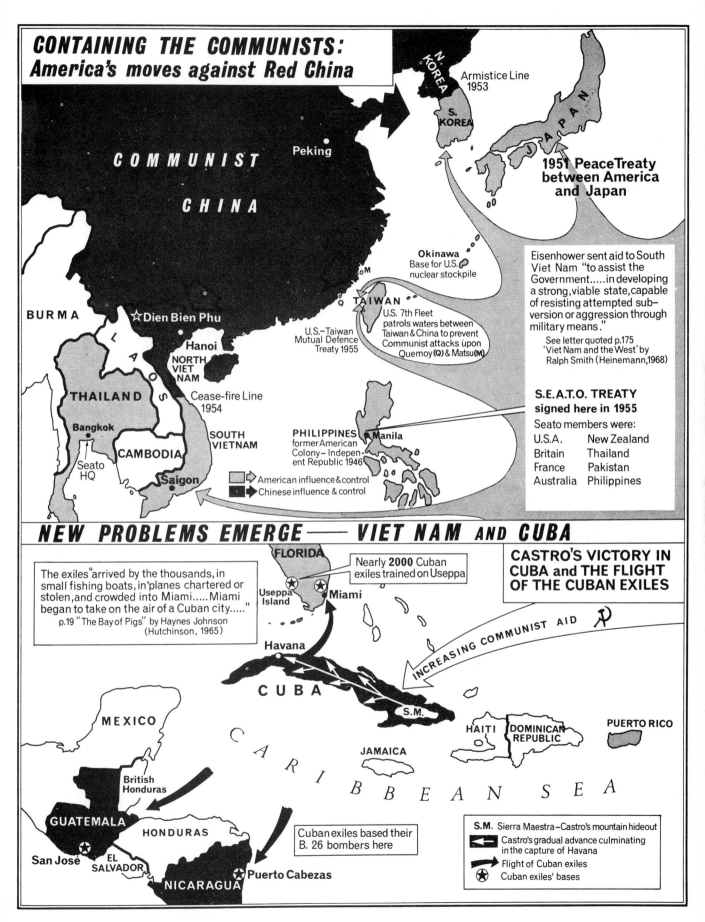

CONTAINING THE COMMUNISTS:
America's moves against Red China

N. KOREA

Armistice Line 1953

S. KOREA

JAPAN

1951 PeaceTreaty between America and Japan

COMMUNIST

Peking

CHINA

Okinawa
Base for U.S.
nuclear stockpile

BURMA

☆Dien Bien Phu

TAIWAN

U.S.–Taiwan
Mutual Defence
Treaty 1955

Q

M

U.S. 7th Fleet
patrols waters between
Taiwan & China to prevent
Communist attacks upon
Quemoy **(Q)** & Matsu**(M)**

Hanoi

NORTH
VIET
NAM

LAOS

THAILAND

Cease-fire Line
1954

Bangkok

SOUTH
VIETNAM

CAMBODIA

PHILIPPINES
formerAmerican
Colony– Indepen-
ent Republic 1946

Manila

Seato
HQ

Saigon

⬜➡ American influence & control
◼➡ Chinese influence & control

Eisenhower sent aid to South
Viet Nam "to assist the
Government.....in developing
a strong, viable state, capable
of resisting attempted subversion or aggression through
military means."

See letter quoted p.175
'Viet Nam and the West' by
Ralph Smith (Heinemann,1968)

**S.E.A.T.O. TREATY
signed here in 1955**

Seato members were:

U.S.A.	New Zealand
Britain	Thailand
France	Pakistan
Australia	Philippines

NEW PROBLEMS EMERGE —— VIET NAM AND CUBA

FLORIDA

Nearly **2000** Cuban
exiles trained on Useppa

CASTRO'S VICTORY IN
CUBA and THE FLIGHT
OF THE CUBAN EXILES

The exiles "arrived by the thousands, in
small fishing boats, in'planes chartered or
stolen, and crowded into Miami..... Miami
began to take on the air of a Cuban city....."
p.19 "The Bay of Pigs" by Haynes Johnson
(Hutchinson, 1965)

Useppa
Island

Miami

INCREASING COMMUNIST AID

Havana

CUBA

S.M.

MEXICO

HAITI

DOMINICAN
REPUBLIC

PUERTO RICO

C A R I B B E A N   S E A

JAMAICA

British
Honduras

GUATEMALA

HONDURAS

Cuban exiles based their
B. 26 bombers here

San José

EL
SALVADOR

NICARAGUA

Puerto Cabezas

S.M. Sierra Maestra–Castro's mountain hideout

◄◼ Castro's gradual advance culminating
in the capture of Havana

➤ Flight of Cuban exiles

★ Cuban exiles' bases

42: 'The Thousand Days': the Kennedy administration, 1961–1963

On 20 January 1961 John F. Kennedy became President of the United States of America. Before long he had involved himself in a military escapade which might well have destroyed the political career of a lesser man.

The Bay of Pigs 1961
Kennedy had inherited Eisenhower's CIA scheme for the overthrow of Fidel Castro and the young President let the plan go ahead on 17 April 1961. Cubans of 'Brigade 2506' landed at the Bay of Pigs, confident that the peasants would welcome them as liberators. But their mission failed. Castro's two T-33 jets shot their obsolete bombers out of the air and the Cuban people made no move to help them. Within a few days the Brigade had surrendered. It had been a fiasco and, as Kennedy openly admitted, the responsibility was his.

The Berlin Crisis 1961
He was thus at a disadvantage when he made his first effort to improve relations with the Soviet Union. He urged Khrushchev to halt all nuclear tests: 'Let us call a truce to terror!' During June they met in Vienna but Kennedy made very little headway. Khrushchev was more concerned about the number of East Germans who were finding asylum in West Berlin and when Kennedy refused to hinder the entry of these refugees the summit ended. On 13 August 1961 the *Volkspolizei* (East German People's Police) set up road blocks at all crossing points into East Berlin. On 17 August they began the construction of a wall to turn Berlin into a permanently divided city. Deciding that a show of US strength was now essential for the morale of the West Berliners, Kennedy ordered the 1st Battle Group to drive from Mannheim into the isolated Allied sectors. The Battle Group crossed East Germany without incident. Kennedy awaited Khrushchev's next move.

Cuba 1962
Early on Tuesday morning, 16 October 1962, McGeorge Bundy, Special Assistant to the President for National Security Affairs, had urgent news for Kennedy. 'Mr. President, there is now hard photographic evidence . . . that the Russians have offensive missiles in Cuba.' U-2s had brought back pictures of at least 9 missile sites; in addition, the Cubans were uncrating *Ilyushin-28* nuclear bombers in Havana. Kennedy wasn't sure of the nature of the threat: was it aimed specifically at the US mainland, or had Khrushchev created a trump card for

future negotiations over Berlin? Whatever Khrushchev's intentions were, Kennedy resolved to impose a 'quarantine' on all Russian offensive shipments coming into Cuba and, if necessary, to invade Cuba itself. Every weapon in the US nuclear armoury—scores of Polaris, Titan, Atlas and Minutemen missiles, hundreds of SAC bombers—now pointed at the USSR. Any incident could trigger off the nuclear holocaust. Soviet ships—about 25 were strung out across the Atlantic—were nearing Task Force 136. The first one, the oil tanker *Bucharest*, approached the American ships; but Kennedy allowed it to come through as it was carrying petroleum. The rest began to turn away—but the threat of nuclear war remained. Then Khrushchev lost his nerve. He agreed to dismantle the missile sites and remove the rockets from Cuba. The greatest post-war crisis was over.

'Hot line' and Test Ban Treaty 1963
After the Cuban crisis, America and Russia worked towards a relationship which would avoid the miscalculations that led to near-catastrophe in October 1962. In April 1963 Russia agreed to instal the 'hot line'—a direct telephone link between Moscow and Washington; and in August Britain joined America and Russia in signing the *Partial Test Ban Treaty* which, as far as those countries were concerned, meant the end of atmospheric nuclear tests.

'Operation Sunrise' 1962–3
In Viet Nam, President Kennedy was responsible for a radical change in the nature and quantity of US aid. In March 1962 US 'advisers' began *Operation Sunrise* to pacify the country. US planes strafed Viet Cong hideouts; US helicopters air-lifted ARVN troops.* 'We are going to win this war', said Robert Kennedy** during a visit to Saigon. 'We will remain here until we do'. *Sunrise* met with little success; the Viet Cong gained in strength. On 1 November 1963 ARVN troops overthrew the corrupt Diem government; Diem, they said, died of 'accidental suicide'. Twenty-two days later Kennedy himself was dead, gunned down in Dallas, Texas. He had never wished to involve America troops indiscriminately in Viet Nam; but he had sent in 14,000 'advisers' and was responsible for beginning the escalation that his successor, Lyndon Johnson, would continue.

*Army of the Republic of Viet Nam (i.e. South Viet Nam).
**The President's brother.

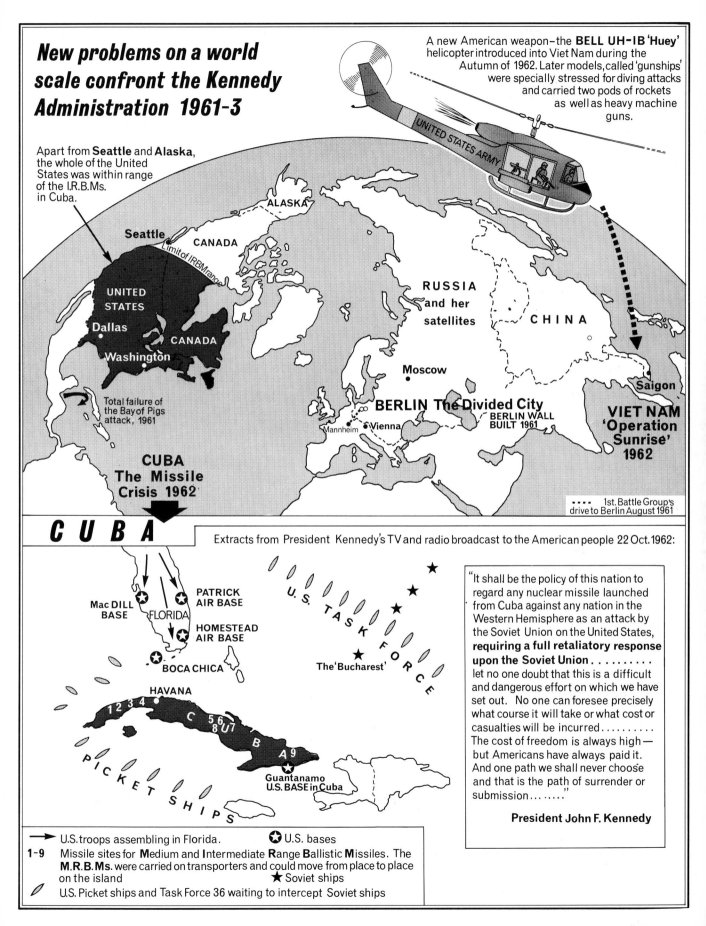

New problems on a world scale confront the Kennedy Administration 1961-3

A new American weapon–the **BELL UH–IB 'Huey'** helicopter introduced into Viet Nam during the Autumn of 1962. Later models, called 'gunships' were specially stressed for diving attacks and carried two pods of rockets as well as heavy machine guns.

UNITED STATES ARMY

Apart from **Seattle** and **Alaska**, the whole of the United States was within range of the I.R.B.Ms. in Cuba.

ALASKA

Seattle
CANADA
Limit of IRBM range

UNITED STATES
Dallas
CANADA
Washington

RUSSIA and her satellites

CHINA

Moscow

Total failure of the Bay of Pigs attack, 1961

BERLIN The Divided City
BERLIN WALL BUILT 1961
Mannheim • Vienna

Saigon

VIET NAM 'Operation Sunrise' 1962

CUBA The Missile Crisis 1962

···· 1st. Battle Group's drive to Berlin August 1961

C U B A

Extracts from President Kennedy's TV and radio broadcast to the American people 22 Oct. 1962:

MacDILL BASE
FLORIDA
PATRICK AIR BASE
HOMESTEAD AIR BASE
BOCA CHICA

U.S. TASK FORCE

The 'Bucharest'

HAVANA
1 2 3 4
C 5 6 U 7
8 B
A 9
Guantanamo U.S. BASE in Cuba

P I C K E T   S H I P S

"It shall be the policy of this nation to regard any nuclear missile launched from Cuba against any nation in the Western Hemisphere as an attack by the Soviet Union on the United States, **requiring a full retaliatory response upon the Soviet Union** . . . . let no one doubt that this is a difficult and dangerous effort on which we have set out. No one can foresee precisely what course it will take or what cost or casualties will be incurred . . . . The cost of freedom is always high — but Americans have always paid it. And one path we shall never choose and that is the path of surrender or submission . . . . "

President John F. Kennedy

→ U.S. troops assembling in Florida.   ✪ U.S. bases

1-9 Missile sites for **M**edium and **I**ntermediate **R**ange **B**allistic **M**issiles. The **M.R.B.Ms.** were carried on transporters and could move from place to place on the island   ★ Soviet ships

∅ U.S. Picket ships and Task Force 36 waiting to intercept Soviet ships

43: President Johnson and the war in Viet Nam

The new President: Lyndon Baines Johnson

Two days after Kennedy's assassination, President Johnson assured the South Vietnamese that they could still count upon American help. However, he left the conduct of the war to Secretary Robert McNamara. The President was far more interested in a peaceful solution to the Viet Nam problem—in contrast to his political opponents, such as Richard Nixon, who wanted the war to be carried into North Vietnamese (NVN) territory.

The Tonkin Gulf Resolution 7 August 1964

Then came the event that transformed Johnson's attitude to the war—the Tonkin Gulf incident 2 August 1964. That night NVN torpedo boats attacked the USS *Maddox*; two days later, it reported a second attack. This enraged Johnson who asked Congress for permission to retaliate. Congress responded with the Tonkin Gulf Resolution which stated that 'all measures will be taken to repulse aggression'. One senator commented: 'I believe history will record that we have made a great mistake in subverting and subventing the Constitution... we are in effect giving the President... war-making powers in the absence of a declaration of war.'

Escalation

American planes now attacked NVN targets; the Viet Cong plastered US air bases with mortar fire; US reinforcements arrived in Viet Nam; thousands of NVN troops swarmed down the Ho Chi Minh trail. Escalation meant that the Americans had to modify their tactics: bombing raids in the north tried to reduce the flow of NVN troops and supplies; armoured gunboats—the first they had used since Civil War days—patrolled the Mekong. But the toughest task of all went to the ground troops. They had to defeat an elusive enemy lurking in hamlets, paddy-fields and jungles where every Vietnamese—friend or foe—looked alike. For the thousands of young GIs brought out to man General Westmoreland's 'search and destroy' missions, it was a brutalizing experience. They had enormous fire power; if they were pinned down by an unseen enemy they could radio for help from a cruising jet or a low-flying gunship even though their use would cause the deaths of innocent civilians.

The Tet Offensive January–February 1968

The Viet Cong's Tet Offensive illustrated the savage nature of the struggle. About 2000 Viet Cong entered Saigon on scooters or in taxis. They occupied office blocks and residential areas; one suicide squad forced its way into the US embassy. Appalling battles raged inside the city. Most other provincial capitals suffered similar attacks; in Hué the Viet Cong executed 3000 civilians. And just below the demilitarized zone, NVN troops attacked the fortified US base at Khe Sanh and there was a danger that it might suffer the fate of Dien Bien Phu. The power of the enemy attacks made a strong impression upon the President and on 13 May representatives of both sides met to begin the Paris Peace Talks. Johnson—realizing the extent to which his policies had failed—decided not to stand for the Presidency again.

Pinkville (the My Lai Massacre) 1968

Pinkville was the name given by American soldiers to areas shaded pink on a map of the large village of Son My. One of the shaded areas was the hamlet of My Khe; intelligence reports indicated that this was a base used by the 48th Local Field Battalion, one of the toughest and most experienced of Viet Cong units. US helicopters ferried two companies of infantry into the area on 16 March 1968. Gunships and artillery pulverized the target and then the infantry attacked. But there was no response—the Americans had attacked the wrong hamlet. They were at Xom Lang, coded 'My Lai (4)' on their maps. Yet when civilians emerged from cover, the Americans kept on firing and killed more than 400 men, women and children in a senseless, protracted massacre. More than all the tales of napalm, defoliation* and gas warfare, Pinkville persuaded the American people that the War in Viet Nam was exceedingly difficult to justify.

*American planes sprayed the jungles with weedkiller to reduce the cover under which the Viet Cong hid.

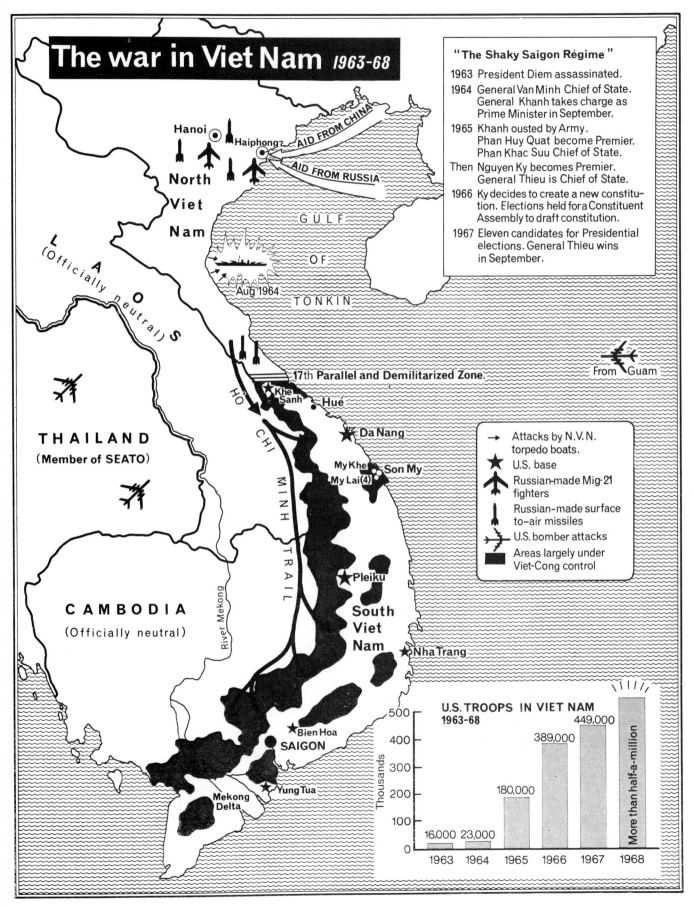

The war in Viet Nam 1963-68

Hanoi ◉
Haiphong

AID FROM CHINA

AID FROM RUSSIA

North Viet Nam

GULF OF TONKIN

Aug 1964

L A O S (Officially neutral)

HO CHI MINH TRAIL

17th Parallel and Demilitarized Zone.

From Guam

Khe Sanh ● Hué ●

★ Da Nang

My Khe
My Lai(4) ● Son My

THAILAND
(Member of SEATO)

★ Pleiku

South Viet Nam

CAMBODIA
(Officially neutral)

River Mekong

★ Nha Trang

★ Bien Hoa

SAIGON

Mekong Delta

★ Yung Tua

"The Shaky Saigon Régime"

1963 President Diem assassinated.

1964 General Van Minh Chief of State.
General Khanh takes charge as
Prime Minister in September.

1965 Khanh ousted by Army.
Phan Huy Quat become Premier.
Phan Khac Suu Chief of State.
Then Nguyen Ky becomes Premier.
General Thieu is Chief of State.

1966 Ky decides to create a new constitution. Elections held for a Constituent
Assembly to draft constitution.

1967 Eleven candidates for Presidential
elections. General Thieu wins
in September.

Legend

→ Attacks by N.V.N.
torpedo boats.

★ U.S. base

Russian-made Mig-21
fighters

Russian-made surface
to-air missiles

U.S. bomber attacks

Areas largely under
Viet-Cong control

U.S. TROOPS IN VIET NAM 1963-68

Thousands

Year	Troops
1963	16,000
1964	23,000
1965	180,000
1966	389,000
1967	449,000
1968	More than half-a-million

44: Nixon and the Communists

Vietnamization

During his Presidential election campaign, Richard Nixon made a solemn pledge to end his country's involvement in Viet Nam. He knew how deeply Americans resented the war, how much they regretted the death of 31,000 young men in what now seemed to be a 'lost crusade'*. So Nixon offered the people a way out of the dilemma; ARVN troops would gradually take over the ground fighting and he would withdraw US troops from Viet Nam. He called this 'Vietnamization'.

The 'credibility gap'

Somehow, events seemed to belie his statements. News of the My Lai Massacre**—first released in November 1969—intensified the anti-war feeling in the United States. The President therefore astounded the people when, in April 1970, he announced the invasion of Cambodia. The war was supposed to be running down; so why was the President trying to expand it? Nixon explained that it was vital to eliminate Viet Cong bases in Cambodia. If he did not do this, America might have 'to accept defeat for the first time in its 190 year history.' Later on Nixon claimed that not only had the invasion of Cambodia achieved its aims but, as the majority of troops employed were ARVNs, it was proof that Vietnamization was working. But if Cambodia was a success then the invasion of Laos was a disaster. In January 1971 ARVN troops, supported by US jets and helicopters, tried to cut the Ho Chi Minh Trail in Laos. NVN troops overwhelmed them, forced them to retreat and shot down 105 US helicopters. Echoing the words of millions of Americans, Senator Fulbright described the invasion of Laos as a 'massive misjudgment'. And to make matters worse, the *New York Times* published the *Pentagon Papers* during June 1971. These were secret documents which showed that although America's original aim in Viet Nam had been to contain the Communists, the dominant American objective between 1964 and 1968 had been the 'defence, power, influence and prestige of the United States . . . *irrespective of conditions in Viet Nam.*' The Pentagon Papers revealed, for example, that far from being the victim of the Tonkin Gulf incident the *Maddox* had in fact provoked it!

*See *The Lost Crusade* by Chester L. Cooper (MacGibbon & Kee 1971).
**Enquiries showed that estimates of civilian casualties at 'My Lai' varied considerably. See *One Morning in the War* by Richard Hammer (Rupert Hart-Davis 1970) for a detailed account.

Disclosures such as this widened the 'credibility gap'—the extent to which Americans could safely believe the statements uttered by their political and military leaders. Nevertheless, Nixon made good his promise to withdraw troops from Viet Nam. Substantial numbers left during 1970—2 and those who remained behind played a relatively minor rôle in ground operations.

SALT—Strategic Arms Limitation Talks

Meanwhile, the President had begun to explore with the Soviet Union ways of reducing the array of sophisticated nuclear weapons assembled over the last twenty years. Both America and Russia had installed complex and highly expensive ABM (Anti-Ballistic Missile) systems and were in the process of developing space rockets capable of ejecting a number of guided nuclear missiles—the hideous MIRVs (Multiple Independently Targeted Re-entry Vehicles). The Strategic Arms Limitation Talks—which some have called the 'most momentuous in diplomatic history'—began in Helsinki late in 1969 before moving to Vienna in 1970.

A realistic attitude towards China

Clearly, President Nixon had broken away from the rigid thinking that had characterized other American Presidents during the Cold War. He reasoned that 'we must deal with governments . . . as they really are'. This was why he chose to 'normalize' his country's relations with the Chinese People's Republic. The first cautious contacts came in June 1971 when an American table-tennis team visited Peking. Chou En-lai welcomed them and remarked that 'when people travel to foreign countries they find new friends everywhere'. Dr. Henry Kissinger, the President's adviser on National Security affairs, took the hint and secretly flew to Peking in July. He returned to the USA with an invitation for President Nixon to visit Communist China. Next month, America announced that she now supported the admission of Communist China to the United Nations, an event which took place in October 1971 though not as Nixon had imagined. The Chinese wouldn't join the UN while Taiwan remained a member. The UN therefore expelled Taiwan, an act which inflicted an humiliating defeat on the USA. Despite this setback, President Nixon visited Peking in February 1972 and spent a week talking to the Chinese leaders. He called it 'the week that changed the world'; it certainly reduced tension between China and the USA and to that extent made an important contribution towards a stable and enduring peace.

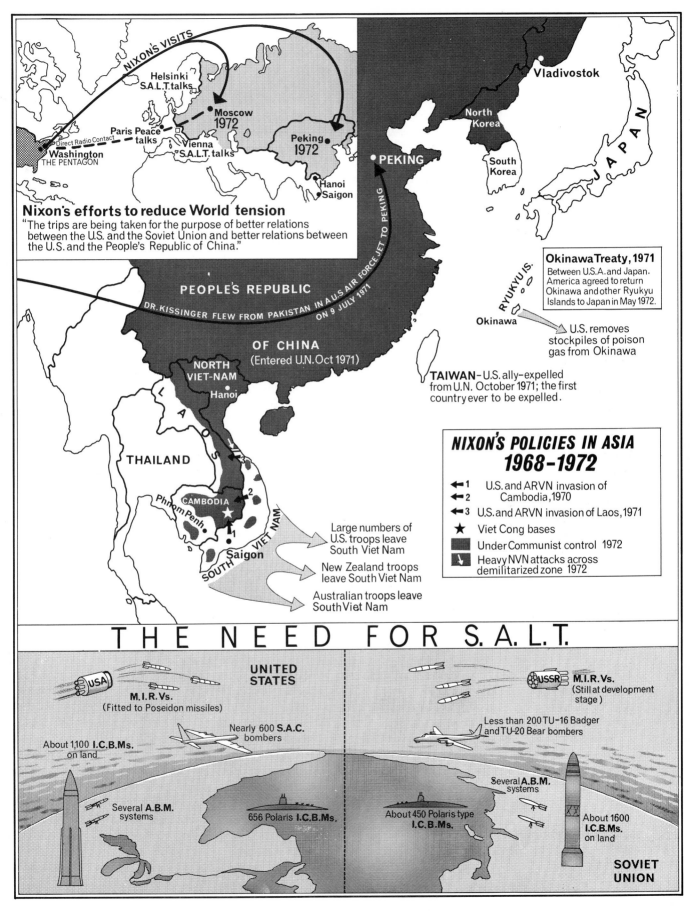

Nixon's efforts to reduce World tension

"The trips are being taken for the purpose of better relations between the U.S. and the Soviet Union and better relations between the U.S. and the People's Republic of China."

NIXON'S VISITS

Helsinki
S.A.L.T. talks

Moscow
1972

Peking
1972

Paris Peace talks

Vienna
S.A.L.T. talks

Washington
THE PENTAGON

Direct Radio Contact

Hanoi
Saigon

Vladivostok

North Korea

South Korea

JAPAN

PEKING

PEOPLE'S REPUBLIC

DR. KISSINGER FLEW FROM PAKISTAN IN A U.S. AIR FORCE JET TO PEKING ON 9 JULY 1971

OF CHINA
(Entered U.N. Oct 1971)

NORTH VIET-NAM
Hanoi

LAOS

THAILAND

CAMBODIA

Phnom Penh

Saigon

SOUTH VIET NAM

Okinawa Treaty, 1971
Between U.S.A. and Japan. America agreed to return Okinawa and other Ryukyu Islands to Japan in May 1972.

RYUKYU IS.

Okinawa

U.S. removes stockpiles of poison gas from Okinawa

TAIWAN–U.S. ally–expelled from U.N. October 1971; the first country ever to be expelled.

NIXON'S POLICIES IN ASIA 1968-1972

←1 U.S. and ARVN invasion of Cambodia, 1970

←2 U.S. and ARVN invasion of Laos, 1971

★ Viet Cong bases

■ Under Communist control 1972

Heavy NVN attacks across demilitarized zone 1972

Large numbers of U.S. troops leave South Viet Nam

New Zealand troops leave South Viet Nam

Australian troops leave South Viet Nam

THE NEED FOR S.A.L.T.

UNITED STATES

M.I.R.Vs.
(Fitted to Poseidon missiles)

Nearly 600 S.A.C. bombers

About 1,100 I.C.B.Ms. on land

Several A.B.M. systems

656 Polaris I.C.B.Ms.

USSR M.I.R.Vs.
(Still at development stage)

Less than 200 TU-16 Badger and TU-20 Bear bombers

Several A.B.M. systems

About 450 Polaris type I.C.B.Ms.

About 1600 I.C.B.Ms. on land

SOVIET UNION

45:   The Middle East: America's search for peace

In January 1973 President Nixon ended his country's participation in the War in Viet Nam. Now he had the chance to change America's policies and priorities. However, his own indiscretions over the Watergate affair* forced him to resign in 1974, by which time America was feeling the effects of another distant conflict—the Fourth Arab-Israeli War.

The Yom Kippur War 6–24 October 1973

At first, the dramatic military events in Sinai camouflaged what was happening among Middle East members of OPEC—the Organization of Petroleum Exporting Countries. As Egyptian troops made their famous amphibious assault across the Suez Canal and startled Israelis cried out for US missiles to combat the MiG-23s, OPEC members were learning to deploy their new weapon—oil. Led by Sheikh Yamani of Saudi Arabia, OPEC not only reduced oil exports to any country aiding Israel but actually placed an embargo on supplies to the USA. America's energetic Dr Kissinger worked tirelessly for peace; while Nixon declared a nuclear alert to deter Russia from sending troops into Egypt. Eventually, the negotiators secured a cease-fire and the Fourth Arab-Israeli War ended. The fighting had precipitated a world energy crisis; this now worsened as OPEC pushed up oil charges. For example, in December the Shah of Iran announced a 100 per cent increase: oil would now cost $11.65 a barrel.

The effects

Because America depended on oil imports she had no option but to pay out huge sums to the Middle East producers. After five years of escalating prices President Carter spelt out the effects: 'The massive oil price increase in 1973-4 contributed to the double-digit inflation of 1974 and to the worst recession in forty years. The US has no choice but to adjust to a new era of expensive energy ... If we act today we have time to make a gradual transition to more effective energy use.' American industrialists were hard hit by the recession and desperate to fill their order books. They wanted to trade with Middle East countries and win back some of the 'petro-dollars'. Nowhere did they try harder than in Iran where the Shah, engaged in his westernizing 'White Revolution', was obsessed with creating the most advanced war machine east of Suez. Carter justified the sale of US arms to Iran on the grounds that the Shah was the bastion of the West against possible Soviet expansion.

The Treaty between Egypt and Israel

America believed that the key to stable oil imports was peace in the Middle East. This meant not only bringing Egypt and Israel together but also grasping the nettle of a homeland for the Palestinian people. Heartened by President Sadat's visit to Jerusalem and Prime Minister Begin's visit to Ismailya (November–December 1977), Carter invited the two leaders to Camp David, Washington in 1978. There the three men worked out the 'Camp David accords' designed to end a long enmity and begin Israel's withdrawal from Sinai. In 1979 Sadat and Begin returned to Washington to sign the 'Treaty of Peace between the Arab Republic of Egypt and the State of Israel'. Both men won a Nobel Peace Prize and the Nobel Committee praised the 'positive initiative taken by the US President Jimmy Carter ...'

America and Iran

Although Iran's new affluence brought Western consumer goods within the grasp of millions, it also brought frustration, especially among those who had abandoned their farms in favour of a squalid life in overcrowded cities. Said one Iranian, 'They're cramming this so-called Western culture down our throats ... our people won't accept it.' He was right. A grass-roots rebellion forced the Shah to flee in January 1979.** The next month, the Ayatollah Khomeini returned from exile to become Iran's self-appointed leader. He proclaimed the Islamic Republic while his student supporters overran the US embassy in Teheran and took its inmates hostage. Carter now put an embargo on Iranian oil and froze Iranian bank assets—worth about $6000 million. He also made one attempt to rescue the hostages. Special forces—the Blue Light Squad from Fort Bragg, North Carolina—took off in eight helicopters from the nuclear-powered aircraft carrier *Nimitz*, on station in the Arabian Sea. Six Hercules aircraft carrying fuel and equipment joined them at 'Desert One', south-east of Teheran. Accidents wrecked several helicopters and a Hercules so that, with eight men dead, Carter had to call off the mission (April 1980). Not until January 1981 did the last fifty-two hostages return to America in exchange for gold payments arranged by Algerian mediators. By then Carter's career as President had ended. Russia had invaded Afghanistan in 1979; the Gulf War between Iran and Iraq had flared up in 1980. America's world position had visibly declined, a fact which helped Ronald Reagan to win the 1980 US Presidential election.

**Iran had insisted that he return to Teheran, one of the conditions for the release of the hostages. But the Shah died in a Cairo hospital, July 1980.

* See p. 122.

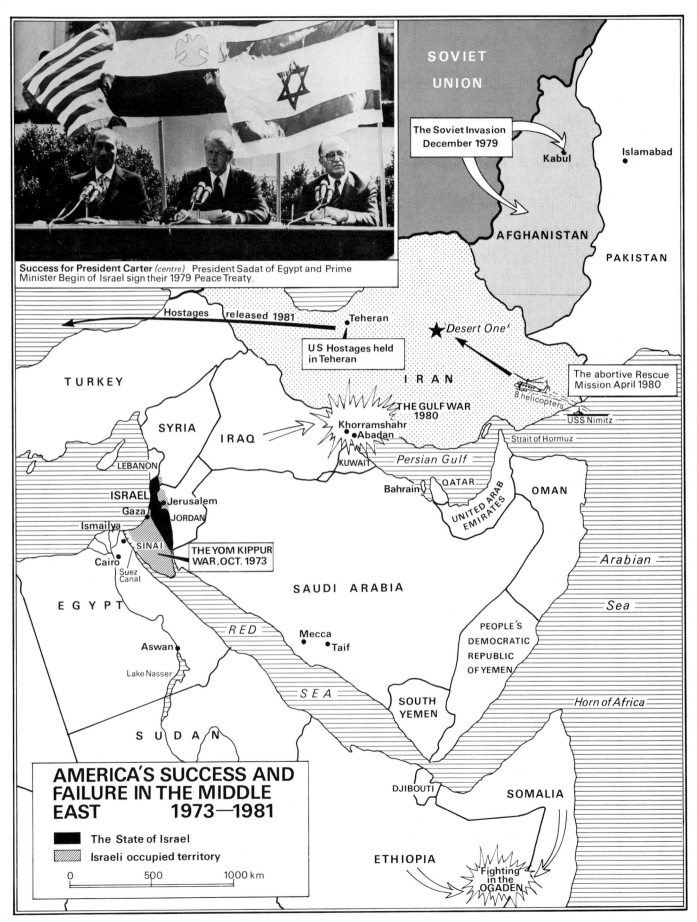

Success for President Carter *(centre)* President Sadat of Egypt and Prime Minister Begin of Israel sign their 1979 Peace Treaty.

SOVIET UNION

The Soviet Invasion December 1979

Kabul

Islamabad

AFGHANISTAN

PAKISTAN

Hostages released 1981

Teheran

Desert One'

US Hostages held in Teheran

IRAN

The abortive Rescue Mission April 1980

TURKEY

THE GULF WAR 1980

8 helicopters

USS Nimitz

SYRIA

IRAQ

Khorramshahr

Abadan

Strait of Hormuz

LEBANON

KUWAIT

Persian Gulf

ISRAEL

Bahrain

QATAR

OMAN

Jerusalem

UNITED ARAB EMIRATES

Gaza

JORDAN

Ismailya

SINAI

THE YOM KIPPUR WAR, OCT. 1973

Cairo

Suez Canal

Arabian

SAUDI ARABIA

EGYPT

RED

Mecca

Sea

Aswan

Taif

Lake Nasser

SEA

PEOPLE'S DEMOCRATIC REPUBLIC OF YEMEN

SOUTH YEMEN

Horn of Africa

SUDAN

DJIBOUTI

SOMALIA

AMERICA'S SUCCESS AND FAILURE IN THE MIDDLE EAST 1973—1981

■ The State of Israel

▨ Israeli occupied territory

ETHIOPIA

Fighting in the OGADEN

0   500   1000 km

46: Defence problems, 1972–1981

SALT: Strategic Arms Limitation Talks

Nixon's meeting with President Brezhnev in Moscow (1972) had led to the signing of the SALT I *Treaty on the Limitation of Defensive Anti-Ballistic Missiles*. This gave real meaning to the expression *détente*, a word used to describe the reduction in tension between Russia and America. And when President Ford supported the *Final Act* of the 1975 Helsinki Conference, which recognized the permanence of Europe's post-war frontiers, this too represented another step forward in the cause of international peace. President Carter, however, was fearful of Russia's real intentions. The USSR was stepping up production of nuclear and conventional weapons and, simultaneously, extending her influence in Africa and South-East Asia through her support of Cuban soldiers and advisers operating in these areas. Carter made two important speeches in 1978. The first was his so-called 'Cold War' speech in March when he pledged that the USA would match all Russia's military capabilities. The second, in August, hinted that NATO might have to accept world-wide responsibilities: 'Our alliance centres on Europe but our vigilance cannot be limited to the continent. In recent years, expanding Soviet power has increasingly penetrated beyond the North Atlantic area. As I speak today, the activities of the Soviet Union and Cuba in Africa are preventing individual nations from charting their own courses.'

The fate of Salt II

Salt I should have been renewed in 1977 but arguments between the superpowers delayed any cut-back in the arms race. Russia objected to America's decision to develop the *Cruise* missile and the enhanced radiation 'neutron' bomb. President Carter insisted that dissidents inside the USSR should be allowed their 'human rights'. Both countries accused one another of fanning the dispute between Ethiopia and Somalia, key territories in the strategically vital 'Horn of Africa'. After two years of disagreement, Carter met Brezhnev in Vienna and on 18 June 1979 signed Salt II, a treaty designed to limit the number of nuclear missiles to be deployed by the superpowers up to 1985. But under Article II, Section 2, of the US Constitution, Senate had to ratify this treaty—and it delayed doing this. Russia's invasion of Afghanistan in 1979 then made ratification less likely and by 1981 America's new leaders were boosting the defence budget to build more nuclear-powered aircraft carriers and revive the B-1 manned supersonic bomber project.*

America, they argued, could not afford to take second place in the new arms race.

The old trouble spots

Korea, Berlin, Cuba, Viet Nam no longer dominated America's defence thinking. In South Korea, a 'lorry-borne American reaction force' was on a two-minute alert, ready to deal with any repetition of the North Korean invasion of 1950. In Berlin, neither superpower had seriously challenged the *status quo* since the Wall went up in 1961. For Cuba, America kept Public Law 87-733 on the statute book: she would stop Cuba's bases being used to endanger the USA; and would use force, if necessary, to prevent Marxist-Leninism spreading into mainland America. In Viet Nam, America accepted her first-ever defeat when she signed the Paris Peace agreement in January 1973. The longest war in the history of the twentieth century finally ended in 1975 when North Vietnamese soldiers entered the suburbs of Saigon—now named Ho Chi Minh City. Thousands of US personnel and South Vietnamese sympathizers had to flee the city either by air or aboard the huge task force of aircraft carriers and troopships assembled to carry out the final act in America's 'lost crusade'.

New defence dilemmas 1979-81

The Iranian Revolution of 1979 and the Gulf War the following year had endangered oil supplies to America, Japan, Western Europe and much of the Third World. Both Carter and Reagan considered the idea of a *Rapid Deployment Force (RDF)* to 'defend the oil fields' and assist 'any friendly power which called for help'. Similar words had been used by Kennedy in 1961; but the policies they represented were hard to implement in the complex world of the 1980s. How could America influence events in Poland or Afghanistan or Namibia without risking the nuclear war her treaties with Russia were supposed to prevent? How could America keep the oil flowing through the Strait of Hormuz? America hadn't been able to save the Shah in 1979, hadn't been able to persuade Iran and Iraq to settle their territorial disputes in 1980—not even the *Islamic Summit Conference* in Taif (1981) managed to do this. Huge expenditure on the US armed forces might maintain the *status quo* in Europe but there was little evidence, and Iraq was quite positive about this, that the oil-producing world of Islam wanted to be defended by any kind of RDF.

* This project had been cancelled by Carter in 1977.

AMERICA'S DEFENCE PROBLEMS —OLD AND NEW

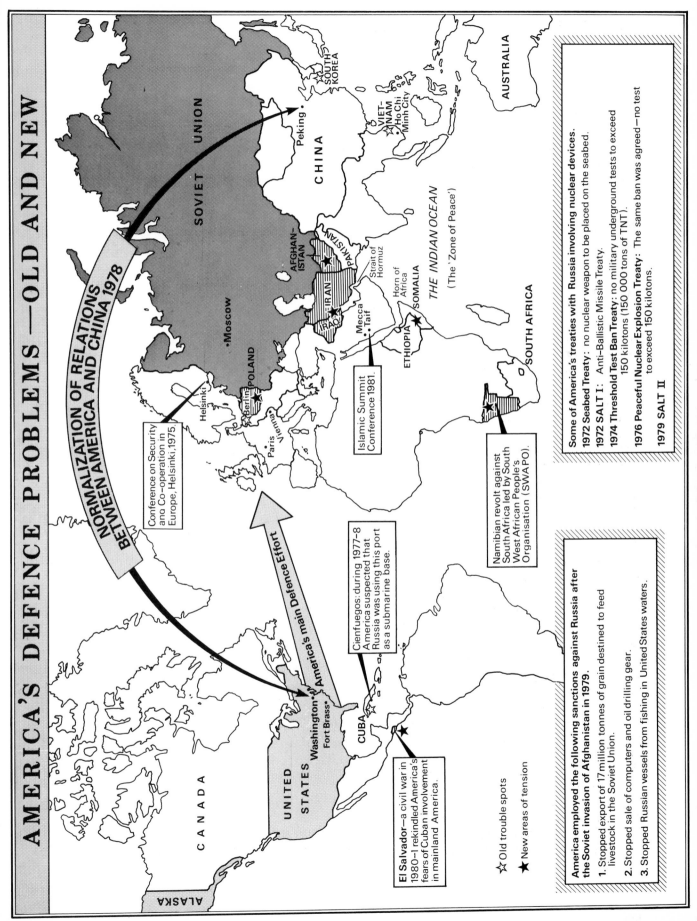

NORMALIZATION OF RELATIONS BETWEEN AMERICA AND CHINA 1978

America's main Defence Effort

Conference on Security and Co-operation in Europe, Helsinki, 1975.

Islamic Summit Conference 1981.

Cienfuegos: during 1977–8 America suspected that Russia was using this port as a submarine base.

Namibian revolt against South Africa led by South West African People's Organisation (SWAPO).

El Salvador—a civil war in 1980–1 rekindled America's fears of Cuban involvement in mainland America.

CANADA

UNITED STATES

Washington. Fort Brass.

CUBA

ALASKA

SOVIET UNION

•Moscow

POLAND
•Berlin

Helsinki

Paris Vienna

AFGHAN- ISTAN

IRAN
IRAQ

PAKISTAN

Mecca
•Taif

Horn of Africa
SOMALIA

ETHIOPIA

THE INDIAN OCEAN
(The 'Zone of Peace')

SOUTH AFRICA

Strait of Hormuz

CHINA

Peking.

SOUTH KOREA

VIET-NAM
•Ho Chi Minh City

AUSTRALIA

☆ Old trouble spots

★ New areas of tension

Some of America's treaties with Russia involving nuclear devices.

1972 Seabed Treaty: no nuclear weapon to be placed on the seabed.

1972 SALT I: Anti-Ballistic Missile Treaty.

1974 Threshold Test Ban Treaty: no military underground tests to exceed 150 kilotons (150 000 tons of TNT).

1976 Peaceful Nuclear Explosion Treaty: The same ban was agreed—no test to exceed 150 kilotons.

1979 SALT II

America employed the following sanctions against Russia after the Soviet invasion of Afghanistan in 1979.

1. Stopped export of 17 million tonnes of grain destined to feed livestock in the Soviet Union.

2. Stopped sale of computers and oil drilling gear.

3. Stopped Russian vessels from fishing in United States waters.

Further Reading

Theme 6 – America and the Cold War

Spread

36. The coming of the Cold War, 1945–7 — *Truman Memoirs—Year of Decision*, Harry S. Truman, Doubleday, 1955

37. Crisis in Europe—the German problem — *Decision in Germany*, Lucius Clay, Heinemann, 1950
City on leave, Philip Windsor, Chatto & Windus, 1963

38. America and Asia, 1945–1950 — *The Challenge of Red China*, Gunther Stein, Pilot Press, 1945
The China White Paper (Department of State Publication), Stanford University Press, 1967, Vols I & II
The United States and the Sino-Soviet Bloc in South East Asia, Oliver Chubb, Brookings Institution, 1962

39. War in Korea — *The War in Korea*, Matthew Ridgway, Cresset Press, 1967

40. The Eisenhower Years (i) the arms race — *The Age of Containment*, David Rees, Papermac, 1967

41. The Eisenhower Years (ii) new problems appear — *America, Russia and the Cold War*, Walter La Feber, John Wiley, 1967
The Invisible Government, Wise and Ross, Cape, 1965

42. 'The Thousand Days' — *Bay of Pigs*, Haynes Johnson, Hutchinson, 1965
Kennedy, T. C. Sorensen, Hodder & Stoughton, 1965
A Thousand Days, A. Schlesinger, Deutsch, 1965

43. President Johnson and the war in Viet Nam — *The Lost Crusade*, Chester L. Cooper MacGibbon & Kee, 1971

44. Nixon and the Communists — *The Pentagon Papers*, N. Sheehan, Bantam Books, 1971
One morning in the war, Richard Hammer, Hart-Davis 1970
American Foreign Policy since World War II, John Spanier, Nelson, (4th Edition) 1972

45. The Middle East: America's search for peace — *Cold War and Détente*, Paul Y. Hammond, Harcourt Brace (1975) Ch. 11

46. Defence problems, 1972–81 — *The Possibilities of Arms Control,* Duncan L. Clarke, Dialogue, US Information Service (1977) Vol 10, No. 2.

THEME 7

The Great Society:
America since 1945

Because the United States is a supreme example of an 'open society', the mass media have publicized America's problems far more than those of other major industrial nations. This means that America's domestic difficulties are well known and subject to a great deal of criticism and comment. The greatest paradox inside this supposedly opulent and confident society is the extent to which poverty touches upon about 20% of the people. Certainly America enjoys a high level of private affluence tolerating far too much public squalor.

The United States has the resources to wipe out poverty; but her critics state that, since 1945, she has been unable to do this because of the dollars spent on the nuclear deterrent, the Apollo space programme and—above all—the longest struggle in American history, the war in Viet Nam. There is no doubt that poverty has been a major cause of urban riot; it has been a driving force in the Civil Rights movement; and it is a constant drain on the existing resources of the nation. A poor region in America—such as the notorious 'old coal' country in Appalachia—raises a welter of subsidiary social problems. Its people tend to migrate—which is largely why South Side Chicago has a massive number of poor Appalachian whites in its slum areas. Those who remain are deprived of fair educational and employment opportunities. During the late Fifties and early Sixties, for example, the Department of Agriculture had to hand out vast quantities of 'commodity dole' or 'hunger rations' to farmers trying—and failing—to raise their families on subsistence agriculture.

Protest against this sort of urban and rural problem has taken many forms in recent American history and the people have come to recognize that the Federal government must act quickly if it is to ensure the peaceful survival of their 'Great Society'. Consequently, Americans have been and still are engaged in a painful re-assessment of how to treat human beings. As President Nixon said: '. . . let us put the money where the needs are. And let us put the power to spend it where the people are.'*

The results of the Watergate Affair destroyed his Presidential career. Those who followed him—Ford, Carter, Reagan—for the first time since 1945 had to contend with an energy crisis and a world-wide economic depression.

*In his speech on the state of the Union, 22 January 1971.

47: The prosperous majority: America after World War II

The years of opportunity 1945–61

Though not the biggest country in the world, the United States is the richest and its people are the most affluent. Since 1945, American families have come to form the world's biggest property-owning democracy whose inclination has been to move away from the manual drudgery of the factories and fields into the richly rewarded aero-space, automobile and service industries. Their ambition has led to continuous migration and resettlement throughout the USA. For example, California's population has increased until it is now* the most populous state in the Union. General Motors Corporation of Detroit has become the biggest manufacturing company in the world and has 696,000 workers on its payroll. Despite persistent inflation, real wages have increased so that the average American family earning $4,200 in 1950 was bringing in an extra $2000 by 1961. And by then 15% of American families were in the professional class earning over $11,000 annually while another 22% were in the skilled worker's bracket between $7,500 and $10,500 annually. The Eisenhower years (1953–61) were clearly years of opportunity for many Americans.

Reasons for their prosperity

The forty-eight States of the American Union had been very lucky in World War II. They escaped the air raids** and this meant that Americans could exploit their natural resources and their unrivalled technological and commercial skills without interruption. Of course, these advantages do not in themselves explain their amazing success since 1945. In fact, pessimists who remembered the Twenties and the Depression saw ruination round the corner when inflation hit America after the Japanese surrender. Some years were difficult, partly because of the unpredictable effects of international crises, but the general prosperity of the country grew faster than that of any other industrialized nation. Several reasons explain this:

(i) *Inflation* didn't halt industrial growth because the Federal government invested in the nation's industrial future. Consequently, US industrialists had plenty of

Federal aid to help them convert from a wartime to a peacetime economy.

(ii) *Consumer spending* increased, despite price rises, because most Americans had accumulated wartime savings and had won higher rates of pay. This meant that they could now buy the luxuries that had vanished during the war. Moreover, most ex-servicemen had money to spend; the GI's 'Bill of Rights' (the *1944 Servicemen's Readjustment Act*) gave educational grants, unemployment benefits and a helping hand to veterans searching for a new job.

(iii) *Higher wages* were paid because industry had few overseas competitors. Federal spending on the armed services maintained employment in aircraft and munitions factories. But far more important was the effect of Marshall Aid. This guaranteed a perpetual demand for US goods so that the American export business was never healthier. Proof of this was in the 4% annual increase in the Gross National Product – *GNP* = the value of the goods and services produced by the whole nation.

(iv) *Strike action* by the powerful trade unions never throttled industrial production. The *1947 Labour-Management Relations Act* (the 'Taft-Hartley Act') included among its many regulations the ruling that strikes which could 'imperil the national health and safety' must be subject to a 'cooling-off period' or restraint imposed by the President for a period of 80 days. The unions accepted this in return for stronger bargaining rights when negotiating wage increases.

Poverty amidst affluence

Serious pockets of poverty existed in America, especially in rural areas and in the abandoned mining regions of Appalachia. In the twenty years after Pearl Harbor, more than 17 million Americans left the farms in search of a better life in the cities. But in *every* community it was the elderly and the sick who suffered the most. Social Security gave them a retirement pension but did not pay the doctor's bills. Not until 1965, when *Medicare* became law, did the elderly have to meet only a fraction of their hospitalization costs. Medicare isn't free— Americans distrust anything that smacks of socialism— and neither is the more recent *Medicaid* designed to help everyone on a low income. But at least the Americans were taking important steps towards the creation in the USA of a truly humane society.

*The 1970 Decennial Census gave a figure of 19,696,840 for the population of California.
**There were, of course, air raids on Pearl Harbor (Hawaii) and the Aleutians (Alaska). But Alaska and Hawaii did not become the 49th and 50th States of the Union until 1959.

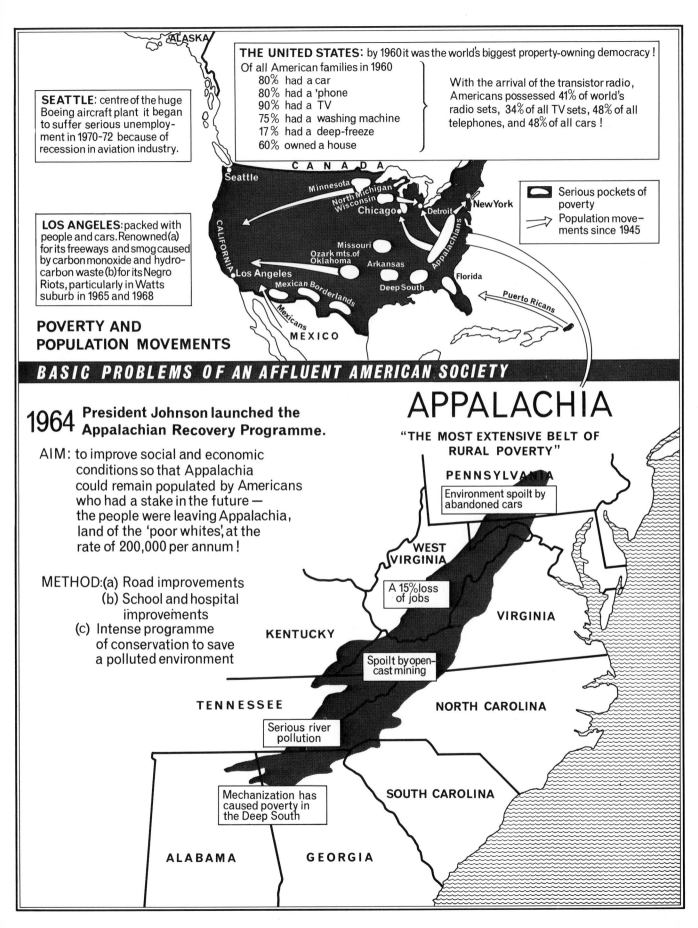

SEATTLE: centre of the huge Boeing aircraft plant it began to suffer serious unemployment in 1970-72 because of recession in aviation industry.

THE UNITED STATES: by 1960 it was the world's biggest property-owning democracy!
Of all American families in 1960
- 80% had a car
- 80% had a 'phone
- 90% had a TV
- 75% had a washing machine
- 17% had a deep-freeze
- 60% owned a house

With the arrival of the transistor radio, Americans possessed 41% of world's radio sets, 34% of all TV sets, 48% of all telephones, and 48% of all cars!

LOS ANGELES: packed with people and cars. Renowned (a) for its freeways and smog caused by carbon monoxide and hydrocarbon waste (b) for its Negro Riots, particularly in Watts suburb in 1965 and 1968

Serious pockets of poverty

Population movements since 1945

POVERTY AND POPULATION MOVEMENTS

BASIC PROBLEMS OF AN AFFLUENT AMERICAN SOCIETY

1964 **President Johnson launched the Appalachian Recovery Programme.**

AIM: to improve social and economic conditions so that Appalachia could remain populated by Americans who had a stake in the future — the people were leaving Appalachia, land of the 'poor whites', at the rate of 200,000 per annum!

METHOD: (a) Road improvements
(b) School and hospital improvements
(c) Intense programme of conservation to save a polluted environment

APPALACHIA
"THE MOST EXTENSIVE BELT OF RURAL POVERTY"

Environment spoilt by abandoned cars

A 15% loss of jobs

Spoilt by open-cast mining

Serious river pollution

Mechanization has caused poverty in the Deep South

48: Aid to the needy; and its consequences

Charity begins at home

By American standards, 15 million people live below the poverty line in the United States. In the years between 1950 and 1965 it was not uncommon for farmers, cursed by high overheads and low market prices, to have an annual income of less than $1000. Nearly a million closed down their farms and for those who remained in the countryside two options remained: either *(a)* to seek work in a nearby town—'every day, in Tennessee, you may see hill-billies driving down from their cabins in the mountains to the aluminium works at Alcoa'* or *(b)* to accept Federal hand-outs. Unemployed families would drive into government depots for food-vouchers, a sack of flour and some cans of dried milk. This can cause a serious problem— some 'poor whites' are quite content to live an aimless but leisurely life on government charity.

Overseas aid

America has poured vast sums of money into most countries in the world. Her motives haven't been entirely charitable for the USA understands that as long as there is mass-poverty in the world, the American people will never enjoy to the full the fruits of their own affluence. Uncontrolled social and political revolution in the Middle East, Africa, Asia and Latin America can be— and has been—harmful to American interests. That is why, since 1945, America has helped underdeveloped countries to modernize their economies. Aid sometimes leads to wastefulness and corruption; *military* aid can lead to American involvement. During 1957 President Eisenhower promised to help Middle East countries threatened by Communist pressures, but he was very unhappy about exporting arms to them.** President Kennedy had no such scruples—in fact he created a government office to handle the sale of American arms abroad. Fifteen years later, President Carter was placing far more faith in words than in weapons; his success in bringing Egypt and Israel together during 1978 was quite remarkable.

Latin America

The USA has been extraordinarily slow to aid the peoples of Latin America. It created the *1947 Rio Pact* for mutual defence purposes but made no attempt to offer the advantages of Marshall Aid. Eisenhower persuaded Congress to donate aid worth $600 million but it wasn't until Kennedy became President in 1961 that interest focussed upon Latin America. He offered a package deal: the Peace Corps, military aid and the Alliance for Progress. *(a)* The *Peace Corps*, Kennedy promised, would be a 'pool of trained men and women sent overseas by the US government to help foreign countries meet their urgent needs for skilled manpower. We will send Americans abroad who are qualified to do a job . . . It will not be easy. None of the men and women will be paid a salary. They will live at the same level as the citizens of the country which they are sent to, doing the same work, eating the same food, speaking the same language. We are going to put particular emphasis on those men and women who have skills in teaching, agriculture and in health. . .' *(b) Military aid* was to help Latin America republics to combat Communist guerrillas. US troops set up jungle warfare schools in the Panama Canal Zone and in Fort Bragg. *(c)* The *Alliance for Progress* was born at the Punta del Este Conference in August 1961. Kennedy promised Latin America aid worth $20,000 million on condition that recipients worked towards peaceful, social and political reform. But it was unrealistic for America to expect progress through *gradual* change in countries such as Peru, Chile and the Dominican Republic. Almost invariably, it took the form of *revolutionary* change and whenever the USA objected she gained fresh enemies in Latin America. The year 1965 saw the appearance of deep hatred for Americans. President Johnson sent in 23,000 marines to quell a suspected Communist revolt in Santo Domingo. This clumsy intervention in the domestic affairs of the Dominican Republic has never been forgiven. Latin American leaders feared that any revolutionary move to promote social advance would invite the arrival of a division of marines. However, fears dwindled when the US refrained from intervention in Chile after the Marxist Salvador Allende won a democratically contested Presidential election in 1970. Sadly, Allende died in September 1973—killed in a counter-revolution which, according to some sources, was master-minded by the US secret service.

*P. 72 Gerald Priestland, *America—the Changing Nation* (Eyre & Spottiswoode, 1968).
**In 1957 Eisenhower wanted to prop up King Hussein of Jordan. First he sent $10,000,000; then he followed this up with a demonstration of the power of the US Sixth Fleet in the Mediterranean.

U.S. OVERSEAS AID SINCE 1945

DOLLAR AID

FOOD SURPLUSES

OVERSEAS AID

MILITARY AID

$125,000,000,000 since 1945 !

GIFT FROM THE PEOPLE OF THE UNITED STATES OF AMERICA.

McDonnell F–4 Phantom Supersonic jet aircraft
(one third of all U.S. aid is military)

UNITED STATES
ALCOA○ ■FORT BRAGG
(Tennessee) (N.Carolina)

CUBA

Guatemala

Santo Domingo 1965

Panama Canal Zone

Venezuela

Colombia

Peru

Bolivia

Chile

■ Communist States
■ U.S. Jungle warfare school
★ Anti-American guerrilla units operating in Latin America immediately after the U.S. landing at Santo Domingo in 1965.
⤵ The American intervention in the Dominican Republic , 1965.

Peru: a typical problem facing the U.S.A.
1. America had sent Peru $21 million in aid 1962–1968
2. 3 October 1968 – REVOLUTION.
3. New government expropriates U.S. owned International Petroleum Co. and refuses to pay compensation to U.S.A.
4. May 1970- U.S.A. suspends sale of arms to Peru.

On 7 November 1971 Alistair Cooke made these points about U.S. Foreign Aid in a B.B.C. broadcast:

1. America was exasperated by Latin-American companies who expropriate U.S. copper and oil holdings.

2. America was exasperated by Afro–Asian countries who feel they have a birthright to the U.S. dollar.

3. America was exasperated by European countries with booming economies who still assume America will foot their arms bills.

4. America's exasperation amounted to nausea when the Afro-Asian delegates clapped the admission of Communist China to, and the expulsion of Taiwan from the United Nations General Assembly.

Punta del Este Conference held in URUGUAY during August, 1961.

Symbol of hope to the people of Chile:

A picture of Che Guevara, the Guerilla fighter killed in Bolivia.

49: The struggle for Civil Rights

Integration in the armed services

Since 1945 the Blacks—as American Negroes now prefer to call themselves—have sought social, economic and political equality with white citizens and an end to the degrading discrimination from which they had so often suffered. In 1948 President Truman made an important contribution by ordering that the US armed services must be fully integrated by 1954—a process often speeded up among hard-pressed American units during the Korean War.*

The demand for Civil Rights

(a) *The Supreme Court Judgment 1954:* in the case of Brown v the Topeka Board of Education, Chief Justice Earl Warren ruled that segregation in schools was contrary to the US Constitution. His decision appalled many Americans. Senator Eastland warned that Southerners would not accept it; Governor Faubus said Arkansas was not ready for a 'complete and sudden mixing of the races'. Trouble began in Arkansas when Faubus used his National Guardsmen to stop Black children entering Little Rock's Central High School during 1957—an action that compelled President Eisenhower to send in Federal troops to enforce the law in Little Rock.

(b) *Bus boycotts and Freedom Riders:* on 1 December 1955 Mrs. Rosa Parks, member of the National Association for the Advancement of Coloured People (NAACP), boarded the Cleveland Avenue bus on her way home from work in a Montgomery department store. As usual, she sat in the rear section—white people sat in the front. Before long, the conductor asked her to give up her seat to a white passenger. She refused—and was arrested as a Communist agitator! Her individual protest led to the Montgomery bus boycott, organized by a newly arrived divinity graduate—Martin Luther King. He also went to jail—but he won the issue. Segregation of Blacks on municipal transport became illegal in 1956. The next task was to desegregate restaurants and the Congress of Racial Equality (CORE—founded in 1942) began 'sit-ins' at Woolworth's lunch counters. Soon sit-ins, run by the Student's Non-violent Co-ordinating Committee (Snick), became common throughout the South. Heartened by this support, CORE's director—James Farmer—arranged a 'Freedom Ride' in 1961. 'Integrated' buses,

with Blacks in the front seats, would drive across the South where 'riders' would ignore segregation restrictions in bus terminal waiting-rooms. This was guaranteed to provoke trouble and as soon as the Freedom Riders reached Alabama the Ku Klux Klansmen and white youths attacked them. Their brutality forced the riders to abandon their demonstration—but enough people took part in later Freedom Rides to win another victory: on 1 November 1961 segregation in waiting-rooms became illegal.

(c) *The March on Washington 1963:* now the Blacks demanded drastic action from the Federal government and in August 1963 200,000 people—black and white—marched towards the Washington statue of Abraham Lincoln. After singing led by Joan Baez and Bob Dylan, Martin Luther King spoke: 'I have a dream. I have a dream that one day this nation will rise up and live out the true meaning of its creed: "We hold these truths to be self evident, that all men are created equal."'

Legislation and race riots

The Washington March won immense publicity for the cause and President Johnson's 1964 *Civil Rights Act* prohibited discrimination in employment. But this wasn't enough for Blacks living in the Northern cities—they wanted financial help in order to secure better jobs and housing. They sneered at Martin Luther King's 'non-violence' and turned instead to riot. There was serious trouble in New York during 1964 and when Johnson offered new political rights and educational aid (*Education Act* and *Voting Rights Act*—1965) he received scant respect. Blacks burnt and looted Watts District, their own Los Angeles suburb, during 1965 and, two years later, similar race riots erupted in Newark, New Jersey. Here the rioters chanted 'Black Power!'—a phrase detested by King—which was the warcry of the Black Moslems who believed that integration was futile. Black Panther extremists produced their own political programme: 'We want land, we want bread, we want housing, we want clothing, we want education, we want justice and we want peace'. But they didn't want—and neither could they have—the leadership of Martin Luther King. A Klansman, James Earl Ray, shot him in Memphis on 4 April 1968. King's untimely death and the demands of the rioters spurred on more legislation and Congress hurriedly passed the 1968 Civil Rights Act which protected Civil Rights workers, forbade discrimination in the sale of houses and made encouragement of riot a Federal offence.

*Even then, it was not always welcome. See Tim Carew, *The Korean War* (Pan Book, 1970) pp. 276–7.

Stages in the Struggle for Civil Rights.......

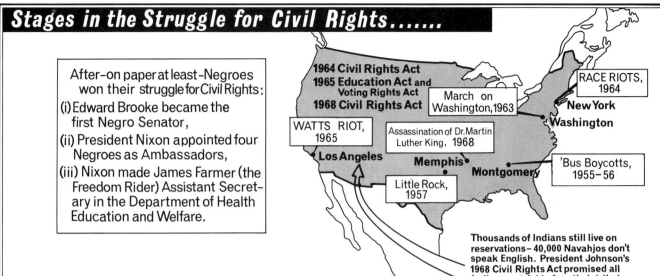

After-on paper at least-Negroes won their struggle for Civil Rights:

(i) Edward Brooke became the first Negro Senator,

(ii) President Nixon appointed four Negroes as Ambassadors,

(iii) Nixon made James Farmer (the Freedom Rider) Assistant Secretary in the Department of Health Education and Welfare.

1964 Civil Rights Act
1965 Education Act and Voting Rights Act
1968 Civil Rights Act

RACE RIOTS, 1964

March on Washington, 1963

New York

Washington

WATTS RIOT, 1965

Assassination of Dr. Martin Luther King, 1968

Los Angeles

Memphis

Montgomery

'Bus Boycotts, 1955–56

Little Rock, 1957

Thousands of Indians still live on reservations– 40,000 Navahjos don't speak English. President Johnson's 1968 Civil Rights Act promised all Indians on trial before their tribal courts the rights and privileges of all United States citizens.

The mood of defiance permeates the colleges
–a Massachusetts demonstrator is forced to leave a black 'sit-in'.

" Black Power has nothing to do with violence. Black Power is when Black People respect themselves. Black Power is when Black men stop allowing themselves to be duped into filling the jailhouses while White men fill the Colleges. Black Power is when we refuse to fight thousands of miles away from home (i.e. in Viet Nam) for freedoms over there that we cannot enjoy here......" Hosea Williams, Negro Leader

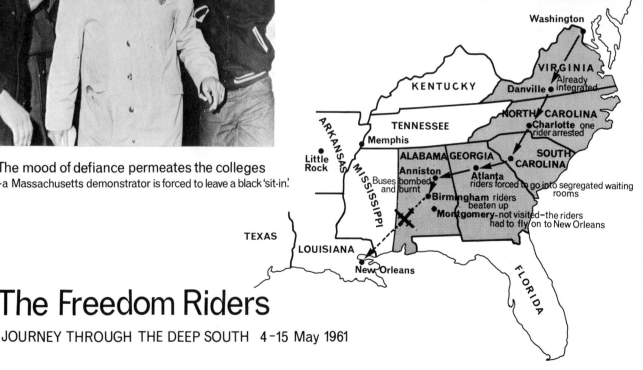

Washington

VIRGINIA
Already integrated

KENTUCKY

Danville

NORTH CAROLINA
Charlotte one rider arrested

TENNESSEE

Memphis

Little Rock

ARKANSAS

MISSISSIPPI

ALABAMA GEORGIA

SOUTH CAROLINA

Anniston

Atlanta riders forced to go into segregated waiting rooms

Buses bombed and burnt

Birmingham riders beaten up

Montgomery-not visited-the riders had to fly on to New Orleans

TEXAS

LOUISIANA

New Orleans

FLORIDA

The Freedom Riders

JOURNEY THROUGH THE DEEP SOUTH 4-15 May 1961

50: Violence in America: the law and order problem

The ghettos

Appalled by the rapid increase in violent crime during the 1960s, Americans readily agreed that the absence of law and order was the most desperate problem facing their society. The National Advisory Commission on Civil Disorders admitted in its 1968 Report that the 'racial disorders of last summer reflect the failure of *all* levels of government . . . to come to grips with the problems of our cities. The ghetto symbolizes the dilemma.' Blacks were increasing in numbers much faster than the Whites—from 18,900,000 (10.6% of the population) in 1960 to 22,700,000 (11.2%) in 1970. This meant that New York had to absorb 396,000 Blacks. California saw its Black population rise another 272,000 while Michigan, Illinois and New Jersey found their city centres swarming with Blacks seeking a better way of life. Discrimination forced the Blacks to gather together in their own communities—or *ghettos*—where poor housing, high unemployment and fierce hatred of the local police force were fairly common. But these dismal facts do not entirely explain why American cities are more prone to violence than others. Alistair Cooke has commented that Watts, for example, was 'a place that many slum dwellers, in the old cities of the earth, would gladly settle for. The houses may be frowzy now, after thirty years of neglect . . . But they are small bungalows built on their own half lots, with bathrooms and bedrooms and some with little lawns and backyards and garages.'* He felt that *envy* was a major cause of the rioting—violence was brought on by Blacks who wanted new furniture and a television set as much as they wanted the right to vote. A riot, with its many opportunities for looting, was one way of getting the 'good' things in life for nothing.

Guns and assassination

Another tragedy of the Sixties was the sickening murder of important public figures, black and white. Medgar Evers, an NAACP officer was killed in 1963. In November that year President Kennedy was assassinated by Lee Harvey Oswald (he in turn was shot by Jack Ruby). In April 1968 Martin Luther King was shot in Memphis. During June a Jordanian Arab killed Robert Kennedy. Too late to prevent this spate of killings, Congress passed the *1968 Gun Act* which ordered the licensing of all firearms and limited the sale of weapons through mail-order catalogues. But millions of Americans already own firearms—and they justify this under the *Second Amendment to the Constitution (1791)*: '. . . the right of the people to bear Arms, shall not be infringed'.

Student protest

The revolt of youth took many forms during the Sixties. Many young people made passionate demonstrations against war. Men destroyed their draft cards and went to prison rather than go into the armed services. Negro youths protested that though the proportion of Blacks to Whites in the USA was 11:100 in the combat zones of Viet Nam it was 23:100. An unfair proportion of Black Americans had fought and died in that detested war. But it was in May 1970 that a particularly tragic incident occurred. Students of Kent State University in Ohio were protesting against Nixon's invasion of Cambodia. On 4 May 1970 the Ohio National Guard arrived and, amidst great confusion, opened fire with their carbines. 'My God—they're killing us!' screamed one girl—and four students lay dead on the university campus.

Talk About America (The Bodley Head, 1968) pp. 206–10.

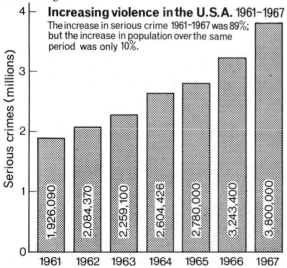

Increasing violence in the U.S.A. 1961–1967
The increase in serious crime 1961-1967 was 89%; but the increase in population over the same period was only 10%.

Serious crimes (millions)

1961	1962	1963	1964	1965	1966	1967
1,926,090	2,084,370	2,259,100	2,604,426	2,780,000	3,243,400	3,800,000

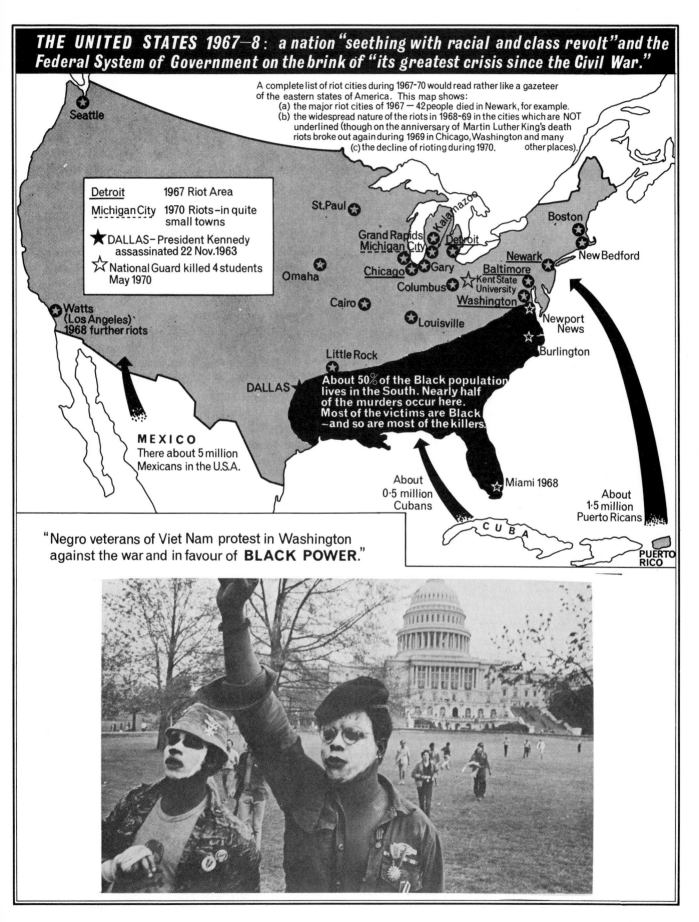

THE UNITED STATES 1967—8: a nation "seething with racial and class revolt" and the Federal System of Government on the brink of "its greatest crisis since the Civil War."

A complete list of riot cities during 1967-70 would read rather like a gazeteer of the eastern states of America. This map shows:
(a) the major riot cities of 1967 — 42 people died in Newark, for example.
(b) the widespread nature of the riots in 1968-69 in the cities which are NOT underlined (though on the anniversary of Martin Luther King's death riots broke out again during 1969 in Chicago, Washington and many other places).
(c) the decline of rioting during 1970.

| Detroit | 1967 Riot Area |
| Michigan City | 1970 Riots – in quite small towns |

★ DALLAS – President Kennedy assassinated 22 Nov. 1963

☆ National Guard killed 4 students May 1970

Seattle

St. Paul

Boston

Grand Rapids
Michigan City
Detroit

Newark
New Bedford

Omaha

Chicago
Gary

Baltimore
Kent State University
Columbus
Washington

Cairo

Newport News

Louisville

Burlington

Watts (Los Angeles) 1968 further riots

Little Rock

DALLAS

About 50% of the Black population lives in the South. Nearly half of the murders occur here. Most of the victims are Black — and so are most of the killers.

MEXICO
There about 5 million Mexicans in the U.S.A.

About 0·5 million Cubans

Miami 1968

About 1·5 million Puerto Ricans

CUBA

PUERTO RICO

"Negro veterans of Viet Nam protest in Washington against the war and in favour of **BLACK POWER**."

51: Men on the Moon

NASA and Apollo

Spurred on by the unexpected success of Russia's Sputniks, President Eisenhower readily approved the creation of NASA (National Aeronautics and Space Administration) in 1958. By 1960 NASA had prepared plans for the exploration of the Moon, Mars and Venus—an idea which so appealed to President Kennedy that he promised in 1961 that there would be a 'major national commitment of scientific manpower, material and facilities' in order to put a man on the Moon by the end of the decade. Although it would be the most expensive and technologically difficult operation ever undertaken by the American people in peace-time, Congress gave the idea its blessing and Project Apollo* was born.

The test missions

Disaster on the Cape Kennedy launch pad wrecked plans for the first manned flight of the Apollo spacecraft. Three astronauts—White, Grissom and Chaffee—died when a flash-fire gutted their Command Module on 27 January 1967. Extensive modifications delayed the first flight until October 1968 when Apollo 7 tested the Command and Service Modules in a low Earth orbit. By Christmas, Apollo 8 was in orbit around the Moon and beaming TV pictures of the lunar surface to millions of viewers on Earth. Apollo 9 perfected the complex docking procedures in March 1969 while Apollo 10, launched in May, tested the Lunar Module a mere nine miles above the Sea of Tranquillity. Everything was ready to send a man to the Moon.

Apollo 11

On 16 July 1969 three astronauts—Neil Armstrong, Michael Collins and Edward Aldrin—blasted off from Cape Kennedy in Apollo 11. Three days later they were in lunar orbit and Armstrong and Aldrin entered the Lunar Module to begin their hair-raising descent. After a perfect landing on the edge of the Sea of Tranquillity, Armstrong crawled through the hatch and rigged up the TV camera. 'I'm going to step off the Lunar Module now. That's one small step for a man, one giant leap for mankind.' The first men were on the Moon. And before they left it the two astronauts placed on its surface the badges of five dead spacemen—three Americans and two Russians.**

Later missions

Five more moonshots left Cape Kennedy during the next three years. In November 1969 Apollo 12 landed in the Ocean of Storms. Apollo 13 blasted off in April 1970 and the three crew members were lucky to survive. 'We've got a problem here,' came the laconic message through space. An oxygen tank had exploded and the three astronauts were in distress. Britain, France and Russia, signatories of the *1966 Outer Space Treaty*, immediately offered assistance but Mission Control was confident that they could bring Apollo 13 home. They guided the spacemen through a Moon orbit and a successful splash-down in the Pacific. Said President Nixon, '. . . never before . . . have more people watched together, prayed together and rejoiced together at your safe return. . . You did not reach the Moon but you reached the hearts of millions of people on Earth by what you did.' Apollo 14 had an eventful journey before it landed in Fra Mauro during February 1971 and in August that year Apollo 15 carried a lunar roving vehicle to help the astronauts explore Hadley Rille. Then in April 1972 Apollo 16 set off on a potentially dangerous mission to the craggy mountains surrounding Descartes Crater. Technical faults compelled the astronauts and Mission Control to delay the Lunar Module descent for six dangerous hours. But the spacemen landed safely, fervently agreeing that 'It's been a hard day's night. . . !'

The expense

Money was supposed to have been no object in implementing the Apollo programme. But devaluation of the dollar (December 1971), a new awareness of the true extent of poverty in the United States and, above all, the daily waste of millions of dollars' worth of bombs over Thailand, Laos and Viet Nam, forced a reconsideration of Apollo. President Nixon decided to cut short all space exploration and to funnel the cash he saved into research designed to improve the quality of life upon Earth. In his State of the Union message to Congress (22 January 1971), he outlined his 'Six Great Goals'.

*Apollo was the twin brother of Artemis, the Moon goddess.
**Vladimir Komorov died when his spacecraft, Soyuz 1, crashed in April 1967; Yuri Gagarin died in an air crash near Moscow in 1968.

APOLLO MOON SHOTS
(Manned Spacecraft Landings)

Apollo 11   Sea of Tranquility, July 1969
Apollo 12   Ocean of Storms, November 1969
Apollo 13   ABORTED
Apollo 14   Fra Mauro Highlands, February 1971
Apollo 15   Sea of Rains (Hadley Rille), July 1971
Apollo 16   Lunar Highlands (Descartes Crater), April 1972

'In-flight configuration'
Lunar Module
Command Module
Service Module

Project Apollo

'Splash-down'

PACIFIC OCEAN

UNITED STATES

Huntsville, Alabama
Space Research Centre

Houston
Mission Control

Mississippi Test Site

Michoud Assembly Site

Cape Kennedy Launch Site

Atlantic Ocean

Progress in Space Exploration before the Apollo Moon Landings

1957   **(i) Sputnik I** first artificial satellite launched by Russia on 4 October
     (ii) Sputnik II 3 November

1958   U.S. 'Atlas' missile in orbit and used as the first communications satellite

1959   **(i) Russian Lunik I** in orbit round the Sun
     (ii) U.S. Pioneer 4 in orbit round the Sun
     (iii) Lunik 2 hit Moon
     (iv) Lunik 4 photographed hidden side of Moon

1961   **(i)** Alan Shepard made first 'sub-orbital lob' of **300** miles
     (ii) Yuri Gagarin first man to orbit the Earth 6 August

1962   John Glenn, the first American to orbit the Earth

1964   **(i) Russian Zond** probe to Mars
     (ii) 'Voshkod' 3-man satellite in orbit

1966-7 'Surveyor' spacecraft land on Moon and beam back TV pictures of surface
Apollo landing sites chosen

Bay of Rainbows
SEA of RAINS
SEA of SERENITY
SEA of CRISIS
Hadley Rille 15
Kepler
OCEAN of STORMS
Copernicus
SEA of TRANQUILITY
SEA of FERTILITY
Fra Mauro
Descartes
SEA of NECTAR
Tycho

52: New attitudes

Roughly seventy years have passed since large numbers of British people emigrated to the USA. Meanwhile, almost every nation in the world has contributed to the stream of American immigrants (45,000,000 between 1820 and 1970) so that the United States no longer conforms to the 'White Anglo-Saxon Protestant' image so carefully nurtured by Hollywood. Yet it is only quite recently that this fact has received general recognition. When Kennedy became President in 1961 millions of Americans were amazed that a Roman Catholic had managed to enter the White House. Ten years later President Nixon made the revealing statement that 'For the Black American, the Indian, the Mexican-American, and for those others in our land who have not had an equal chance, the nation has AT LAST begun to confront the need to press open the door of full and equal opportunity, and of human dignity.'

The revolt of youth

Hostility to authority and rejection of the 'rat race' were the watchwords of the 'Beat Generation' of the 1950s—a movement led by Jack Kerouac and Allen Ginsberg, two ex-Columbia University students. Then, in the Sixties a 'Hippie' culture replaced the Beatniks and concerned itself, among other things, with long hair, marijhuana and protest against the war in Viet Nam. The Hippies coincided with the period of urban riot in which young Blacks expressed their dissatisfaction with the ghettos by resorting to violence. These two quite different strands became united on the university campuses where thousands of young Americans* went through profound educational experiences not always related to their academic studies. They discovered, for example, that they had to take forceful action if they wanted to play a democratic, participatory role in university life and there is no doubt that their demonstrations and sit-ins effectively changed many people's views about the nature of education in America. But when the students applied the same methods to political demands for peace and city slum improvement they were not so successful. They found out that instant information—the gift of television—was not the same thing as instant understanding. Most of America's problems could not be solved overnight no matter how desirable this might be. But the demonstrations did underline the urgency of these problems. At the 1969 Woodstock Festival, for example, the students adopted

John Lennon's words:

> 'All we are saying is
> Give peace a chance'

and then assembled in Washington in November to make their protest felt. Undoubtedly, the actions of so many young Americans formed one of several factors that encouraged the President to produce a programme of radical reform in order to meet the needs and wishes of an increasingly articulate population.

'Six Great Goals'—and the desire for Peace

This impressive programme for social, economic and political improvement was the theme of Nixon's State of the Union speech to Congress on 22 January 1971. It coincided with his plans to reduce the number of US troops in Viet Nam (there were less than 95,000 there by March 1972) so that by the time of the Presidential elections (November 1972) they would simply constitute a force of 'military advisers'. However, he continued America's air support of South Viet Nam and economists criticized the President's 'misuse' of funds in fighting a non-stop war in East Asia. 'Had those ... dollars been spent at home on roads, hospitals, schools and mass transport facilities, they would have drastically reduced unemployment and produced new institutions that might have created millions of jobs (and new income taxes) for generations'.** President Nixon countered these criticisms by claiming that 'Our cities are no longer engulfed in civil disorders. Our colleges and universities have again become places of learning instead of battlefields. A beginning has been made on preserving and protecting our environment. The rate of increase in crime has been slowed ...' and '... as our involvement in the war in Viet Nam comes to an end, we must go on to build a generation of peace'.***

The new realism

America has realized that she could no longer be the world's policeman. In 1961 Kennedy, using grand but ill-advised rhetoric, had promised the American people that 'We shall pay any price, bear any burden, meet any hardship, oppose any foe, to assure the survival and the success of liberty'. But Nixon understood that he could afford to make only those commitments which the American people were willing and able to meet.

---

*By 1970 the majority of young Americans had between 14 and 19 years of formal education.

**Harlow Unger (New York) writing in *The Sunday Times*, 30 January 1972.
****State of the Union, 1972*, US Information Service, p. 3. American military involvement in Viet Nam formally ended in 1973.

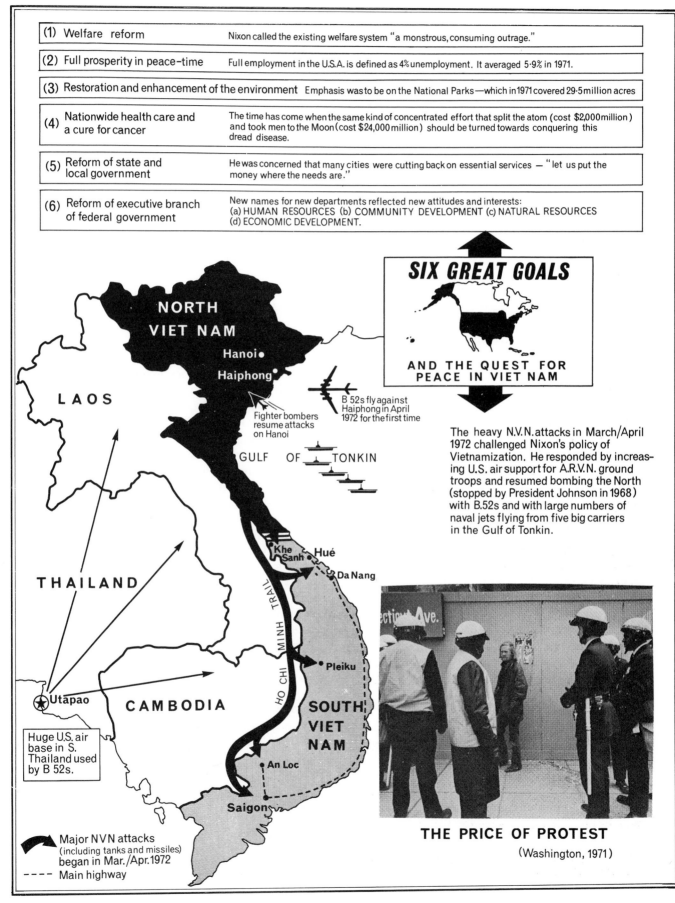

(1)	Welfare reform	Nixon called the existing welfare system "a monstrous, consuming outrage."
(2)	Full prosperity in peace-time	Full employment in the U.S.A. is defined as 4% unemployment. It averaged 5·9% in 1971.
(3)	Restoration and enhancement of the environment	Emphasis was to be on the National Parks—which in 1971 covered 29·5 million acres
(4)	Nationwide health care and a cure for cancer	The time has come when the same kind of concentrated effort that split the atom (cost $2,000 million) and took men to the Moon (cost $24,000 million) should be turned towards conquering this dread disease.
(5)	Reform of state and local government	He was concerned that many cities were cutting back on essential services — "let us put the money where the needs are."
(6)	Reform of executive branch of federal government	New names for new departments reflected new attitudes and interests: (a) HUMAN RESOURCES (b) COMMUNITY DEVELOPMENT (c) NATURAL RESOURCES (d) ECONOMIC DEVELOPMENT.

SIX GREAT GOALS

AND THE QUEST FOR PEACE IN VIET NAM

NORTH VIET NAM

Hanoi●

Haiphong●

Fighter bombers resume attacks on Hanoi

B 52s fly against Haiphong in April 1972 for the first time

LAOS

GULF OF TONKIN

The heavy N.V.N. attacks in March/April 1972 challenged Nixon's policy of Vietnamization. He responded by increasing U.S. air support for A.R.V.N. ground troops and resumed bombing the North (stopped by President Johnson in 1968) with B.52s and with large numbers of naval jets flying from five big carriers in the Gulf of Tonkin.

THAILAND

Khe Sanh ● Hué

Da Nang

● Pleiku

Utapao

CAMBODIA

SOUTH VIET NAM

Huge U.S. air base in S. Thailand used by B 52s.

HO CHI MINH TRAIL

● An Loc

Saigon

Major NVN attacks (including tanks and missiles) began in Mar./Apr. 1972

- - - - Main highway

THE PRICE OF PROTEST
(Washington, 1971)

53: New directions: America since 1973

Social change

Perhaps the most significant change in America has been the speed at which the country has 'grown together' or 'integrated'. Though the terrible racial divisions of the past have not entirely vanished, America no longer excludes her black citizens from playing a full part in society because of their colour. Racial issues still bedevil education, however. Thousands of black families have moved into city centres; simultaneously, thousands of white families have moved into the suburbs. As you can see from the diagram opposite, this has made compulsory educational integration very difficult in huge cities such as Detroit. To administrators, 'bussing' seemed to be a good solution, though unpopular with the people. Blacks and whites wrecked Boston's Hyde Park High School during an anti-bussing demonstration in 1974; while the decision in Louisville (1975) that no school would have less than 12 per cent or more than 40 per cent black children on roll meant bussing for 23,000 students and a great deal of protest from parents. It became an election issue in California during 1980: 'No more bussing. Vote for Reagan.' But at least the recession and high unemployment did not discriminate solely against black families. During the first years of economic decline (1974–5) there was a sense of common predicament. Blacks and whites alike had to depend on food stamps and social security as unemployment went up to 8.9 per cent—over 8 million people!

Technological challenges

America's technology leads the world, though it has encountered lots of problems as these two examples show:

Nuclear energy: In the search for alternative forms of energy, American technologists have turned to light-water nuclear reactors—mainly because they seemed less of a health hazard than other types. But the accident at the Three Mile Island reactor* (March 1979) reduced public confidence in nuclear energy, especially as repairs were still going on two years later. Moreover, natural forces can endanger reactor sites particularly if they are located in earthquake zones as America's biggest reactor is. The reality of the threat came home in May 1980 when Mount St Helens exploded with the force of a hydrogen bomb, killed a hundred people and made part of the north-west an official disaster area.

Space: The link-up in July 1975 between three Apollo astronauts and two Soyuz cosmonauts demonstrated new possibilities in space technology. So while NASA continued to investigate the planets—Voyager 2, launched in 1977, was photographing Jupiter in 1979—its main objective became the development of a re-usable space-shuttle, Columbia. This was a space ship designed to take astronauts and satellites into orbit and then return to Earth. A shuttle would be cheaper than the usual expensive Titan rockets and it could also earn money by ferrying foreign satellites into space. Unfortunately, engine fires and the failure of the silica foam tiling on the heat shield plagued Columbia and kept delaying its launch date.

South of the border

The United States has begun to show more sympathy towards the individual political aspirations of the countries that make up the Organization of American States (OAS). This has meant accepting the growth of grass-roots democracy, especially after revelations that the CIA had helped to overthrow Allende's government in Chile (1973). President Carter loudly supported human rights—the right of Latin American and Caribbean peoples to exercise their democratic freedoms and not, as a consequence, to suffer imprisonment, torture and murder at the hands of military rulers who dominated so many OAS countries. Happily, his ideas coincided with those of Lopez Portillo, President of Mexico, now the fifth most important oil-producer in the world. His advice to Carter and Reagan was: 'Don't interfere. Respect the internal processes.' So President Carter did not openly interfere when Marxist-led Sandinistas overthrew Nicaragua's dictator, Somoza, in 1979. However, he saw the El Salvador revolution differently. Both he and Reagan thought this was inspired by 'international communism', i.e. by Russia and Cuba. Both Presidents sent in advisers and political commentators were quick to point out that this was the road America had taken twenty years earlier, a road that had led to the war in Viet Nam. One long-standing issue, the ownership of the Panama Canal, was settled. In 1977 Carter signed the *Panama Canal Treaties*, which took effect in 1979. They abolished the Canal Zone and handed over 58 per cent of its area to the Panamanians. A Canal Commission, five Americans and four Panamanians, would control the remainder until 31 December 1999, when it would all pass to Panama. Meanwhile, America would provide for the defence of this crucial link between the Atlantic and Pacific Oceans.

*Fitted with a Babcock & Wilson PWR (Pressure Water Reactor).

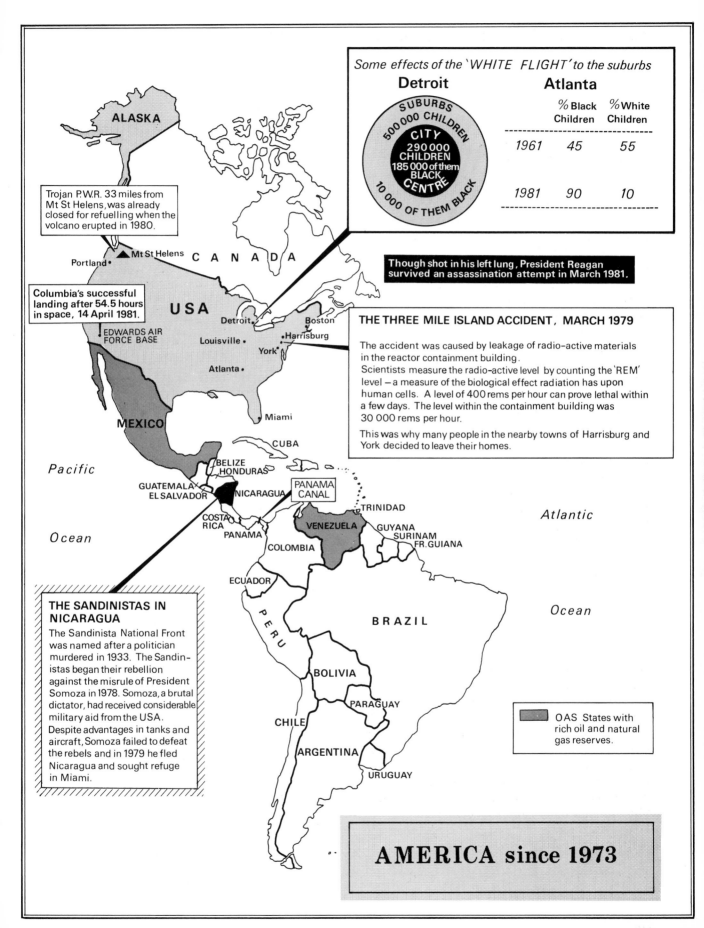

Some effects of the 'WHITE FLIGHT' to the suburbs

Detroit

SUBURBS
500 000 CHILDREN
CITY
290 000 CHILDREN
185 000 of them
BLACK
CENTRE
10 000 OF THEM BLACK

Atlanta

	% Black Children	% White Children
1961	45	55
1981	90	10

Trojan P.W.R. 33 miles from Mt St Helens, was already closed for refuelling when the volcano erupted in 1980.

Though shot in his left lung, President Reagan survived an assassination attempt in March 1981.

Columbia's successful landing after 54.5 hours in space, 14 April 1981.

EDWARDS AIR FORCE BASE

ALASKA

Portland •
▲ Mt St Helens
C A N A D A

U S A

Detroit •
Boston •
Louisville •
• Harrisburg
York •
Atlanta •

Miami

THE THREE MILE ISLAND ACCIDENT, MARCH 1979

The accident was caused by leakage of radio-active materials in the reactor containment building.

Scientists measure the radio-active level by counting the 'REM' level — a measure of the biological effect radiation has upon human cells. A level of 400 rems per hour can prove lethal within a few days. The level within the containment building was 30 000 rems per hour.

This was why many people in the nearby towns of Harrisburg and York decided to leave their homes.

Pacific

MEXICO

CUBA

BELIZE
HONDURAS
GUATEMALA
EL SALVADOR
NICARAGUA
PANAMA CANAL
TRINIDAD

Ocean

COSTA RICA
PANAMA
VENEZUELA
GUYANA
SURINAM
FR. GUIANA
COLOMBIA

Atlantic

ECUADOR

P E R U

B R A Z I L

Ocean

THE SANDINISTAS IN NICARAGUA

The Sandinista National Front was named after a politician murdered in 1933. The Sandinistas began their rebellion against the misrule of President Somoza in 1978. Somoza, a brutal dictator, had received considerable military aid from the USA. Despite advantages in tanks and aircraft, Somoza failed to defeat the rebels and in 1979 he fled Nicaragua and sought refuge in Miami.

BOLIVIA

PARAGUAY

CHILE

ARGENTINA

URUGUAY

OAS States with rich oil and natural gas reserves.

AMERICA since 1973

Further Reading

Theme 7 – The Great Society: America since 1945

Spread

47. The prosperous majority

America: the Changing Nation, Gerald Priestland, Eyre & Spottiswoode, 1968

48. Aid to the needy

Latin America, Peter Calvert, Macmillan 1969
Since Columbus: Pluralism and Poverty in the Americas, Peter d'A. Jones, Heinemann, 1975 (Ch. 8)

49. The struggle for Civil Rights

Desegregation and the Supreme Court, Benjamin Ziegler, Heath & Co, 1958
The Negro Revolt, Louis Lomax, Harper, 1962

50. Violence in America

America: the Changing Nation, Gerald Priestland, Eyre & Spottiswoode, 1968
The City in American History, Blake McKelvey, Allen & Unwin, 1969
Violence in America, H. D. Graham and T. R. Gurr, Sage Publications, 1979, especially Ch. 2

51. Men on the Moon

Project Apollo, Booker, Frewer and Pardoe, Chatto & Windus, 1969

52. New attitudes

Youth and Foreign Policy, Steven Kelman, Dialogue No. 4 1971 (US Information Service)
Social Change in Industrial Society—America in the Twentieth Century, Thomas C. Cochran, Allen & Unwin, 1972
Report on the State of the Union 1971, 1972 (US Information Service)
Report from Iron Mountain—on the possibility and desirability of peace (a satirical account of a mythical committee's report. Originally anonymous, now known to be the work of Leonard C. Lewin), Penguin, 1968

53. New directions: America since 1973

The Case for Nuclear Power, Samuel McCracken, Dialogue No. 3 1978 (US Information Service)
Retreat to the Ghetto, Thomas L. Blair, Wildwood House, 1977

The United States Constitution

The United States Constitution is a set of laws written in 1787 by the Founding Fathers—men such as George Washington, John Dickinson and Benjamin Franklin —and modified by additional laws or AMENDMENTS, the first ten of which came into force in 1791 as the Bill of Rights.

The Constitution defines the activities of government and the rights of the people. It is a FEDERAL Constitution because the original Thirteen Colonies wished to federate or join together for certain purposes of government e.g. DEFENCE but to remain separate for other purposes e.g. EDUCATION. The Constitution therefore divides the LEGISLATIVE, EXECUTIVE and JUDICIAL powers of government between the Federal government in Washington and the 50 State governments. This means that the US citizen is subject to two sets of laws. If he breaks FEDERAL LAW he has committed a Federal offence and may be arrested by a Federal officer and prosecuted by a US attorney in a Federal court. If he breaks STATE LAW he may be arrested and prosecuted by officers appointed by the State.

Congress exercises legislative power to pass Federal law. Congress consists of the Upper House or SENATE to which each State sends two SENATORS and the Lower House or HOUSE OF REPRESENTATIVES to which States send CONGRESS-MEN elected by proportional representation. The President exercises executive power to ensure that Federal law is obeyed, but he and his Cabinet officers are not members of Congress. The American people elect their President for a four-year term* by popular vote. The Supreme Court exercises judicial power and its judges are there to interpret the written Constitution in the light of the current needs of the people. The Constitution is regarded as one of the most remarkable legal documents in history: 'It ranks above every other written constitution for the intrinsic excellence of its scheme, its adaptation to the circumstances of the people, the simplicity, brevity and precision of its language, its judicious mixture of definiteness in principle with elasticity in detail.'**

*Since 1951 no President may serve more than two four-year terms. President Roosevelt was elected for four consecutive terms in 1932, 1936, 1940 and 1944.
**These words were written by an Englishman, James Bryce, in his *The American Commonwealth* published by Macmillan in 1889.

54: The US Constitution as a source of controversy

The power of the President

'I will faithfully execute the office of President of the United States and will to the best of my ability preserve, protect and defend the Constitution of the United States.' With these words the new President begins his term as the most powerful executive officer in any of the world's democracies. Though he is not a member of Congress, he can exert a very real pressure on the American legislature. Every year, he delivers a speech on the State of the Union and the message it contains will strongly influence the kind of laws Congress will pass. No Congressional bill can become law until the President signs it—so the President has a veto. But if Congress can muster a 2/3 majority it can override this veto as it did in the 1917 immigration controversy. The President is Commander-in-Chief of the armed services and makes all the important federal appointments. He has charge of American foreign policy but he may neither declare war nor accept a peace treaty. Today his central interest is the welfare of the mass of the people. Truman once said—and Kennedy repeated him word for word—that 'There are 14 or 15 million Americans who have the resources to have representatives in Washington to protect their interests and that the interests of the great mass of the *other* people—the 150 or 160 million—is the responsibility of the President of the United States.'

Congressional Committees of Inquiry

The power of Congress to conduct investigations is 'inherent in the legislative process'. Exercise of this power is a constant source of controversy. Some Senators achieve distinction in this work—Truman did as a World War II chairman of a Defence Industry committee; so did Nixon when he chaired the Un-American Activities committee in 1948. But Senator McCarthy turned the committee system into a Communist witch-hunt. In a speech at Wheeling, West Virginia (December 1950), McCarthy said he had the names of 205 Communists working *inside* the State Department. He never proved this but his investigations ruined the careers of men such as Robert Oppenheimer, the atomic physicist. McCarthy harassed his witnesses with unrelenting questions. Of course, a witness could plead the Fifth Amendment (No person ... shall be compelled in a criminal case to be a witness against himself) but such a plea is sometimes interpreted as a sign of guilt.

The Supreme Court

The Supreme Court sits in judgement upon all law passed by Congress and can, by declaring a law 'unconstitutional', frustrate the work of a dedicated President. To Roosevelt's disgust, the Supreme Court declared the entire National Recovery Administration illegal because, in one case, it was exercising unconstitutional powers. The following year (1936), the Supreme Court treated the Agricultural Adjustment Administration in exactly the same way.

National Security

Here the President's principal adviser is the Defence Secretary. But in 1947 Congress passed the *National Security Act* which created a National Security Council to advise the President on the integration of 'domestic, foreign and military policies relating to national security'. Defence decisions can be taken inside the Secretary's Pentagon headquarters after the CIA has fed in intelligence data gathered from all over the world. The National Security Council then debates policy with the President inside the White House.

The Watergate scandal

In June 1972 five agents broke into the Democratic Party's HQ in the *Watergate Building*, Washington DC. They planted some 'bugging devices' and were then arrested. This event began the Watergate scandal, which broke just before the 1972 presidential election campaign. Gradually, it seemed that President Nixon himself was implicated in an attempt to discredit the Democrats and when Senate prepared articles of impeachment against him Richard Nixon resigned (June 1974)—the first US President to have done so.

New Presidential attitudes

Gerald Ford was determined to bring back honour to the office of President: 'Our Constitution works. Our great Republic is a government of laws ... As we bind up the internal wounds of Watergate, more painful ... than those of foreign wars, let us restore the golden rule of the political process.' Then, in 1976, President Ford lost the election to Jimmy Carter who quickly showed the world quite new presidential priorities by supporting civil rights in Russia* and the conservation of dwindling energy reserves at home. When Ronald Reagan took office in 1981 he gave priority to rebuilding America's power and prestige, and ending economic decline at home.

*See *A Map History of Russia*, Spread 50.

THE 1964 ELECTORAL VOTE

Each state has electors (the number is based upon the state populations) who cast their votes in the Electoral College in favour of the candidate who wins their state Presidential election.

Although the total popular vote achieved, for example, by Kennedy in 1960 was a mere 127,000 ahead of Nixon, Kennedy had an Electoral College majority of 84 out of a total of 537 Electors.

The map below shows the result of individual state elections during the 1964 Presidential campaign. 44 states voted for Johnson (Democrat 486 votes) and 6 for Goldwater (Republican 52 votes) but Johnson's popular vote was 43,000,000 compared to Goldwater's 27,000,000.

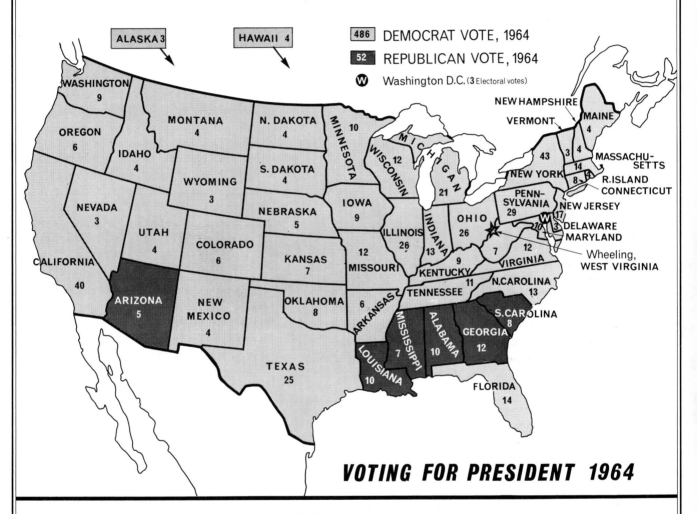

486 DEMOCRAT VOTE, 1964
52 REPUBLICAN VOTE, 1964
Ⓦ Washington D.C. (3 Electoral votes)

ALASKA 3
HAWAII 4

WASHINGTON 9
OREGON 6
MONTANA 4
N. DAKOTA 4
MINNESOTA 10
WISCONSIN 12
MICHIGAN 21
NEW HAMPSHIRE
VERMONT
MAINE 4
43
3 4
14
NEW YORK
8
MASSACHU-SETTS
R.ISLAND
CONNECTICUT
IDAHO 4
S. DAKOTA 4
IOWA 9
PENN-SYLVANIA 29
NEW JERSEY 17
W 3 DELAWARE
10 MARYLAND
WYOMING 3
NEBRASKA 5
ILLINOIS 26
INDIANA 13
OHIO 26
7
VIRGINIA 12
Wheeling, WEST VIRGINIA
NEVADA 3
UTAH 4
COLORADO 6
KANSAS 7
MISSOURI 12
KENTUCKY 9
N.CAROLINA 13
11
TENNESSEE 11
CALIFORNIA 40
ARIZONA 5
NEW MEXICO 4
OKLAHOMA 8
ARKANSAS 6
S.CAROLINA 8
MISSISSIPPI 7
ALABAMA 10
GEORGIA 12
LOUISIANA 10
TEXAS 25
FLORIDA 14

VOTING FOR PRESIDENT 1964

THE PRESIDENT CHOOSES HIS EXECUTIVE OFFICERS
Example: THE KENNEDY ADMINISTRATION 1961

President:
John F. Kennedy (elected)

Vice President:
Lyndon B. Johnson (elected)

Secretary of STATE — DEAN RUSK
Secretary of TREASURY — CLARENCE DILLON
Secretary of DEFENCE — ROBERT McNAMARA
ATTORNEY-GENERAL — ROBERT F. KENNEDY
POSTMASTER — EDWARD DAY
Secretary of INTERIOR — STEWART L. UDALL
Secretary of AGRICULTURE — ORVILLE FREEMAN
Secretary of COMMERCE — LUTHER HODGES
Secretary of LABOUR — ARTHUR GOLDBERG
Secretary of HEALTH, EDUCATION & WELFARE — ABRAHAM RIBICOFF

The Constitution of the United States of America

We, The People of the United States, in Order to form a more perfect Union, establish Justice, insure domestic Tranquility, provide for the common defence, promote the general Welfare, and secure the Blessings of Liberty to ourselves and our Posterity, do ordain and establish this Constitution for the United States of America.

ARTICLE I

SECTION I All legislative Powers herein granted shall be vested in a Congress of the United States, which shall consist of a Senate and a House of Representatives.

SECTION 2 The House of Representatives shall be composed of Members chosen every second Year by the People of the several States, and the Electors in each State shall have the Qualifications requisite for Electors of the Most numerous Branch of the State Legislature.

No Person shall be a Representative who shall not have attained to the Age of twenty-five Years, and been seven Years a Citizen of the United States, and who shall not, when elected, be an Inhabitant of that State in which he shall be chosen.

Representatives and direct Taxes shall be apportioned among the several States which may be included within this Union, according to their respective Numbers, which shall be determined by adding to the whole Number of free Persons, including those bound to Service for a Term of Years, and excluding Indians not taxed, three fifths of all other Persons. The actual Enumeration shall be made within three Years after the first Meeting of the Congress of the United States, and within every subsequent Term of ten Years, in such Manner as they shall by Law direct. The Number of Representatives shall not exceed one for every thirty Thousand, but each State shall have at Least one Representative; and until such enumeration shall be made, the State of New Hampshire shall be entitled to chuse three, Massachusetts eight, Rhode-Island and Providence Plantations one, Connecticut five, New-York six, New Jersey four, Pennsylvania eight, Delaware one, Maryland six, Virginia ten, North Carolina five, South Carolina five, and Georgia three.

When vacancies happen in the Representation from any State, the Executive Authority thereof shall issue Writs of Election to fill such Vacancies.

The House of Representatives shall chuse their Speaker and other Officers; and shall have the sole Power of Impeachment.

SECTION 3 The Senate of the United States shall be composed of two Senators from each State, chosen by the Legislature thereof, for six Years; and each Senator shall have one Vote.

Immediately after they shall be assembled in Consequence of the first Election, they shall be divided as equally as may be into three Classes. The Seats of the Senators of the first Class shall be vacated at the Expiration of the second Year, of the second Class at the Expiration of the fourth Year, and of the third Class at the Expiration of the sixth Year, so that one-third may be chosen every second Year; and if Vacancies happen by Resignation, or otherwise, during the Recess of the Legislature of any State, the Executive thereof may make temporary Appointments until the next Meeting of the Legislature, which shall then fill such Vacancies.

No Person shall be a Senator who shall not have attained to the Age of thirty Years, and been nine Years a Citizen of the United States, and who shall not when elected, by an Inhabitant of that State for which he shall be chosen.

The Vice President of the United States shall be President of the Senate, but shall have no Vote, unless they be equally divided.

The Senate shall chuse their other Officers, and also a President pro tempore, in the Absence of the Vice President, or when he shall exercise the Office of President of the United States.

The Senate shall have the sole Power to try all Impeachments. When sitting for the Purpose, they shall be on Oath or Affirmation. When the President of the United States is tried, the Chief Justice shall preside; And no Person shall be convicted without the Concurrence of two-thirds of the Members present.

Judgment in Cases of Impeachment shall not extend further than to removal from Office, and disqualification to hold and enjoy any Office of honor, Trust, or Profit under the United States; but the Party convicted shall nevertheless be liable and subject to Indictment, Trial, Judgment and Punishment, according to Law.

SECTION 4 The Times, Places and Manner of holding Elections for Senators and Representatives, shall be prescribed in each State by the Legislature thereof; but the Congress may at any time by Law make or alter such Regulations, except as to the Places of chusing Senators.

The Congress shall assemble at least once in every Year, and such Meeting shall be on the first Monday in December, unless they shall by Law appoint a different Day.

SECTION 5 Each House shall be the Judge of the Elections, Returns and Qualifications of its own Members, and a Majority of each shall constitute a Quorum to do Business; but a smaller Number may adjourn from day to day, and may be authorized to compel the Attendance of absent Members, in such Manner, and under such Penalties as each House may provide.

Each House may determine the Rules of its Proceedings, punish its Members for disorderly Behavior, and, with the Concurrence of two-thirds, expel a Member.

Each House shall keep a Journal of its Proceedings, and from time to time publish the same, excepting such Parts as may in their Judgment require Secrecy; and the Yeas and Nays of the Members of either House on any question shall, at the Desire of one-fifth of those present, be entered on the Journal.

Neither House, during the Session of Congress, shall, without the Consent of the other, adjourn for more than three days, nor to any other Place than that in which the two Houses shall be sitting.

SECTION 6   The Senators and Representatives shall receive a Compensation for their Services, to be ascertained by Law, and paid out of the Treasury of the United States. They shall in all Cases, except Treason, Felony and Breach of the Peace, be privileged from Arrest during their Attendance at the Session of their respective Houses, and in going to and returning from the same; and for any Speech or Debate in either House, they shall not be questioned in any other Place.

No Senator or Representative shall, during the Time for which he was elected, be appointed to any civil Office under the Authority of the United States, which shall have been created, or the Emoluments whereof shall have been encreased during such time; and no Person holding any Office under the United States, shall be a Member of either House during his Continuance in Office.

SECTION 7   All Bills for raising Revenue shall originate in the House of Representatives; but the Senate may propose or concur with Amendments as on other Bills.

Every Bill, which shall have passed the House of Representatives and the Senate, shall, before it become a Law, be presented to the President of the United States; If he approve he shall sign it, but if not he shall return it, with his Objections to that House in which it shall have originated, who shall enter the Objections at large on their Journal, and proceed to reconsider it. If after such Reconsideration two-thirds of that House shall agree to pass the Bill, it shall be sent, together with the Objections, to the other House, by which it shall likewise be reconsidered, and if approved by two-thirds of that House, it shall become a Law. But in all such cases the Votes of both Houses shall be determined by Yeas and Nays, and the Names of the Persons voting for and against the Bill shall be entered on the Journal of each House respectively. If any Bill shall not be returned by the President within ten Days (Sundays excepted) after it shall have been presented to him, the Same shall be a Law, in like Manner as if he had signed it, unless the Congress by their Adjournment prevent its Return, in which Case it shall not be a Law.

Every Order, Resolution, or Vote to which the Concurrence of the Senate and House of Representatives may be necessary (except on a question of Adjournment) shall be presented to the President of the United States; and before the Same shall take Effect, shall be approved by him, or being disapproved by him, shall be repassed by two-thirds of the Senate and House of Representatives, according to the Rules and Limitations prescribed in the Case of a Bill.

SECTION 8   The Congress shall have Power to lay and collect Taxes, Duties, Imposts and Excises, to pay the Debts and provide for the common Defence and general Welfare of the United States; but all Duties, Imposts and Excises shall be uniform throughout the United States;

To borrow Money on the credit of the United States:

To regulate Commerce with foreign Nations, and among the several States, and with the Indian Tribes;

To establish an uniform Rule of Naturalization, and uniform Laws on the subject of Bankruptcies throughout the United States;

To coin Money, regulate the Value thereof, and of foreign Coin; and fix the Standard of Weights and Measures;

To provide for the Punishment of counterfeiting the Securities and current Coin of the United States;

To establish Post Offices and post Roads;

To promote the Progress of Science and useful Arts, by securing for limited Times to Authors and Inventors the exclusive Right to their respective Writings and Discoveries;

To constitute Tribunals inferior to the supreme Court;

To define and punish Piracies and Felonies committed on the high Seas, and Offences against the Law of Nations;

To declare War, grant Letters of Marque and Reprisal, and make Rules concerning Captures on Land and Water;

To raise and support Armies, but no Appropriation of Money to that Use shall be for a longer Term than two Years;

To provide and maintain a Navy;

To make Rules for the Government and Regulation of the land and naval Forces;

To provide for calling forth the Militia to execute the Laws of the Union, suppress Insurrections and repel Invasions;

To provide for organizing, arming, and disciplining

the Militia, and for governing such Part of them as may be employed in the Service of the United States, reserving to the States respectively, the Appointment of the Officers, and the Authority of training the Militia according to the discipline prescribed by Congress;

To exercise exclusive Legislation in all Cases whatsoever, over such District (not exceeding ten Miles square) as may, by Cession of particular States, and the Acceptance of Congress, become the Seat of the Government of the United States, and to exercise like Authority over all Places purchased by the Consent of the Legislature of the State in which the Same shall be, for the Erection of Forts, Magazines, Arsenals, dock-Yards, and other needful Buildings;—And

To make all Laws which shall be necessary and proper for carrying into Execution the foregoing Powers, and all other Powers vested by this Constitution in the Government of the United States, or in any Department or Officer thereof.

SECTION 9 The Migration or Importation of such Persons as any of the States now existing shall think proper to admit, shall not be prohibited by the Congress prior to the Year one thousand eight hundred and eight, but a Tax or duty may be imposed on such Importation, not exceeding ten dollars for each Person.

The Privilege of the Writ of Habeas Corpus shall not be suspended, unless when in Cases of Rebellion or Invasion the public Safety may require it.

No Bill of Attainder or ex post facto Law shall be passed.

No Capitation, or other direct, tax shall be laid, unless in Proportion to the Census or Enumeration herein before directed to be taken.

No Tax or Duty shall be laid on Articles exported from any State.

No Preference shall be given by any Regulation of Commerce or Revenue to the Ports of one State over those of another: nor shall Vessels bound to, or from, one State, be obliged to enter, clear, or pay Duties in another.

No Money shall be drawn from the Treasury, but in Consequence of Appropriations made by Law; and a regular Statement and Account of the Receipts and Expenditures of all public Money shall be published from time to time.

No Title of Nobility shall be granted by the United States: And no Person holding any Office of Profit or Trust under them, shall, without the Consent of the Congress, accept of any present, Emolument, Office, or Title, of any kind whatever, from any King, Prince, or foreign State.

SECTION 10 No State shall enter into any Treaty, Alliance, or Confederation; grant Letters of Marque and Reprisal; coin Money; emit Bills of Credit; make any Thing but gold and silver Coin a Tender in Payment of Debts; pass any Bill of Attainder, ex post facto Law, or Law impairing the Obligation of Contracts, or grant any Title of Nobility.

No State shall, without the Consent of the Congress, lay any Imposts or Duties on Imports or Exports, except what may be absolutely necessary for executing its inspection Laws: and the net Produce of all Duties and Imposts, laid by any State on Imports or Exports, shall be for the Use of the Treasury of the United States; and all such Laws shall be subject to the Revision and Control of the Congress.

No State shall, without the Consent of Congress, lay any Duty of Tonnage, keep Troops, or Ships of War in time of Peace, enter into any Agreement of Compact with another State, or with a foreign Power, or engage in War, unless actually invaded, or in such imminent Danger as will not admit of delay.

ARTICLE II

SECTION 1 The executive Power shall be vested in a President of the United States of America. He shall hold his Office during the Term of four Years, and, together with the Vice President, chosen for the same Term, be elected, as follows.

Each State shall appoint, in such Manner as the Legislature thereof may direct, a Number of Electors, equal to the whole Number of Senators and Representatives to which the State may be entitled in the Congress: but no Senator or Representative, or Person holding an Office of Trust or Profit under the United States, shall be appointed an Elector.

The electors shall meet in their respective States, and vote by ballot for two Persons, of whom one at least shall not be an Inhabitant of the same State with themselves. And they shall make a List of all the Persons voted for, and of the Number of Votes for each; which List they shall sign and certify, and transmit sealed to the Seat of the Government of the United States, directed to the President of the Senate. The President of the Senate shall, in the Presence of the Senate and House of Representatives, open all the Certificates, and the Votes shall then be counted. The Person having the greatest Number of Votes shall be the President, if such Number be a Majority of the whole Number of Electors appointed; and if there be more than one who have such Majority, and have an equal Number of Votes, then the House of Representatives shall immediately chuse by Ballot one of them for President; and if no Person have a Majority, then from the five highest on the List the said House shall in like Manner chuse the President. But in chusing the President, the Votes shall be taken by States, the Representation from each State having one Vote; a

Quorum for this Purpose shall consist of a Member or Members from two-thirds of the States, and a Majority of all the States shall be necessary to a Choice. In every Case, after the Choice of the President, the Person having the greatest Number of Votes of the Electors shall be the Vice President. But if there should remain two or more who have equal Votes, the Senate shall chuse from them by Ballot the Vice President.

The Congress may determine the Time of chusing the Electors, and the Day on which they shall give their Votes; which Day shall be the same throughout the United States.

No Person except a natural born Citizen, or a Citizen of the United States, at the time of the Adoption of this Constitution, shall be eligible to the Office of President; neither shall any Person be eligible to that Office who shall not have attained to the Age of thirty five Years, and been fourteen Years a Resident within the United States.

In Case of the Removal of the President from Office, or of his Death, Resignation or Inability to discharge the Powers and Duties of the said Office, the same shall devolve on the Vice President, and the Congress may by Law provide for the Case of Removal, Death, Resignation or Inability, both of the President and Vice President, declaring what Officer shall then act as President, and such Officer shall act accordingly, until the Disability be removed, or a President shall be elected.

The President shall, at stated Times, receive for his Services, a Compensation, which shall neither be encreased nor diminished during the Period for which he shall have been elected, and he shall not receive within that Period any other Emolument from the United States, or any of them.

Before he enter on the Execution of his Office, he shall take the following Oath or Affirmation:—'I do solemnly swear (or affirm) that I will faithfully execute the Office of President of the United States, and will to the best of my Ability, preserve, protect and defend the Constitution of the United States.'

SECTION 2   The President shall be Commander in Chief of the Army and Navy of the United States, and of the Militia of the several States, when called into the actual Service of the United States; he may require the Opinion, in writing, of the principal Officer in each of the executive Departments, upon any Subject relating to the Duties of their respective Offices, and he shall have Power to grant Reprieves and Pardons for Offences against the United States, except in Cases of Impeachment.

He shall have Power, by and with the Advice and Consent of the Senate, to make Treaties, provided two thirds of the Senators present concur; and he shall nominate, and by and with the Advice and Consent of the Senate, shall appoint Ambassadors, other public Ministers and Consuls, Judges of the supreme Court, and all other Officers of the United States, whose Appointments are not herein otherwise provided for, and which shall be established by Law: but the Congress may by Law vest the Appointment of such inferior Officers, as they think proper, in the President alone, in the Courts of Law, or in the Heads of Departments.

The President shall have Power to fill up all Vacancies that may happen during the Recess of the Senate, by granting Commissions which shall expire at the End of their next Session.

SECTION 3   He shall from time to time give to the Congress Information of the State of the Union, and recommend to their Consideration such Measures as he shall judge necessary and expedient; he may, on extraordinary Occasions, convene both Houses, or either of them, and, in Case of Disagreement between them, with Respect to the Time of Adjournment, he may adjourn them to such Time as he shall think proper; he shall receive Ambassadors and other public Ministers; he shall take Care that the Laws be faithfully executed, and shall Commission all the Officers of the United States.

SECTION 4   The President, Vice President and all civil Officers of the United States, shall be removed from Office on Impeachment for, and Conviction of, Treason, Bribery, or other high Crimes and Misdemeanors.

ARTICLE III

SECTION 1   The Judicial Power of the United States, shall be vested in one supreme Court, and in such inferior Courts as the Congress may from time to time ordain and establish. The Judges, both of the supreme and inferior Courts, shall hold their Offices during good Behaviour, and shall, at stated Times, receive for their Services, a Compensation, which shall not be diminished during their Continuance in Office.

SECTION 2   The judicial Power shall extend to all Cases, in Law and Equity, arising under this Constitution, the Laws of the United States, and Treaties made, or which shall be made, under their Authority;—to all Cases affecting Ambassadors, other public Ministers and Consuls;—to all Cases of admiralty and maritime Jurisdiction;—to Controversies to which the United States shall be a Party;—to Controversies between two or more States;—between a State and Citizens of another State;—between Citizens of different States,—between Citizens of the same State claiming Lands under Grants of different States, and between a State, or the Citizens thereof, and foreign States, Citizens or Subjects.

In all Cases affecting Ambassadors, other public

Ministers and Consuls, and those in which a State shall be Party, the supreme Court shall have original Jurisdiction. In all the other Cases before mentioned, the supreme Court shall have appellate Jurisdiction, both as to Law and Fact, with such Exceptions, and under such Regulations as the Congress shall make.

The Trial of all Crimes, except in Cases of Impeachment, shall be by Jury; and such Trial shall be held in the State where the said Crimes shall have been committed; but when not committed within any State, the Trial shall be at such Place or Places as the Congress may by Law have directed.

SECTION 3   Treason against the United States, shall consist only in levying War against them, or in adhering to their Enemies, giving them Aid and Comfort. No Person shall be convicted of Treason unless on the Testimony of two Witnesses to the same overt Act, or on Confession in open Court.

The Congress shall have Power to declare the Punishment of Treason, but no Attainder of Treason shall work Corruption of Blood, or Forfeiture except during the life of the Person attainted.

ARTICLE IV

SECTION 1   Full Faith and Credit shall be given in each State to the public Acts, Records, and judicial Proceedings of every other State. And the Congress may by general Laws prescribe the Manner in which such Acts, Records and Proceedings shall be proved, and the Effect thereof.

SECTION 2   The Citizens of each state be entitled to all Privileges and Immunities of Citizens in the several States.

A person charged in any State with Treason, Felony, or other Crime, who shall flee from Justice, and be found in another State, shall on Demand of the executive Authority of the State from which he fled, be delivered up, to be removed to the State having Jurisdiction of the Crime.

No Person held to Service or Labour in one State, under the Laws thereof, escaping into another, shall, in Consequence of any Law or Regulation therein, be discharged from such Service or Labour, but shall be delivered up on Claim of the Party to whom such Service or Labour may be due.

SECTION 3   New States may be admitted by the Congress into this Union; but no new State shall be formed or erected within the Jurisdiction of any other State; nor any State be formed by the Junction of two or more States, or Parts of States, without the Consent of the Legislatures of the States concerned as well as of the Congress.

The Congress shall have Power to dispose of and make all needful Rules and Regulations respecting the Territory or other Property belonging to the United States; and nothing in this Constitution shall be so construed as to Prejudice any Claims of the United States, or of any particular State.

SECTION 4   The United States shall guarantee to every State in this Union a Republican Form of Government, and shall protect each of them against Invasion; and on Application of the Legislature, or of the Executive (when the Legislature cannot be convened) against domestic Violence.

ARTICLE V

The Congress, whenever two thirds of both Houses shall deem it necessary, shall propose Amendments to this Constitution, or, on the Application of the Legislatures of two thirds of the several States, shall call a Convention for proposing Amendments, which, in either Case, shall be valid to all Intents and Purposes, as Part of this Constitution, when ratified by the Legislatures of three fourths of the several States, or by Conventions in three fourths thereof, as the one or the other Mode of Ratification may be proposed by the Congress; Provided that no Amendment which may be made prior to the Year One thousand eight hundred and eight shall in any Manner affect the first and fourth Clauses in the Ninth Section of the first Article; and that no State, without its Consent, shall be deprived of its equal Suffrage in the Senate.

ARTICLE VI

All Debts contracted and Engagements entered into, before the Adoption of this Constitution, shall be as valid against the United States under this Constitution, as under the Confederation.

This Constitution, and the Laws of the United States which shall be made in Pursuance thereof; and all Treaties made, or which shall be made, under the Authority of the United States, shall be the supreme Law of the Land; and the Judges in every State shall be bound thereby, any Thing in the Constitution or Laws of any State to the Contrary notwithstanding.

The Senators and Representatives before mentioned, and the Members of the several State Legislatures, and all executive and judicial Officers, both of the United States and of the several States, shall be bound by Oath or Affirmation, to support this Constitution; but no religious Test shall ever be required as a Qualification to any Office or public Trust under the United States.

ARTICLE VII

The Ratification of the Conventions of nine States, shall be sufficient for the Establishment of this Constitution between the States so ratifying the Same.

DONE in Convention by the Unanimous Consent of the States present the Seventeenth Day of September in the Year of our Lord one thousand seven hundred and Eighty seven and of the Independence of the United States of America the Twelfth.

AMENDMENTS

ARTICLE I   1791

Congress shall make no law respecting an establishment of religion, or prohibiting the free exercise thereof; or abridging the freedom of speech, or of the press; or the right of the people peaceably to assemble, and to petition the Government for a redress of grievances.

ARTICLE II   1791

A well regulated Militia, being necessary to the security of a free State, the right of the people to keep and bear Arms, shall not be infringed.

ARTICLE III   1791

No Soldier shall, in time of peace, be quartered in any house, without the consent of the Owner, nor in time of war, but in a manner to be prescribed by law.

ARTICLE IV   1791

The right of the people to be secure in their persons, houses, papers, and effects, against unreasonable searches and seizures, shall not be violated, and no Warrants shall issue, but upon probable cause, supported by Oath or affirmation, and particularly describing the place to be searched, and the persons or things to be seized.

ARTICLE V   1791

No person shall be held to answer for a capital, or otherwise infamous crime, unless on a presentment or indictment of a Grand Jury, except in cases arising in the land or naval forces, or in the Militia, when in actual service in time of War or public danger; nor shall any person be subject for the same offence to be twice put in jeopardy of life or limb; nor shall be compelled in any Criminal Case to be a witness against himself, nor be deprived of life, liberty, or property, without due process of law; nor shall private property be taken for public use, without just compensation.

ARTICLE VI   1791

In all criminal prosecutions, the accused shall enjoy the right to a speedy and public trial, by an impartial jury of the State and district wherein the crime shall have been committed, which district shall have been previously ascertained by law, and to be informed of the nature and cause of the accusation; to be confronted with the witnesses against him; to have compulsory process for obtaining Witnesses in his favor, and to have the Assistance of Counsel for his defence.

ARTICLE VII   1791

In suits at common law, where the value in controversy shall exceed twenty dollars, the right of trial by jury shall be preserved, and no fact tried by a jury shall be otherwise re-examined in any Court of the United States, than according to the rules of the common law.

ARTICLE VIII   1791

Excessive bail shall not be required, nor excessive fines imposed, nor cruel and unusual punishments inflicted.

ARTICLE IX   1791

The enumeration in the Constitution, of certain rights, shall not be construed to deny or disparge others retained by the people.

ARTICLE X   1791

The powers not delegated to the United States by the Constitution, nor prohibited by it to the States, are reserved to the States respectively, or to the people.

ARTICLE XI   1798

The Judicial power of the United States shall not be construed to extend to any suit in law or equity, commenced or prosecuted against one of the United States by Citizens of another State, or by Citizens or Subjects of any Foreign State.

ARTICLE XII   1804

The Electors shall meet in their respective states, and vote by ballot for President and Vice President, one of whom, at least, shall not be an inhabitant of the same state with themselves; they shall name in their ballots the person voted for as President, and in distinct ballots the person voted for as Vice President, and they shall make distinct lists of all persons voted for as President, and of all persons voted for as Vice-President, and of the number of votes for each, which lists they shall sign and certify, and transmit sealed to the seat of the Government of the United States, directed to the President of the Senate;—The President of the Senate shall, in the presence of the Senate and House of Representatives, open all the certificates and the votes shall then be counted;—The person having the greatest number of votes for President, shall be the President, if such number be a majority of the whole number of Electors appointed; and if no person have such majority, then from the persons having the highest numbers not exceeding three on the list of those voted for as President, the House of Representatives shall choose immediately, by ballot, the President. But in choosing the President, the votes shall be taken by states, the representation from each state having one vote; a quorum for this purpose shall consist of a member or members from two thirds of the states, and a majority of all the states shall be necessary to a choice. And if the House of Representatives shall not choose a President whenever the right of choice shall devolve upon them, before the fourth day of March next following, then the Vice President shall act as President, as in the case of the death or other constitutional disability of the President. The person having the greatest number of votes as Vice President, shall be the Vice President, if such number be a majority of the whole number of Electors appointed, and if no person have a majority, then from the two highest numbers on the list, the Senate shall choose the Vice President; a quorum for the purpose shall consist of two-thirds of the whole number shall be necessary to a choice. But no person constitutionally ineligible to the office of President shall be eligible to that of Vice President of the United States.

ARTICLE XIII   1865

SECTION 1   Neither slavery nor involuntary servitude, except as a punishment for crime whereof the party shall have been duly convicted, shall exist within the United States, or any place subject to their jurisdiction.

SECTION 2   Congress shall have power to enforce this article by appropriate legislation.

ARTICLE XIV   1868

SECTION 1   All persons born or naturalized in the United States, and subject to the jurisdiction thereof, are citizens of the United States and of the State wherein they reside. No State shall make or enforce any law which shall abridge the privileges or immunities of citizens of the United States; nor shall any State deprive any person of life, liberty, or property, without due process of law; nor deny to any person within its jurisdiction the equal protection of the laws.

SECTION 2   Representatives shall be apportioned among the several States according to their respective numbers, counting the whole number of persons in each State, excluding Indians not taxed. But when the

right to vote at any election for the choice of electors for President and Vice President of the United States, Representatives in Congress, the Executive and Judicial officers of a State, or the members of the Legislature thereof, is denied to any of the male inhabitants of such State, being twenty-one years of age, and citizens of the United States, or in any way abridged, except for participation in rebellion, or other crime, the basis of representation therein shall be reduced in the proportion which the number of such male citizens shall bear to the whole number of male citizens twenty-one years of age in such State.

SECTION 3   No person shall be a Senator or Representative in Congress, or elector of President and Vice President, or hold any office, civil, or military under the United States, or under any State, who, having previously taken an oath, as a member of Congress, or as an officer of the United States, or as a member of any State legislature, or as an executive or judicial officer of any State, to support the Constitution of the United States, shall have engaged in insurrection or rebellion against the same, or given aid or comfort to the enemies thereof. But Congress may by a vote of two thirds of each House, remove such disability.

SECTION 4   The validity of the public debt of the United States, authorized by law, including debts incurred for payment of pensions and bounties for services in suppressing insurrection or rebellion, shall not be questioned. But neither the United States nor any State shall assume or pay any debt or obligation incurred in aid of insurrection or rebellion against the United States, or any claim for the loss or emancipation of any slave; but all such debts, obligations and claims shall be held illegal and void.

SECTION 5   The Congress shall have power to enforce, by appropriate legislation, the provisions of this article.

ARTICLE XV   1870

SECTION 1   The right of citizens of the United States to vote shall not be denied or abridged by the United States or by any State on account of race, color, or previous condition of servitude.

SECTION 2   The Congress shall have power to enforce this article by appropriate legislation.

ARTICLE XVI   1913

The Congress shall have power to lay and collect taxes on incomes, from whatever source derived, without apportionment among the several States and without regard to any census or enumeration.

ARTICLE XVII   1913

The Senate of the United States shall be composed of two senators from each State, elected by the people thereof, for six years; and each Senate shall have one vote. The electors in each State shall have the qualification requisite for electors for the most numerous branch of the State legislature.

When vacancies happen in the representation of any State in the Senate, the executive authority of such State shall issue writs of election to fill such vacancies: PROVIDED, That the legislature of any State may empower the executive thereof to make temporary appointments until the people fill the vacancies by election as the legislature may direct.

This amendment shall not be so construed as to affect the election or term of any senator chosen before it becomes valid as part of the Constitution.

ARTICLE XVIII   1919

After one year from the ratification of this article, the manufacture, sale, or transportation of intoxicating liquors within, the importation thereof into, or the exportation thereof from the United States and all territory subject to the jurisdiction thereof for beverage purposes is hereby prohibited.

The Congress and the several States shall have concurrent power to enforce this article by appropriate legislation.

This article shall be inoperative unless it shall have been ratified as an amendment to the Constitution by the legislatures of the several States, as provided in the Constitution, within seven years from the date of the submission hereof to the States by the Congress.

ARTICLE XIX   1920

The right of citizens of the United States to vote shall not be denied or abridged by the United States or by any States on account of sex.

The Congress shall have power, by appropriate legislation, to enforce the provisions of this article.

ARTICLE XX   1933

SECTION 1   The terms of the President and Vice President shall end at noon on the twentieth day of January, and the terms of Senators and Representatives at noon on the third day of January, of the years in which such terms would have ended if this article had not been ratified; and the terms of their successors shall then begin.

SECTION 2   The Congress shall assemble at least once in every year, and such meeting shall begin at noon on the third day of January, unless they shall by law appoint a different day.

SECTION 3   If, at the time fixed for the beginning of the term of the President, the President elect shall have died, the Vice President elect shall become President. If a President shall not have been chosen before the time fixed for the beginning of his term, or if the President elect shall have failed to qualify, then the Vice President elect shall act as President until a President shall have qualified; and the Congress may by law provide for the case wherein neither a President elect nor a Vice President elect shall have qualified, declaring who shall then act as President, or the manner in which one who is to act shall be selected, and such person shall act accordingly until a President or Vice President shall have qualified.

SECTION 4   The Congress may by law provide for the case of the death of any of the persons from whom the House of Representatives may choose a President whenever the right of choice shall have devolved upon them, and for the case of the death of any of the persons from whom the Senate may choose a Vice President whenever the right of choice shall have devolved upon them.

SECTION 5   Sections 1 and 2 shall take effect on the 15th day of October following the ratification of this article.

SECTION 6   This article shall be inoperative unless it shall have been ratified as an amendment to the Constitution by the legislatures of three fourths of the several States within seven years from the date of its submission.

ARTICLE XXI   1933

SECTION 1   The eighteenth article of amendment to the Constitution of the United States is hereby repealed.

SECTION 2   The transportation or importation into any State, Territory or possession of the United States for delivery or use therein of intoxicating liquors, in violation of the laws thereof, is hereby prohibited.

SECTION 3   This article shall be inoperative unless it shall have been ratified as an amendment to the Constitution by convention in the several States, as provided in the Constitution, within seven years from the date of the submission hereof to the States by the Congress.

ARTICLE XXII   1951

No person shall be elected to the office of the President

more than twice, and no person who has held the office of President, or acted as President, for more than two years of a term to which some other person was elected President shall be elected to the office of the President more than once.

But this article shall not apply to any person holding the office of President when this article was proposed by the Congress, and shall not prevent any person who may be holding the office of President, or acting as President, during the term within which this article becomes operative from holding the office of President or acting as President during the remainder of such term.

This article shall be inoperative unless it shall have been ratified as an amendment to the Constitution by the legislatures of three-fourths of the several States within seven years from the date of its submission to the States by the Congress.

ARTICLE XXIII 1961

SECTION 1   The District constituting the seat of Government of the United States shall appoint in such manner as the Congress may direct:

A number of Electors of President and Vice President equal to the whole number of Senators and Representatives in Congress to which the District would be entitled if it were a State, but in no event more than the least populous State; they shall be in addition to those appointed by the States, but they shall be considered, for the purposes of the election of President and Vice President, to be Electors appointed by a State; and they shall meet in the District and perform such duties as provided by the Twelfth Article of amendment.

SECTION 2   The Congress shall have power to enforce this article by appropriate legislation.

ARTICLE XXIV 1964

SECTION 1   The right of citizens of the United States to vote in any primary or other election for President or Vice President, for Electors for President or Vice President, or for Senator or Representative in Congress, shall not be denied or abridged by the United States or any State by reason of failure to pay any poll tax or other tax.

SECTION 2   The Congress shall have the power to enforce this article by appropriate legislation.

ARTICLE XXV 1967

SECTION 1   In case of the removal of the President from office or his death or resignation, the Vice President shall become President.

SECTION 2   Whenever there is a vacancy in the office of the Vice President, the President shall nominate a Vice President who shall take office upon confirmation by a majority vote by both Houses of Congress.

SECTION 3   Whenever the President transmits to the President *pro tempore* of the Senate and the Speaker of the House of Representatives his written declaration that he is unable to discharge the powers and duties of his office, and until he transmits to them a written declaration to the contrary, such powers and duties shall be discharged by the Vice President as Acting President.

SECTION 4   Whenever the Vice President and a majority of either the principal officers of the Executive Departments or of such other body as Congress may by law provide, transmit to the President *pro tempore* of the Senate and the Speaker of the House of Representatives their written declaration that the President is unable to discharge the powers and duties of his office, the Vice President shall immediately assume the powers and duties of the office as Acting President.

Thereafter, when the President transmits to the President *pro tempore* of the Senate and the Speaker of the House of Representatives his written declaration that no inability exists, he shall resume the powers and duties of his office unless the Vice President and a majority of either the principal officers of the Executive Department or of such other body as Congress may by law provide, transmit within four days to the President *pro tempore* of the Senate and the Speaker of the House of Representatives their written declaration that the President is unable to discharge the powers and duties of his office. Thereupon Congress shall decide the issue, assembling within 48 hours for that purpose if not in session. If the Congress, within 21 days after receipt of the later written declaration, or, if Congress is not in session, within 21 days after Congress is required to assemble, determines by $\frac{2}{3}$ vote of both Houses that the President is unable to discharge the powers and duties of his office, the Vice President shall continue to discharge the same as Acting President; otherwise the President shall resume the powers and duties of his office.

Further Reading

Brief account: *Modern Forms of Government*, Michael Stewart, Allen & Unwin, 1964
Detailed accounts: *American Government*, Richard H. Pear, MacGibbon & Kee, 1963
American Democracy in Theory and Practice, Carr, Bernstein and Morrison, Holt, Rinehart & Winston 1961

Glossary

ARKIES and OKIES Epithets used to describe the unfortunate migrants from Arkansas and Oklahoma during the years of the Depression.

CONESTOGA WAGONS The Conestoga were Indians (now extinct) who had lived in Maryland and Pennsylvania. The heavy freight wagons coming out of these states were termed 'Conestoga'.

FORTY-NINERS These were the 100,000 hopeful prospectors who arrived in California during the 1849 gold rush. They came by ship and wagon-train from all over the world. They were already a year late—the first strike had been made in the Sacramento Valley during the spring of 1848.

HOOVERVILLES These were shanty towns built outside cities by the thousands of homeless during the early years of the Depression when Herbert Hoover was President (1929–33). Ironically, Hoover had been America's Relief Administrator in Europe after World War I.

KAMIKAZE The highest expression of *bushido*, the Japanese code of warrior conduct. Kamikaze literally means 'the divine wind' which had once before saved Japan from a seaborne invasion. The name was taken by Japanese Army and Navy aircrew who trained to undertake suicide attacks on American and British warships during the last months of World War II. About 5000 Japanese committed suicide in kamikaze attacks.

MINUTEMEN The name given to volunteers who were instantly ready for battle during the American War of Independence. Today, '*Minuteman*' is the name of an American ICBM.

WAR HAWKS A derisive name given by Congressmen to their younger and more militant colleagues during 1810–1811. The War Hawks wanted to fight Britain in order to capture Canada and Florida; they helped to push America into the War of 1812. More recently, 'hawks' favoured the escalation of war in Viet Nam; the 'doves' opposed it.

YANKEES This is probably a corruption of a Dutch name 'Jan Kes'. Southerners used this expression to describe Northerners and during the eighteenth century corrupted it to 'Yankees'.

ZERO This was the first name that the Allies used to describe the Mitsubishi Type 0 fighter. Later on, they called it 'Zeke'.

Presidents of the United States

(Their political parties are indicated for the post-Civil War period)

George Washington, 1789–97
John Adams, 1797–1801
Thomas Jefferson, 1801–9
James Madison, 1809–17
James Monroe, 1817–25
John Quincy Adams, 1825–9
Andrew Jackson, 1829–37
Martin Van Buren, 1837–41
William Henry Harrison, 1841
John Tyler, 1841–5
James Polk, 1845–9
Zacchary Taylor, 1849–50
Millard Fillmore, 1850–3
Franklin Pierce, 1853–7
James Buchanan, 1857–61
Abraham Lincoln, 1861–5*
Andrew Johnson, Unionist (Republican), 1865–9
Ulysses, S. Grant, Republican, 1869–77
Rutherford B. Hayes, Republican, 1877–81
James A. Garfield, Republican, 1881*
Chester A. Arthur, Republican, 1881–5
Grover, Cleveland, Democrat, 1885–9
Benjamin Harrison, Republican, 1889–93
Grover Cleveland, Democrat, 1893–7
William McKinley, Republican, 1897–1901*
Theodore Roosevelt, Republican, 1901–9
William H. Taft, Republican, 1909–13
Woodrow Wilson, Democrat, 1913–21
Warren G. Harding, Republican, 1921–3
Calvin Coolidge, Republican, 1923–9
Herbert Hoover, Republican, 1929–33
Franklin D. Roosevelt, Democrat, 1933–45
Harry S. Truman, Democrat, 1945–53
Dwight D. Eisenhower, Republican, 1953–61
John F. Kennedy, Democrat, 1961–3*
Lyndon B. Johnson, Democrat, 1963–68
Richard Nixon, Republican, 1968–74
Gerald Ford, Republican, 1974–76
James E. Carter, Democrat, 1976–80
Ronald Reagan, Republican 1980–

*Assassinated

INDEX